Surviving with Dignity

SURVIVING WITH DIGNITY

HAUSA COMMUNITIES OF NIAMEY, NIGER

Scott M. Youngstedt

LEXINGTON BOOKS
Lanham • Boulder • New York • Toronto • Plymouth, UK

Published by Lexington Books
A wholly owned subsidiary of The Rowman & Littlefield Publishing Group, Inc.
4501 Forbes Boulevard, Suite 200, Lanham, Maryland 20706
www.rowman.com

10 Thornbury Road, Plymouth PL6 7PP, United Kingdom

British Library Cataloguing in Publication Information Available

Library of Congress Cataloging-in-Publication Data

Youngstedt, Scott M.
Surviving with dignity : Hausa communities of Niamey, Niger / Scott M. Youngstedt.
p. cm.
Includes bibliographical references and index.
ISBN 978-0-7391-7350-3 (cloth : alk. paper) — ISBN 978-0-7391-7351-0 (electronic)
1. Hausa (African people)—Niger—Niamey—Social conditions. 2. Hausa (African people)—Niger—Niamey—Economic conditions. 3. Rural-urban migration—Niger. I. Title.
HN824.N53Y67 2013
362.8493706626—dc23

2012040502

™ The paper used in this publication meets the minimum requirements of American National Standard for Information Sciences—Permanence of Paper for Printed Library Materials, ANSI/NISO Z39.48-1992.

Printed in the United States of America

To the Hausa of Niamey

Contents

Photographs

Figures & Tables

Acknowledgments

I could not have written this book without the financial, logistical, intellectual, and emotional support of many people and institutions. Saginaw Valley State University generously awarded me Research Grants that covered most of my expenses for work in Niamey in 1998-1999, 2000-2001, 2003, 2005-2006, and 2009-2010. I am also grateful to the West African Research Association (WARA) for providing me with a Post-Doctoral Research Fellowship that allowed me to complete two rounds of fieldwork in Niamey in 2005. I thank the government of Niger and the Ministère de l'Enseignement Supérieur, de la Recherche et de la Technologie for granting me permission to conduct research.

The warmth, generosity, hospitality, and patience of the Nigeriens with whom I worked have always impressed and inspired me. To thank all of the Nigeriens who have helped me would require an entire chapter. I apologize to those individuals who I omit here. I thank Mangoné Niang, who served for many years as the Director of Niger's Union Africaine (AU) delegation and the Centre d'Études Linguistiques et Historiques par Tradition Orale (CELHTO). I appreciated our stimulating conversations and his willingness to host me at the guest apartments for visiting scholars operated by the AU/CELHTO during several visits. I also benefitted from the lively scholarly community at the CELHTO and at the Institut de Recherche en Sciences Humaines (IRSH) located next door.

Mohamadou, Ousseini, Ibrahim, Elhadji Aboubacar, and Elhadji Anas were key participants in my research over many years. I thank each for sharing their knowledge of many things with me, and for their incredibly warm hospitality. The Hima family—particularly Elhadji Maouri, Abdoulrazack, Elhadji Yayé, Garba "d'an Maradi," Moctar, and Madame Kane—has been important scholarly and historical resources for me. They also graciously made me feel like a member of the family during religious holidays, weddings, and funerals.

Among the Nigeriens that have guided me, three stand out above all others. For 20 years, Djibrilla Garba and Koche "Yagi" Dan Jima have shared their sophisticated views of the joy and pain of life in Niamey, patiently answered all of my questions, helped me frame my research and interview schedules, introduced me to dozens of their family members and friends, traveled with me, invited me to many religious, cultural, sports, and musical events, and regularly included me in important family gatherings. I am deeply thankful for all that they have done for me. I value their friendship even more than all of the help that they have given me. Cheifou Idrissa began working as my Research Assistant more than a decade ago. He quickly became more collaborator than assistant, and our productive relationship developed into a wonderful friendship.

I am extremely grateful to Justin Race and Sabah Ghulamali, Editors at Lexington Books, for their extremely helpful suggestions, patience, and support. I feel privileged to have worked with them. I also thank an anonymous reviewer for Lexington Books for her/his very careful reading and enormously useful and constructive criticism. Many scholars influence my thinking in important ways. I owe much to Walter Goldschmidt for helping me to think about the interplay between individual careers and broad socio-historical patterns. I also thank Russell Schuh and Lawan Danladi Yalwa for skillfully introducing me to the Hausa language and people. I sincerely thank Adeline Masquelier, Jeff Kolnick, Paul Stoller, and Jennifer Yanco for very insightful advice on particular chapters. I gratefully acknowledge the encouragement and particularly helpful suggestions on multiple drafts of several chapters provided by Ousseina Alidou, Barbara Cooper, and Rachel Reynolds. They have helped me immeasurably over the years. I also have benefitted from lively exchange and support from many colleagues in WARA.

I sincerely appreciate the patience, love, and inspiration of Jamila Youngstedt, my daughter. I thank her for her helpful suggestions on the first chapter. I am so pleased that she has developed a love for West Africa. My son, Reid Youngstedt, arrived in the world in my final days spent on the book, reminding me of what is really important. I also thank Kiren Ghei for her long-term support on many levels.

I reserve my deepest gratitude for my wife and best friend, Sara Beth Keough. I benefitted greatly from her polished fieldwork skills and companionship during two recent trips to Niger. Despite her busy life as geography professor, scholar, and mother, she has always made time to make excellent suggestions on the book, and offer unfailing support. She has read more versions of the manuscript more times than anyone but me. I cannot thank her enough.

I humbly hope that I am repaying the gracious hospitality of my hosts in some small measure by sensitively and accurately doing justice to the complexity, dignity, and pain of Hausa lived experience in Niamey. I bear responsibility for any flaws in the book.

— 1 —

Introduction: Making Sense of the World

Rashin sani ya hi dare duhu:
Ignorance is darker than the night

Journeys through Time and Space

The Rimbo bus station of Niamey at 5:00 a.m. on a cool day in January 2010 was an utterly chaotic scene. Five hundred people with luggage crowded around ten busses, jostling to get to the front of the lines. Rimbo personnel changed the destination placards (Agadez, Zinder, Lomé, Dakar, Ouagadougou) on several busses over the next few minutes, while other busses with their engines running remained unlabeled. Over the hum of multiple engines and the din of the crowd, we struggled to hear our names on the list being read by an attendant sitting on a bus. Hassane was hosting my wife Sara Beth Keough, a cultural geographer, and me on a visit to Kuka, his home village. We managed to secure the last three open seats, and while they were not nearly as large and comfortable as those on the first private busses that began operating in Niger about a decade ago, I recognized the luxury of bus travel. Our trip involved a four-hour bus ride along Niger's national highway 275 kilometers eastward to the town of Dogondoutchi. From there we completed our journey 25 kilometers northward by bush taxi on a deeply rutted, rocky, dirt road.

I had met Hassane purely by chance on a hot afternoon in 1991 while on a 10-kilometer walk through several neighborhoods of Niamey trying to re-orient myself and assess what had changed in the three years since I had last visited Niger's capital in 1988. I was parched and had just begun to search for something to drink when a roadside vendor with a small thatched hangar for shade and a refrigerator greeted me with a smile and a friendly, "*Bonjour.*" I responded, "*Bonjour,*" before surprising him with a Hausa greeting, "*Ina wuni*?" ("How have you passed the day?"). We then exchanged a typical series of Hausa greetings asking about each other's work, families, and fatigue. I introduced myself as "Chaibou"—a Muslim Hausa name ceremoniously given to me in 1988—and he introduced himself as "Hassane." He offered me a soft-backed chair and a Coke, while he and several other men sat beside me on hard wooden benches. After allowing me a few moments to quench my thirst, Hassane observed, "I have never met a white man who speaks Hausa," and asked, "Where did you learn to speak Hausa and where are you from?" I explained that I first learned Hausa as a university student in the U.S., my home, but that I really learned to speak Hausa during several months of travel and residency across Southern Niger and Northern Nigeria in 1988 and 1989. "*Ikon Allah*" ("By the power of God"), exclaimed Hassane.

I returned to visit Hassane the following day and I have enjoyed a special bond with him ever since. I quickly learned that Hassane was widely respected as a friendly, generous, pious, knowledgeable, engaging conversationalist—an all-around *mutumin kirki* ("good man"). He had built an enormous social network, and was regarded as a focal point in the Kuka migrant community in Niamey. He introduced me to dozens of relatives and friends over the years, many of who became critically important participants in my research. In addition to spending hundred of hours in Hassane's *hira* ("informal street corner conversation") group, we have shared visits to football and wrestling matches, horse races, Islamic sermons, and funerals. For many years, Hassane extended an open invitation to me to accompany him on a visit to his hometown. I had long been intrigued by this opportunity, given my research focus on Hausa migration and diaspora, other remarkably revealing trips with men that I had met in Niamey to their home villages, and our long-term relationship that blossomed as a deep friendship despite our vastly different life experiences. However, we had never been able to coordinate a visit to Kuka until January 2010, and hence I was very excited to finally have this opportunity.

The bus trip to Dogondoutchi reminded me of the importance of sharing and Islam in Nigerien society. As soon as we sat down, a woman struggling with a large duffel bag plopped her baby on Hassane's lap, apparently recognizing the kindness in his friendly smile and demeanor. Hassane gently held the baby for most of the trip. Early into the journey the bus pulled into a station for the morning Muslim prayer. Virtually all passengers grabbed plastic teakettles filled with water provided by Rimbo, performed their ablutions, prayed, and re-entered the bus. I have long been struck by the powerful ways that Islam unites Nigeriens. Hassane recently joined the *'yan Izala*, a strict, reformist Islamist sect whose adherents usually pray together in their own congregations. On this occasion, Hassane simply joined the crowd—undoubtedly consisting of people of various sects—at the makeshift, open-air, mosque at the back of the bus station.

Upon reaching Dogondoutchi, Hassane went to negotiate a ride to Kuka on a bush taxi. He had cell-phoned family and friends before our departure to inform them of our visit, and hence a group of people were waiting to welcome us when the bush taxi arrived in Kuka. Aliou, Moctar, and other men who I had come to know well in Niamey, but had not seen in a decade, were among them. Given that it was nearly three months into the dry season, the village was largely vacant of working-aged men. Only young children, some women, and older residents remained—with a few exceptions. Those able to work had left the village for Niamey and other West and North African cities until the rains returned. Twenty curious, smiling, and giggling children immediately surrounded us. Baso, Hassane's mother and our host, explained that she had heard stories over many years about the American professor that her son had befriended. She thanked God for our visit, and invited us to stay as long as we liked, presenting us with a large bowl of sizzling hot k'osai ("fried bean cakes")—my favorite Hausa snack—and a calabash of cool water.

The Nigerien hospitality that I have always found so humbling was certainly evident in Hassane's village. Salisou, who Hassane had introduced me to Niamey in 1991, greeted me as an old friend, despite the three years that had passed since our last meeting. Hassane and Salisou explained that we would have more privacy if we stayed in the compound Salisou shares with Hampsou, one of his two wives, than in Hassane's family's home, and that both Baso and Hampsou would cook for us. Salisou's bull, guinea fowl, donkeys, and chickens—an entourage that we dubbed, "the animal chorus"— welcomed us as we entered his compound. We greeted Hampsou, their children, and neighbors, and settled into the home that Ibrahim and Hampsou graciously vacated for the duration of our stay. As Hassane called his father in Niamey to let him know that we had arrived safely, I pondered the technological leap forward represented by cell phones in this village of one to two thousand people (depending on the seasons) that had only three electrified homes, a few generators, no running water, and no biomedical health clinic.

Our three days were packed with activities. We greeted dozens of relatives, friends, and neighbors of our hosts, including the *mai gari* ("village headman"); climbed the 500-meter high rock mesa that towers over the village; took long walks in the surrounding countryside to visit farms and granaries, nomadic Fulani camps, neighboring villages, and a lake; ate sumptuous meals; and enjoyed long conversations with our hosts, especially over strong cups of tea late into the night.

As is almost always the case among Hausa, my conversations with Kuka friends and residents were free flowing. In these *hira* groups, we reminisced about our time together in Niamey, mostly laughing at humorous events that we jointly experienced, but also remembering the lean times that the men had endured. We discussed each other's families, and I asked for updates about several Kuka men that I had met in Niamey but had not seen for years. I learned that some had settled in Nigeria, Benin, and Ghana, some had died, and that the whereabouts of others was unknown. After catching up, we covered a wide range of topics, including politics, career trajectories, rural–urban connections, and the relative merits of village and city life.

The men introduced politics to the conversation by informing me that they are ecstatically happy that Barack Obama was elected President of the U.S., and expressed their hope that he would do good things for Africa. I told them that I shared their feelings about Obama, but that I was also curious to hear their take on the political situation in Niger. As we spoke, President Mamadou Tandja was just ten days into his illegal third term in office, after dismantling the Supreme Court and National Assembly and holding bogus elections the previous year. The men agreed that Tandja had done a fair job as President, but that it was time for him to step down. They explained that they had no control over what would happen next and so therefore they would not worry about it. However, they also expressed hope that conflict would be avoided. Hassane explained that, "After all, peace is the most important value in Islam," to which his friends added, "*Amin*."

The men compared their life histories. All were approaching 50 years of age and had spent most of the last 30 years in Niamey and in various West African countries. All had carefully maintained ties to Kuka, particularly by regularly sending money to their parents even during times when they could barely make ends meet. Hassane migrated seasonally between Kuka and Niamey for a few years as a teen and into his early twenties. Over the next 20 years he rarely visited home, but kept in touch. During the last three rainy seasons, however, he began traveling home for weeks at a time to help out during key phases of planting and harvesting. Salisou and Aliou have followed similar paths, though they are more actively preparing to retire in Kuka than Hassane is. Salisou came home for the duration of the past few rainy seasons to resume farm work, and is spending more time in Kuka in dry seasons, as he was when we visited him, repairing mud brick homes that were damaged in previous rainy seasons. Aliou stopped coming to Niamey five years ago, and opened a modest dry goods shop in Kuka.

Hassane has typically been more committed to the city than the others, despite declining opportunities in Niamey. Until a decade ago, he operated a modestly successful dry goods and cold soda trading business seven days a week. Today, aside from occasional odd jobs, he works only one night per week selling milk and honey and other refreshments to crowds of 500 people attending public *'yan Izala* Islamist sermons in his neighborhood. Nevertheless, Hassane had built his reputation in Niamey and considered himself an urbanite. Furthermore, he has kept his two wives and their nine children in Niamey. Hassane is a devout Muslim who sees no contradiction in sending all of his children to public, secular schools because he believes French education will allow them more opportunities in modern Niger than he had. In contrast, Ibrahim and Aliou moved their wives and younger children from Niamey to Kuka.

I asked this group of middle-aged men to compare the merits of the village and the city in light of their current life plans. They all shared a love of Kuka, identifying it as a place of family, friendly neighbors, and community. They emphasized that, unlike the city, there is no need to pay for rent or food in Kuka, and that there is no stench from open sewers and festering trash heaps. Aliou mentioned, "Niamey has grown too large, we enjoy the peace and quiet here." The problem with Kuka, they concurred, is that there is almost no work during the dry season. Aliou explained, "If we could make a living solely through farming, we never would have left home." Hassane added, "But it made no sense for us to stay here with no money when we were young, strong, and ambitious." Salisou explained that the region had grown progressively drier over his lifetime, leading to increasingly frequent famines, "When my father was a child 100 years ago we had forests and many lakes dotted the region, but the one we visited today is the last permanent one that I know about, and as you can see we have few trees except for those that we have planted in the village." He added that local people from several villages fished in this lake and shared irrigation pumps to create year-round vegetable gardens, and wondered aloud what would happen if it dried up. In contrast, they highlighted the economic advantages of Niamey. Hassane explained that the city has much more work and that it is possible to establish relationships there with rich people who are willing to share their money. Salisou added, "A few Kuka men even become rich in Niamey, as you know." Several men interjected that this was counterbalanced by the expensive and rising cost of rent and food. Moctar agreed, and reminded me, "Chaibou, you know that much of the year there are more people from Kuka in Niamey than there are here, and that many of us will never live at home again. But we have managed to reconstruct our Kuka community in Niamey."

Before leaving, dozens of people greeted us, wished us a safe journey to Niamey, and invited us to return. Baso gave Sara Beth large sacks of beans and peanuts as parting gifts. We did our best to thank her and all of our hosts for their gracious hospitality. Hassane, Sara Beth, and I secured a ride in a truck back to the bus station in Dogondoutchi, and said farewell to Salisou, Aliou, Moctar, and the crowd of men, women,

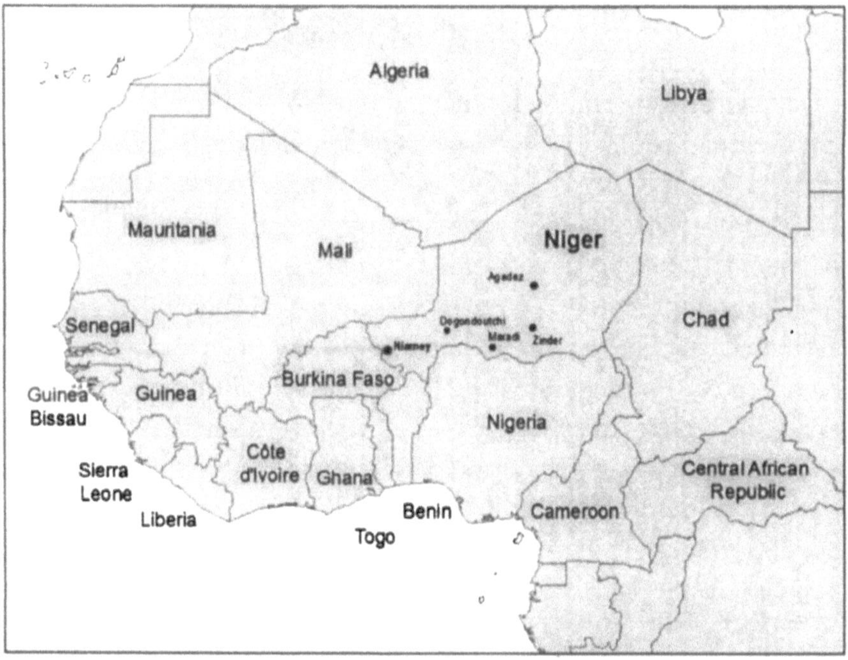

Figure 1.1 Map of Niger, created by Sara Beth Keough.

and children gathered with us by the side of the road. We faced another chaotic crunch to board the bus in Dogondoutchi, and had to sit separately. A group of tired students from Chad en route to Niamey who had already been on busses for a day and a half filled the seats between us. As I reflected on our trip, I realized that I had encountered several significant key issues, namely, hospitality, solidarity, joy, and dignity; migration, diaspora, and urban—rural connections; Islam, careers, conversation, new technologies, and economic decline. The remaining chapters of this book elaborate on these issues and their importance in the lives of contemporary Hausa in Niamey.

Structural Violence, Suffering, and Surviving with Dignity

This book explores three key interconnected themes—structural violence, suffering, and surviving with dignity—through examining the lived experiences of first and second-generation migrant Hausa men in

Niamey over the past two decades in the current neoliberal moment. Colonialism, state mismanagement, structural adjustment, and global neoliberalism have inflicted structural violence on Nigeriens by denying them human and particularly socioeconomic rights and relegating them to a status at—or very near—the bottom of the UN Human Development Index in each year of the past decade (Alidou 2005:11-14; Loftsdottir 2008:26; Masquelier 2000; Stoller 2002:17; UNHDP 2012). As a result of structural violence, most Hausa of Niamey suffer grinding and intractable poverty that has intensified over the past two decades. Suffering is a recurrent and expected condition; it is the normal condition. The central goal of the book is to explain the material (migration and informal economy work) and symbolic (meaning-making) strategies that Hausa individuals and communities have deployed in their struggles not only to literally survive in the face of economic austerity on the outer periphery of the global economy, but also to survive with dignity.

Hausa men's struggles lead to differential outcomes. Some fail and slide into anomie, isolation, depression, and even insanity. However, the fact that the majority succeeds—that is, they are surviving with dignity—is the most interesting and compelling aspect of Hausa life in Niamey. Despite daunting challenges, many Hausa men—like Hassane and his friends—find strength and patience in their humble devotion to Islam, cherish their vibrant sociability and gracious hospitality, deeply value extraordinary conversational virtuosity and knowledge, deploy humor in complex transcendent, defensive, and self-critical ways, perpetuate a sense of hope and optimism for the future, articulate their own modernities, and strive relentlessly to feel connected to the modern world at large. Indeed, for many Hausa of Niamey, "*Rashin sani ya hi duhu dare*" ("Ignorance is darker than the night"), because even a pauper can lead a life of profound intellectual and social satisfaction. *Surviving with Dignity* explains this extraordinary achievement, highlighting the remarkable resilience and subtle resistance of Hausa to annihilation by global forces and a small local elite.

My assertion that many Hausa of Niamey live fulfilling lives of dignity and joy does not avoid the "structural violence" of the neoliberal world order that has disconnected them and left them with difficult daily struggles to survive. Cultural relativism regarding dire poverty is untenable, in that it functions as a "smokescreen or apology for...structural violence" (Farmer 2003:26). Extreme poverty created by socioeconomic injustice constitutes an unacceptable assault on human dignity. Their remarkable strength does not negate the reality of the socioeconomic injustices they face. Their dire poverty in a world of plenty is unacceptable even when they handle it gracefully.

Suffering is multidimensional, complex, and difficult to study. Hausa men are suffering, even though they are committed to enduring it without complaint and even though many manage to enjoy life. Comparative measures—such as the United Nations Human Development Index—offer a basic starting point for understanding Nigeriens' difficult struggles to survive; "But the experience of suffering, it's often noted, is not effectively captured by statistics or graphs" (Farmer 2003:31). I emphasize that the lived experience of suffering must also be represented by the ways that people comment on and try to make sense of their lives. Furthermore, I regard suffering as more than the deep subjective pain of afflicted individuals, following the influential work of anthropologist Arthur Kleinman (Kleinman 1996; Kleinman, Das, and Lock 1997). Suffering is also social. "Social suffering," according to Kleinman (1996:2) refers to "collective and individual human suffering associated with life conditions shaped by powerful social forces." These powerful social forces inflict what Farmer (2003:40) calls "structural violence," because "such suffering is 'structured' by historically given (and often economically driven) processes and forces that conspire...to constrain agency." Suffering is social in that it entails "transpersonal engagement with pain and misery in social relationships" that becomes part of the collective memory and consciousness of people assaulted by structural violence (Kleinman et al. 1997:318). Suffering also has a social dimension because global and local social institutions categorize forms of suffering as objects of intervention to which they respond or deny relief; "Thereby social institutions, through their policies and programs, frequently deepen certain forms of social suffering and become obstacles to their alleviation. Structural adjustment policies of the International

Monetary Fund and the World Bank, which have deepened poverty in Africa, are a case in point" (Kleinman et al. 1997:319).

Suffering in Niamey takes physical forms, such as endemic hunger, illness, and short life spans. Suffering also has cognitive and affective dimensions. I focus on the latter without ignoring the former, and the fact that they are often inextricably linked. Symbolic and psychosocial suffering is expressed through a sense of meaninglessness, bitterness, depression, spitefulness, fear, anger, jealousy, and frustration. Farmer (2003:26) argues that for many reasons, "The silence of the poor is conditioned. To describe it as stoic...is not to be wrong, but rather runs the risk of missing the great eloquence beneath the silence." Hausa people have enormous capacities for patience in the face of virtually any difficult circumstance. Hausa men never cry, whether they have lost a loved one, their home, or their job. They poke fun at men from around the world who cry over what to them seem like trivial matters such as a divorce or losing a World Cup football game. However, this does not mean that Hausa have no feelings or emotions. Farmer (2003:26) suggests that one of the key tasks of the anthropologist is to "scratch at this surface silence to trigger that painful eloquence." I have often left this "second silence" undisturbed out of respect, but through years of fieldwork I also gained access to "painful eloquence" that takes many forms, and which I describe in more detail in later chapters.

In the face of declining economic opportunities and increasing structural violence over the past two decades, increasing numbers of Hausa men express a creeping sense of abjection, dejection, and desperation. They articulate their suffering and frustration regarding poverty and inequality in various ways, including political-economic analysis, climactic arguments, and self-criticism. In a typical conversation, Youssoufou Garba, a key participant in my research over 20 years, explained, "We are actually a rich country with many resources, especially uranium, but also petroleum and gold, but the population does not benefit, most Nigeriens continue to suffer in relentless poverty," highlighting frustrations shared by millions of Nigeriens. His brother responded,

> We are poor but when we talk we insult rich people. We discuss how they use robbery to get rich, and corruption in the ministries. They steal a lot of money to become rich. Currently, they are investigating certain personalities associated with Tandja. They stole a lot of money: $100 billion. They become very, very rich. Those working in the ministries have luxury cars and villas and huge salaries. Even now there is too much injustice. Poor people are very angry.

Their mutual friend added, "Even during the transition period, the government continued to steal money to become rich. This is a very bad disease we have in Africa." Another member of their *hira* group agreed with these assessments, but suggested that these problems could be alleviated by a more favorable climate, "The main problem in the Sahel is the weather. The rains start early and then stop. It is very bad for farming." Shifting climate patterns and global heating are, of course, a form of structural violence since they are caused by activities in the core countries of the global economy.

Hausa men's frustration is also articulated through the increasingly widespread feeling that morality is being lost. This sentiment is found through the accelerating circulation of rumors about nefarious, occult get-rich-quick schemes that Hausa men use to make sense of widening economic disparities, and in daily discussions about the perceived rise in prostitution, petty crime and banditry, vagrancy and glue sniffing, individualism and selfishness, and the commoditization of social relationships. "Today, chasing money drives people crazy," one unemployed man poignantly stated.

In January 2010, Niaméens closely followed media reports of the tragic earthquake in Haiti. One man's question, posed to his *hira* ("conversation") group mates, seemed to be on the minds of many, "Why does God punish poor black people?" Two decades ago, Hausa men in Niamey neither posed such questions nor did they blame themselves for their suffering. Today, some Hausa argue that their own poverty and suffering is deserved, that it is divine punishment for their lack of morality. An important example of this inward-looking perspective is the assessment that violence in Niamey is no longer perpetrated exclusively by foreigners as in the past, but rather by Nigeriens against themselves. As Youssoufou explained to me in 2010,

> Many big African cities are very violent. Niamey is becoming violent, too. Everything is changing now. It is nothing compared to Lagos or Abidjan, but for us it is becoming really violent. Religion [Islam] makes us afraid to make mistakes such as being violent. Niamey is small compared to Cairo, Lagos, Abidjan, or Johannesburg. But bandits here try to imitate big city violence. Recently they started using machine guns.

This book explains what it means to be a dignified Hausa man in the face of abject poverty, pressure, and uncertainty. Moreover, I marshal evidence to demonstrate that many Hausa men in Niamey are indeed surviving with dignity. Dignity means many different things. Dignity involves the proper performance of culturally defined modes of self-presentation. Dignity is also about deeply held personal feelings, self-esteem, and valuing the inherent worth of the individual. Dignified Hausa men do not blame themselves for their poverty. Dignity thus entails many things at once: social skills, an emotion, and strategies for alleviating suffering.

Hausa men demonstrate dignity by handling difficulties gracefully, by never losing their cool or patience, and by keeping face, for example, by never crying, or by cultivating an attitude described thusly by Hassane, "We must laugh or we will cry." In a similar vein, the Guinean writer Williams Sassine, in his interview with Manthia Diawara (1998:53), explains that, "If we do not learn to laugh we will die—we will commit suicide." Hausa men's dignity, however, involves more than stoicism or fatalism. Most Hausa men of Niamey are neither paralyzed by fatalism nor do most simply wish that their lives would improve. Rather, bolstered by strong faith and broad social connections, they actively work to improve their standard of living and to find meaning in their lives. For example, millions of Hausa have left the country in the last 20 years seeking to improve their life chances or that of their families, including many who knowingly risk their lives in the process, particularly those who embark on perilous journeys across the Sahara. Furthermore, dignified

Hausa men experience and demonstrate joy, humor and laughter, serious discussion and debate, and a profound sense that their lives have meaning. They find dignity in constructing their own modernities and by seeking understanding of the complexity of global and local contexts in which they live. Many Hausa of Niamey conceive of enduring suffering with dignity as a potentially character-building process that can lead to spiritual growth and moral achievement. They demonstrate the power of suffering together in solidarity.

One day while sitting on street corner benches sipping coffee with Youssoufou, a particularly obese man lumbered by us. Youssoufou laughed while explaining to me, "fat men cannot fast: that guy would not be able to go more than three or four hours during Ramadan without food!" Fatness is seen as symbolic of wealth in Niger, as only a few people of means can afford to become fat. For the masses of thin Nigeriens, like Youssoufou, fatness and by extension wealth, are also associated with decadence, greed, and moral weakness. In contrast, thinness is seen as symbolic of suffering with moral strength and dignity.

It might seem like Hausa have neither nothing to laugh about at all nor anything worth discussing other than their own suffering in poverty. Nevertheless, laughter fills the streets of Niamey. Most Hausa of Niamey celebrate life—from everyday routines to the births of children and New Year's Eve parties—rather that wallowing in misery or succumbing to defeatism. Many men claim that they have to laugh to keep from crying, but this is not the whole story. They have crafted lives of profound joy, and sense of purpose and meaning.

Anthropologist William F. S. Miles (2008:12), in reflecting on the grinding poverty in rural Hausa communities he has studied since the 1970s, similarly emphasizes the Hausa zest for living,

> Yet for all these grim realities, there is a sense of solidarity and purpose, an exuberance that pulses throughout the rural Hausa village. In Haiti, which is statistically better off than Nigeria and Niger (its GDP per capita is more than that of both countries combined), the local term that encapsulates the struggle for existence is *misère*. That is a defeatist mind frame that you rarely encounter in Hausaland.

In her autobiographical ethnographic novel, *Still Waters in Niger*, Kathleen Hill (1999) also ponders Hausa strength in the midst of hardship. Hill (1999:60), though she does not directly pose the question to anyone, wonders,

> But how do people go on waking to the call to prayer, spooning out the *tuwo*, calling their greetings back and forth all day long; how does Matameye [a largely Hausa town in South Central Niger] get from one day to another, with the children dying behind its walls, beneath its *pagnes*?...Why doesn't it raise its fist against the sky, collapse in despair, lie down in the sand and never get up?

Her daughter, who works in a clinic with malnourished and starving children, answers her mother's unspoken question, "You know... Matameye is a bountiful place. There's an overflow of something here, whatever it is that keeps us all afloat. I suppose you could call it a lot of things: energy, humor, generosity. But the word I use myself...is joy" (Hill 1999:60-61). Indeed, the exuberant *joie de vivre* of many Hausa of Niamey almost obscures their tenuous hold on survival.

As I paused to greet him on New Year's Eve 2009 at his roadside *kilishi* ("beef jerky") stand, Aliou, a 50-year-old Hausa man from Maradi who has spent the last 25 years in Niamey and is another long-time friend, spontaneously declared to me, "We have everything of value here—*hira*, religion, friendship, peace (a man can sleep on the road without being disturbed)—except for money." His seemingly simple summation is actually quite profound, as I believe it articulates the prevailing ethos among Hausa communities of Niamey. He volunteered this statement, explaining that he wants me to inform the world that while Hausa cultural modernity—which in his view draws on "traditional" values such as articulate speech, non-violence, and male social interaction that is appropriate within Islam—is dignified and worthy of global respect, Hausa people unjustly suffer intractable poverty and are cut off from economic modernity. Hausa want the purported fruits of globalization—economic security, consumer goods, and health care. They want to participate in the world as full global citizens. In recent years, dozens of other Hausa men in Niamey have also requested this of me.

"Modernities" refers to the ways that people reflect and act upon globalization processes in their quest to make sense of the world and their place it. According to Hodgson (2001:12), "modernities…are processes with histories. As such they are produced, reproduced, contested, and transformed through the ideas and practices of people operating under shifting structures of constraint and opportunity." *Surviving with Dignity* shows that globalization and modernity "are inherently gendered and that gender is a crucial site of intersection between the 'inside' and the 'outisde'" (Grosz-Ngaté 1997:8). This book focuses on Hausa men's experiences, while recognizing that "the multivalent processes and projects of Modernity provide important sites for the negotiation and experience of gender relations" (Hodgson 2001:9).

In sum, *Surviving with Dignity* does not simplistically celebrate the cultural creativity of Nigeriens outside of the context of the grim material conditions they face (cf. Verrips and Meyer 2008:163, Weiss 2009:238). I reject tired old racist stereotypes about "cultures of poverty" or simple-minded Africans who can be happy with nothing but their stories by highlighting the ways Nigerien Hausa actively articulate meaning, and their sense of rights, security, and social justice in daily life in a very hard place to live.

Appreciating structural violence, suffering, and surviving with dignity in Hausa lived experience in Niamey over the past 20 years requires a broad historical context that considers global, national, and local processes. This book begins, in Chapter 2, by reviewing the history of Niamey, concentrating on the crucial roles played by Hausa migrants in its development and expansion. Then, it examines the key—and in some cases, revolutionary—demographic, economic, political, and technological transformations in Niamey of the past two decades. Chapter 3 focuses on migration as a core adaptive strategy for dealing with poverty, highlighting the important roles played by Hausa communities in Niamey in the maintenance and ongoing creation of the global Hausa diaspora. Chapters 4 and 5 address the central aim of the book by emphasizing the symbolic strategies Hausa use as they strive to survive with dignity.

I analyze the ways Hausa survive, establish communities, build fulfilling social lives, and articulate a wide range of alternative modernities in unique ways on the ground in Niamey through Islam, social networks, popular culture, and the convergence of these social concerns in informal street corner *hira* groups—the most important institution of public culture in Niamey. It also examines the recent emergence and proliferation of formal men's *fada* ("conversation") and women's *foyandi* ("conversation") groups, and their important roles in building solidarity and promoting community development. Chapter 6 considers the links and the divides between the first generation Hausa migrants I met some 20 years ago, and the youth who were born and reared and are now coming of age in Niamey. The Conclusion summarizes the core themes of the book, and discusses the uncertain futures for Hausa of Niamey. In sum, *Surviving with Dignity* offers a longitudinal depiction of the ways Hausa navigate complex, multiple states of continuous liminality, betwixt and between: inclusion and exclusion, home and away, tradition and modernity, joy and pain, surviving and dying, dignity and suffering. The remainder of this introduction outlines the dramatic changes experienced by Hausa of Niamey over the past two decades, describes my research methodology and perspectives, and briefly discusses the fluidity of Hausa ethno-linguistic identity.

No Condition Is Permanent: Hausa Communities in Niamey and Beyond, 1988-2010

By way of Anglophone Nigeria, "No Condition is Permanent" is one of a relatively few English language proverbs used in the vernacular argot and on bumper stickers in Francophone Niger. It is trite or simplistic on the surface, but like all good proverbs it communicates many layers of meaning. It typically refers to the rapidly changing fortunes of individuals. Some use it as a warning to resist gloating, complacency, and taking success for granted as rich people can be pauperized in an instant. Poor men and women employ it as a source of solace, perseverance, and hope. Many people use it more broadly in reference to sweeping global and local social, political, and economic change. *Surviving with Dignity* documents how Hausa in Niamey draw on the polysemic and timeless qualities of this famous proverb to negotiate and comment on confounding transformations.

Many of the contemporary realities described in my visit to Hassane's village were unimaginable in 1988 when I began my research. Four radical transformations since then—and the complex interplay between them—are particularly salient: the tripling of Niamey's population, gradual economic decline and deepening poverty, the transition from autocracy to democracy, and information and communication revolutions. This book highlights the ways by which Hausa individuals and communities have adapted to, engaged with, and strived to make sense of these challenging vortexes of extraordinary change from 1988 to 2010.

First, Niamey's population—about half of whom are Hausa—grew from 400,000 in 1988 to 1.3 million in 2010, as a result of accelerating rural exodus and the first large generation of children born and reared in Niamey. Very few of the Hausa I encountered in Niamey in 1988 were born there. Most were seasonal or recently settled migrants. Tens of thousands of Niamey's young people today—like Hassane's children—have made only brief visits, if any, to their parents' home villages or towns.

Niamey attracts migrants from all regions and ethnic groups of Niger. Niamey's neighborhoods are ethnically integrated, but they are segregated by class. The ethnic demography of Niamey more or less mirrors that of Niger as a whole and "includes the Hausa (50 percent), the Zarma-Songhay (22.8 percent), Fulani (Fulbe) 10.4 percent, Kanuri (8.5 percent), Tuareg (3 percent) and Tubu (0.5 percent)…[and]…a small host of ethnic [Azawagh-Arabs, Gurmance, Buduma] minorities" (Alidou 2005:11). However, as Alidou (2005:11) emphasizes, "These categories and figures totally ignore the reality of *brassage*," or the cultural and ethnic blending that is so prevalent in Niger. In addition, at least 40,000 foreigners—including West Africans representing many ethnic groups, European (particularly French) expatriates, Western aid workers employed by the full gamut of international NGOs, personnel of dozens of foreign embassies, Lebanese businessmen, and most recently, Chinese capitalists, engineers, and construction workers—add to Niamey's diversity.

Second, many of the middle-aged generation of Hausa in Niamey, born primarily in rural Niger, had a brief taste of modestly improving conditions after they arrived in Niamey during the 1980s before enduring downward social mobility ever since. (Hassane is an example of this.) Most of the current Hausa generation 20 years of age and younger in Niamey were born in Niamey, and have known only severe economic crisis and insecurity. Nothing underscores the severity of Nigeriens' predicament more vividly than the fact that there are roughly as many Nigeriens living outside of the country as within it.

Third, Niger's unstable but gradual democratization project began in 1991. Before then, journeys to Dogondoutchi were typically delayed by about ten police checkpoints. We faced only two checkpoints in 2010, travelling far more comfortably in a bus rather than the ever-popular bush taxis that were the only option for most travel in Niger just a decade ago. Prior to 1991, the state exercised monopoly control over the media, providing one radio station, one newspaper, and one television station. Today Niaméens enjoy more than a dozen local private radio stations, a dozen independent newspapers, and five private television stations, and have exponentially expanded access to international radio, television, and video culture. In the late 1980s, Hausa in Niamey cautiously avoided discussing local and international political topics. Today these are common themes of conversational analysis.

Fourth, extraordinary technological developments—the Internet and cell phones—in the midst of Niger's democracy era have further contributed to the exponential acceleration of global and local information and communication exchange. The Internet arrived in the late 1990s. Mobile phone service was introduced in Niamey and other urban areas of Niger in October 2001, and has incrementally spread to offer coverage in most parts of the country with significant population concentrations. The popularity of cell phones for everyday communication rapidly superseded that of computers. By December 2010, cell phones had become part of the taken-for-granted routines of about one-half of Niaméens, and dramatically changed the nature of the Hausa diaspora—that is, the nature of separation and being away from home.

First and second-generation Hausa migrants in Niamey express very different experiential perspectives on these four dramatic transformations. Middle-aged and elderly Hausa of Niamey—who typically grew up as rural farmers in a single-party state with relatively limited access to tools of spatiotemporal compression—have creatively contributed and adapted to remarkable social change. In contrast, the youth of Niamey (about 50% of Nigeriens are aged 14 years or younger) are growing up on urban streets, openly criticizing politicians, channel surfing with friends, and fumbling through the oversized pockets of their global hip hop jeans for their cell phones. They cannot imagine themselves living the life of the previous generation.

These historical transformations did not unfold in a vacuum. The key demographic, economic, political, and techno-cultural changes of Niamey are generated, in large measure, by central contemporary globalization patterns, policies, and forces including: urbanization, the intensification of global structures and processes that create and maintain inequality through global neoliberal policies such as structural adjustment, the worldwide wave of democratization that followed the collapse of the USSR, and corporate-driven technological inventions—the Internet and cell phones—that have accelerated transnational flows of money, ideas, and information. No place on earth is free of these challenges, threats, and opportunities. However, globalization is not a process that leads to simple economic, political, and cultural homogeneity (Appaduruai 1990; Cooper 1999; Beynon and Dunkerley 2000; Inda and Rosaldo 2008). Even though African individuals, communities, and nations sometimes devise similar strategies for dealing with shared constraints of globalization, Africans acting with agency develop unique adaptations, policies, and worldviews, and experience their lives in particular ways in particular places. Global processes always manifest themselves within local contexts, and can only be fully understood by examining local places.

Niamey is more than merely the setting for this book. Niamey, a seriously understudied city, is a window through which the key social processes of contemporary times can be understood—complementing the influential work of Sassen (2007) on "the global city." The Hausa men's lived experiences that are documented in this book could only have unfolded in the ways that they have in Niamey. For Nigeriens in general and Nigerien Hausa in particular, Niamey serves functions analogous to the roles played by the lungs in a human body. Niamey constantly inhales and exhales people, and—just how the biological processes of inhalation and exhalation transform relatively simple oxygen into more complex carbon dioxide—Niamey transforms relatively inexperienced "traditionalists" into sophisticated cosmopolitans. Upon arrival in Niamey with thousands of other migrants, Nigeriens are exposed to swirling and fluid cultures, languages, and alternative—and sometimes conflicting—articulations of modernity. Niamey lures migrants from throughout Niger while simultaneously Niamey serves as the primary place where Nigeriens plot their international travels as well as their returns home. Movement and transience define the ethos of Niamey. It is a city of dreamers and dreams—both realized and frustrated. Sharing the crowded space of Niamey, Nigeriens feel alternatively invigorated and liberated, or overwhelmed by pressures to remit money to family at home and the commoditization of social relationships in the city, and choked by the dust of the harmattan, tens of thousands of wood cooking fires, and the fumes of open sewers. Likewise, the human lungs breathe life into the body while struggling to filter out toxins that inhibit its smooth functioning. Niamey *is* the lungs of Niger.

Modernist Ethnographic Praxis

My research strategies were carefully designed to elucidate the complex ways by which Hausa experience and negotiate personal careers and worldviews or articulations of modernity in their efforts to survive with dignity. My methodologies were developed by considering Hausa experiences of migration, building diasporic communities, and urban life in the context of broad global and national economic and political processes of transformation over the past two decades. My analysis is informed by and aims to contribute to a wide range of social theory regarding globalization, modernity, and urban anthropology, especially pertaining to Africa in general, and to the literature on Hausa culture, migration, and diaspora in particular. My eclectic approach is also inspired by ethnographic styles employed in several recent innovative studies in Niger and Africa (Alidou 2005, Ferguson 1999, Piot 1999, Stoller 2002, Weiss 2009). *Surviving with Dignity* features a mélange of careful ethnographic description (particularly of detailed biographies and extended vignettes) and theoretical analysis, to offer a narrative linking individual experience and globalization.

I focus on Hausa men because as a male scholar I had limited opportunities to meet with women in highly gender-segregated Niger. However, I recognize the importance understanding gendered life experiences of both men and women. Therefore, I draw on scholarship by women that centers on Hausa women, particularly that of Alidou (2005), Cooper (1997, 1999, 2003) and Masquelier (1996, 2000, 2001, 2007, 2009), to supplement my own data regarding the lives of women. I note that most key recent studies of Hausa of Niger have focused on women, which provides me an opportunity to make a special contribution to the literature with my focus on men.

I rely heavily on participant observation in everyday life activities, especially *hira* groups, as well as shopping in city markets, visiting acquaintances both close and distant, and dining nightly with close friends. I have closely followed the trajectories of eight *hira* groups and participated in dozens of others. Over the years, I have carried out more than 400 structured interviews, and recorded three life histories. Four key participants emerged and have remained very helpful and influential to my work over the entire time frame of my research. They helped me construct interview questions, included me in their daily routines, introduced me to broad networks of friends and families, and spent countless hours sharing their analyses of changing local and global cultures. All told, I came to know the career paths of roughly 200 Hausa of Niamey very well; that is, multi-dimensionally through shared time in *hira*, interviews, and important life events over multiple years. Through cultivating close relationships, I have also been invited to attend and participate in the full range of ceremonials in Niamey, including healing rituals, all annual religious and secular holidays, and rites of passage (naming ceremonies, weddings, and funerals).

Through snowball sampling and happenstance, but informed by key participants and local social scientists, I took care to find people who represent all of the major regions and Hausa subgroups of Niger, live and socialize in diverse neighborhoods scattered throughout Niamey, and work primarily in typical occupations—small-scale trading, service jobs such as tea and coffee preparation and selling, manual labor such as water carrying, and trades such as tailoring, repairing, butchering, and leather working. Participants also include a few men and women employed in either high paying or high prestige occupations, such as large-scale merchants, Muslim clerics, and civil servants.

My modernist perspective confronts the challenges of understanding and representing the temporal, the spatial, and disparate voices (Marcus 1998:57-78). *Surviving with Dignity* draws from 13 fieldwork periods in Niamey from 1988 to 2010. This experience has allowed me to develop long-term relationships, chronicle the adaptations of the urban pioneers who first settled in Niamey en masse, witness the coming of age of the first significant generation of Hausa born in Niamey, and gain a diachronic perspective on broad social change.

The highly mobile and fluid nature of Hausa communities required a flexible, innovative, persistent, and patient approach. While many of the Hausa in Niamey that I have come to know are more-or-less settled migrants, most are constantly on the move through circular migrations—intra-national and international—that are both seasonal and last for years. Thus, I regularly meet new people, have lost contact with many others, and often re-unite with friends and acquaintances after years without communication.

Because I regard Niamey both as a place and as a nexus of global processes, I employ a multi-sited perspective drawing from many visits during the past two decades to communities in the Hausa heartland of southern Niger and northern Nigeria as well as diaspora communities in Ghana, Senegal, New York City, Saginaw and Ypsilanti, Michigan, and cyberspace. My migrancy as a researcher has been critical to my understanding of migrants and "traveling cultures" (Clifford 1997). I consider particular individuals' careers and identity performances in multiple places. I accompanied many of the Hausa I met in Niamey on visits to their hometowns. I met others in various diaspora communities before reuniting with them in Niamey.

I emphasize a dialogical approach that highlights the voices of the people, since my goal is to reveal everyday, lived experiences and understandings. Each chapter is named after and considers important popular proverbs that speak to core themes of the book. My ethnographic perspective emphasizes local knowledge and how it is generated by linguistic, symbolic, and material exchange among Hausa in Niamey and between participants and me.

My ethnographic representation emphasizes discourse and dialogue in "naturalistic," quotidian settings, though I also draw from interview material. In particular, I highlight the central themes of analysis and performances in *hira* groups. I was always upfront about my anthropological research, and I was almost always welcomed with remarkably gracious hospitality. I spent hundreds of hours in particular *hira* groups. Like many other participants, I sometimes sat quietly listening to discussions without speaking for long periods of time. However, I had more power than most participants to orient discussions toward topics of interest to me. Furthermore, since participants were sharing their lives with me, I freely shared the details of my life and culture with them. I, nevertheless, strive to be as unobtrusive as possible by refraining from tape recording conversations. I often jotted down a few key words on small scraps of paper. Like Stoller, who followed Desjarlais's strategy, I would go back to my apartment following *hira* sessions "to write down the gist of these exchanges," creating closely paraphrased or "quasi-verbatim accounts" of particularly salient moments (Desjarlais 1997:40-41 cited in Stoller 2002:x).

Connections made through *hira* often lead to informative and complex exchanges. In 1998, for example, Abdoulwahab—a man who was not one of my very closest acquaintances—invited me to serve as the *abokin ango* ("best man") for his wedding. I was very surprised. I asked Abdoulwahab why he did not want one of his lifelong, best friends—some of whom I knew and named—to fill this role. He evaded my question, and emphatically stated that he would be very happy if I accepted. I told him that I wanted a couple of days to consider it. The more I thought about it I came to the conclusion that Abdoulwahab calculated that he would earn prestige from having a relatively wealthy, Hausa-speaking, white, American university professor perform the important *abokin ango* duties. On the one hand, I reckoned that I was being used; on the other hand, I also felt that it could be Aboulwahab's and his *hira* group's way of showing that I was indeed a member of the group. After careful reflection I accepted Abdoulwahab's offer because I decided that this presented an ideal opportunity for me to gain intimate knowledge of the entire marriage process from a position of social honor, including meetings with male elders of Abdoulwahab's family, a series of negotiations with the family of his wife-to-be, and the ritual and social celebrations of the wedding day. This exchange, it seemed, offered mutual benefit.

In addition to the ethnographic complexities of representing the temporal, the spatial, and disparate voices, I faced many difficult practical, emotional, and ethical challenges in the course of my fieldwork. Since I believe that purely positivistic, "objective" data collection in anthropology is unrealistic, often dishonest, distancing, and dehumanizing, I allowed myself room to make deep friendships. This was rewarding both professionally and personally, but it also presented many hurdles and restricted me in some ways. Indeed, this is part of the risks involved in the practice of ethnography.

I believe that many Hausa of Niamey regard me, in a sense, as one of them—that my absence is felt when I don't show up as an *abokin hira* ("conversation partner"). Miles (2008:151; emphasis in original), in his important longitudinal work on the Niger-Nigeria borderlands, describes a similar experience,

> Here in Hausaland there exists a communal bonding that I have not experienced in other places...This bonding is based not on shared class or education or religion. Its core is rather a constant and unqualified embrace of the human condition, actualized through the repeated miracle of "seeing and being seen," and undergirded by an abiding belief in the dignity of life. I fully appreciate the irony: I am so thoroughly accepted here *precisely* because I am an anomaly... I have

earned my friendships in Hausaland...[on]...the basis of...mastery of the Hausa language.

I have long been moved and fascinated by the close relationships that I have forged with people so different from myself through my ability to speak Hausa.

In contrast, in some cases I misread or overestimated several individuals' personal closeness to me, discovering much to my consternation that their primary objective was to extract money from me. Cognitively this was understandable to me, but nevertheless my feelings were hurt. This also caused me to question—sometimes perhaps unfairly—others' motives. I also, at times, inadvertently, deeply offended friends by associating with their enemies. Some people asked me to choose sides in rivalries, leaving me with difficult choices that entailed losing or severely straining at least one connection. I felt awkward and thus discontinued contact and interviews with certain people with whom I became very close.

The ethical dilemma that I found most troubling involves the intersection of positionality, power, and history. I make a living hanging out on street corners with the poorest people in the world. I have found it difficult, at times, to reconcile my scholarly and professional gains with the suffering of so many of the participants in my study. In a way, I represent the rich, white, secular humanist, colonizer, while my participants represent the poor, black, Muslim colonized. It is impossible for me to meet most requests made of me for money, medicine, and visas to the U.S. I humbly hope that I am repaying the gracious hospitality of my hosts in some small measure by sensitively and accurately sharing their joys and pain with the world.

The Fluidity of Hausa Ethno-linguistic Identity

Nigerien *brassage* is intensified in Niamey, as it is the one place in the country where so many different (yet similar) people meet and live together. The Hausa case is particularly revealing and important given their massive presence in Niamey. Following the definition articulated by most Nigeriens I have met over more than two decades (many whose families have only in the last century "become" Hausa), I use the ethnic term "Hausa" very loosely, so as to include any person who speaks Hausa well and who in some contexts announces, or responds affirmatively when questioned, that he is Hausa.[1] Being Muslim can "close the deal," but being a non-Muslim is not a "deal-breaker;" indeed, "'Hausaness'… has always been a multiple and shifting identity" (Alidou 2005:8). For example, the Aderwa are both Hausa and Tuareg, the Damagarawa a blend of Hausa and Kanuri, the Hausa-Fulani peoples ruled much of Northern Nigeria and parts of Southern Niger for the past two centuries, and the Mawri are a new ethnic group consisting of Hausa and Zarma elements (Alidou 2005:8). For many Niaméens, particularly the youth who increasingly are born in inter-ethnic, polyethnic, polygynous families, ethnicity is only one source—and often not the most important one—of affiliation and identity construction, alongside Islam, francophonie, nationalism, and global hip-hop.

Youssoufou Garba's life history illustrates the sorts of complex situational identities that many Nigeriens negotiate. Youssoufou moved to Niamey with his family in 1970 as a teen, and has lived there ever since—save for a five year period when he worked abroad, including 18 months in the U.S. He speaks Hausa with most of his friends in Niamey who typically regard him as Hausa. Yet his father is Kanuri, and his mother is Fulbe, both from Damagaram in South Central Niger. When Youssoufou periodically visits his father's kin, he speaks Kanuri, he is welcomed as Kanuri, and he is Kanuri. When he visits his mother's kin, he speaks Fulfulde, he is welcomed as Fulbe, and he is Fulbe. In addition, Youssoufou speaks Zarma fluently as do almost all Nigeriens who have spent any significant time in Niamey. He also speaks and reads English and French fluently—and uses the latter exclusively with many people in his social network and to read translations of the Qur'an.

Niamey consists of overlapping ethno-linguistic communities. Niaméens on average speak three to four languages. Virtually all speak Hausa and Zarma, while more than one-third speak French. Niaméen's multilingualism is often demonstrated within single sentences that combine words from three or more languages. Youssoufou's flexibility is thus representative; "the average Nigerien, especially in the urban and in the semi-urban space, embodies the many-in-one and, depending on context, can be simultaneously Tuareg, Fulani, Hausa, Zarma, and so forth without implying a crisis or a confusion of identities" (Alidou 2005:9). At times Nigeriens cannot even identify their own ethnic origins (Alidou 2009).

Some Niaméens are chauvinistic regarding ethnic identities and boundaries, however they are becoming fewer and further between. Complex inter-ethnic joking relationships have been used for centuries to mitigate tensions and build harmony, and these remain popular. Twenty years ago, street corner conversation groups were largely segregated by ethnicity (however slippery), and almost entirely segregated by gender. Today's conversation groups—including informal *hira* and formal men's *fada* and formal women's *foyandi* groups—though often consisting of a core of migrants hailing from the same hometown, are almost always multi-ethnic.

Recognizing the fluidity and ambiguity of what it means to be Hausa, as well as the drawbacks to focusing on one ethnic group given pervasive and accelerating *brassage* in Niamey, I assert that the Hausa case is nevertheless useful for understanding the urban, transnational, and global adaptations and modernity-making processes that I explore. Furthermore, I cannot turn back the clock. I sought out Hausa people and almost all of the participants in my research self-identify as Hausa.

— 2 —

Niamey Yesterday and Today

Duniya mai halin d'an mangoro:
Life can surprise you if you don't take care

Putting Niamey on the Map

Niamey emerges from the sparsely populated Sahel as an oasis. Its rolling hills layered with rich golden brown hard-packed dirt, sand, and gnarled thorny trees and bushes meander down to the lush gardens on the banks of the winding and magnificent Niger River. The scent of the river permeates the air, as do the wood and charcoal cooking fires in virtually every compound. Almost all architecture (from multi-story buildings to the humblest abodes) and roads are built with local earth or cement of similar hue, blending practically and artfully into the physical terrain.

The sun and searing dry heat are relentless and daunting almost year round. In Niamey there are, nevertheless, just enough gardens and standing pools of water to create year-round habitat for malarial mosquitoes. When the heat is not oppressive, wind blown sand and dust fill the sky and lead to meningitis epidemics and other pulmonary ailments. Rain brings temporary relief when it falls sporadically from July to October, but squalls transform the streets of Niamey into ankle-deep cesspools.

In defiance of this stark yet subtly beautiful and enormously challenging context, Niaméens proudly press on to construct lives of profound meaning and exuberant joy. Today Niamey is a remarkably vibrant, lively, sociable place featuring a distinctive cosmopolitan, public, outdoor culture. Niamey is simultaneously very calm, peaceful, and relaxed. People are always out and about but very few are in a hurry, except those with motorized vehicles. Most Niaméens saunter through the city in a slow, dignified manner that I call "the Niamey shuffle." The flowing white and blue gowns of men and the bold, bright, multicolored print fabrics worn gracefully by women create striking visual contrasts with the sun-baked brown environment while enriching and beautifying the visual landscape of the city. The most common jobs—in trading, services, and manual labor—take place outdoors. Most prayers are performed in open-air mosques and in sidewalk gatherings that sometimes expand to block off roads. Most men participate several hours daily in street corner conversation groups.

On their daily walking circuits of 10 kilometers for work (or looking for work), prayer, and social networking, Niaméens make eye contact with thousands of others, and see tens of thousands of fellow urbanites, and engage in short and long conversations with dozens of friends and acquaintances. In bustling central districts they encounter high rise buildings occupied by banks and government offices; luxury retail shops; French, Italian, Chinese, Lebanese, Nigerien, Senegalese, and Ghanaian restaurants; mosques; hotels, bars, nightclubs and casinos; markets, ambulatory hawkers and traders occupying any available space; biomedical, Chinese, and traditional pharmacies; international standard sports stadiums, the national museum, and cultural centers; enormous billboards featuring advertisements of four cell phone companies, Western Union, and Maggi (a Nestlé condiment); and streets clogged with motorcycles and bicycles made in China, white Toyota taxis, BMW and Mercedes luxury sedans and SUVs, hand-drawn and animal-driven carts, and people—men and women, old and young, from the fabulously wealthy to desperately poor beggars, of all of Niger's ethnic groups and from around the world.

Wide avenues and roundabouts funnel traffic into the mazes of narrow dirt roads of residential neighborhoods. Here the streets are less crowded, the pace is slower: In many ways it feels like rural Niger. Residents typically know their neighbors and greet dozens of them daily. Most live in modest, densely crowded, rectangular compounds constructed of handmade mud bricks or industrially manufactured cement, but a few ostentatious grand villas, round thatch dwellings, cardboard and plastic shacks are found interspersed in almost every district. Regardless of scale, high walls that face streets and provide residents with a measure of privacy surround most homes. Slightly more than half (54.4%) of residences have electricity while just over one-third (38.3%)

has running water (Hamidou and Ali 2005:7). Almost every block has a small mosque or designated prayer space. Men gather in shady spots along the roads to sell roasted meat, serve coffee and tea, and for conversation. Women—carrying loads atop their heads and babies strapped to their backs—are constantly coming and going to the market, to work, or to visit family and friends. The Muslim call to prayer and public preaching—amplified with electric loudspeakers—shares the "soundscape" with radios blaring the deep bass beats of the rap music preferred by youth today. And children are omnipresent—the median age in Niger is 14 (République du Niger 2010:1)—filling the air with laughter that belies the squalor in which they typically live.

—

Niamey has attracted little scholarly attention, probably for a variety of reasons. It was not an indigenous city historically, and remained small until very recently. The continuing neglect of Niamey in the literature—including the recent proliferation of scholarship on African cities—is more mysterious given its expansion and unique sociocultural development from 30,000 residents in 1960 to a city of 1.3 million today. Perhaps the fact that "urban cultural processes are the most difficult to study" (Coquery-Vidrovitch 2005:15) has deterred some researchers. I have encountered some scholars and many travelers of all sorts who express an aversion to Niamey on the grounds that it lacks the "authentic," "real," or "traditional" culture of rural Niger. Others complain that the in-your-face poverty of Niamey represented by thousands of beggars, glue-sniffing children, open sewers, and sprawling ubiquitous trash heaps together with its heat and congestion make the city an altogether unpleasant place relative to the less public suffering and tranquility of Nigerien village life. When I introduced the title of my paper, "In and Out of Niamey: Cosmopolitanism in the Sahel," at the annual meeting of the American Anthropological Association in 2008, several people in the audience chuckled and I overheard one man say, "I never thought I would hear those words [Niamey and Cosmopolitanism] together in the same phrase."

Whatever the reasons, only a handful of book-length studies of Niamey exist. Most are in French, including Suzanne Bernus' *Niamey:*

Population et Habitat (1962) and *Particularismes Ethnique au Milieu Urbain: L'Example de Niamey* (1969), Sidikou Hamidou's doctoral thesis, *Niamey, Étude de Geographie Socio-Urbaine* (1980), and Boureima Alpha Gado's short, but important, *Niamey: Garin Kaptan Salma (Histoire d'une Ville)* (1997). Ousseina Alidou's, *Engaging Modernity: Muslim Women and the Politics of Agency in Postcolonial Niger* (2005), is the only English language, book-length study set primarily in Niamey.

Niamey is worth studying. In this chapter, I analyze Niamey as a unique place as well as a window for understanding the key social processes of contemporary times. Niaméen peoples and cultures have adapted in distinctive ways to spectacular social change over the past century marked by Niger's accelerating integration into the modern world-system. While Niamey might not be a "global city" by some definitions, it clearly serves as Niger's most important "gateway to the global world" (Hansen 2008:4). As "one of the spaces where major macrosocial trends materialize" (Sassen 2007:100), Niamey offers a strategic site for studying the local faces of globalization.

Niamey is a place of extremes and contrasts. Inspired by Stoller's (2009) thesis articulated in his recent book *The Power of the Between*, I suggest that it is fruitful to think of Niamey as a space between the local and the global, the rural and the urban, the traditional and the modern, the fourth world and the first world, the here and the there, solidarity and impermanence, dreams and realities. That is, I am concerned with how Niaméens have navigated and attempted to reconcile these liminal spaces.

This chapter begins by sketching the history of Niamey from c. 1800 to 1988, as the settlement evolved from a collection of small villages totaling about 600 residents in 1900, became the capital of the French colony of Niger in 1926 and then the capital of independent Niger in 1960, and mushroomed to a city of 400,000 in 1988. Then, the chapter focuses on the last two decades, when Niamey's population tripled to reach 1.3 million inhabitants, the city and the nation suffered gradual economic decline and deepening poverty, the city hosted the nation's transition from autocracy to democracy, and the arrival of the internet and cell phones generated information and communication revolutions. While emphasizing how these profound demographic, economic, political, and technological transformations play out at the local level in Niamey, their relations to current global patterns, connections, and disconnections are explained. The key roles that Hausa migrants played in Niamey's phenomenal growth, particularly after about 1970 and since Hausa became a slight majority in the city after about 1980, are highlighted.

As discussed in the Introduction, my intent is not to just look at these changes in Niamey as such, rather my primary goals involve explaining how Hausa individuals and communities (including first and second generation migrants) have adapted to, engaged with, and strived to make sense of challenging vortexes of extraordinary change from 1988 to 2010. Thus, this chapter sets the context for the development of subsequent chapters.

From Fishing Village to French Colonial Capital, c. 1800-1960

Diverse peoples have shaped Niamey's unique identity and character through time. Gado begins *Niamey: Garin Kaptan Salma (Histoire d'une Ville)* by presenting evidence that Niamey is not solely a French colonial creation. From the 18th century (if not earlier) until the turn of the 20th century Niamey consisted of a collection of small fishing villages—Goudel, Saga, Lamordé, Bitinkidji, and Gamkalé—situated alongside the banks of the Niger River and inhabited by Zarma, Songhay, Mawri, and Fulani peoples (Gado 1997:9,14). These villages later became neighborhoods of the city of Niamey. The countryside surrounding Niamey was (and remains) primarily Zarma country, with some interspersion of Fulani and Tuareg.

Several stories recount the founding of the settlement and the origin of its name (Gado 1997:14). For example, a Mawri story explains that after leaving Neini, their island home on the Niger river, the original Mawri settlers first rested and then settled on the river bank near a huge tree known as a "*Nia*." The tree had magical qualities, and though long since gone, its site on the current location of Hotel Gawaye is still remembered. In one Zarma version of the story that emphasizes domesticity,

Zarma people established Niamey at the "*Nya-me*" ("mother's riverbank") where an old woman regularly collected water. In another variation, some explain that the name "Niamey" is derived from the Zarma expression, "*wa-gnama-ne*," meaning, "settle here." According to this version, a man named Kalley from the village of Sargane in Zarmaganda used this expression to order his followers to camp in a particular spot where a little later the first legal cases of Niamey were arbitrated. Idrissa (2009:162) argues that, "the name Niamey...derives from a Zarma-Songhay word meaning (what else?) 'intermingling.' This name has become over the decades a self-fulfilling prophecy, as other populations taken into the colony and republic of Niger sent in waves of settlers to the capital."

Gawaye, Kalley, Foulan-Kwara, Maourey, and Zongo predate the arrival of Europeans and are the oldest neighborhoods in Niamey (Gado 1997:15). Two brothers from Gao founded Gawaye. The aforementioned Kalley established Kalley. Fulani people formed a new neighborhood within Kalley named Foulan-Kwara. Mawrey was first settled by Mawri people from Neini and later from Matankari and other villages to the east of Niamey. Zongo was established as a foreigner's quarter inhabited primarily by merchants.

Niamey was "not mentioned in any of the accounts of [European] exploration in the 19th century" (Decalo 1989:171), including those of Barth, Monteil, and Toutée (Gado 1997:13). It did not occupy the attention of the French empire until 1898, when the Hourst military reconnaissance mission first recorded the name "Niamey" (Gado 1997:23). The Voulet-Chanoine Mission of 1899 brutally swept eastward across French West Africa, committing horrific atrocities including killing scores of people in Niamey and massacring thousands of people in nearby Sansanne Haoussa and Birnin Konni along the way. Niamey had only 600 residents in 1900 (Gado 1997:27). In the "Mission l'Enfant," French forces took control of Niamey in 1901 and established a military supply post. Later that year, two French officers, Commandant Gouraud and Capitaine Salaman, recognizing the advantageous position of Niamey, proposed that Niamey replace Sorbon as the Chef-Lieu de Cercle du Djerma ("Capital City of the Zarma Administrative Zone") and to expand the zone. According to Gado (1997:25, my translation),

> Only the name of Capitaine Salaman remains in the memory of Niaméens. Still today the old people of Niamey continue to recount to the young the life and times of Capitaine Salaman, considered the founding father of the city, with slogans in Hausa and Zarma: *Nyamey garin kaptan salma* (Niamey: Capitaine Salaman's city) and *kwaara ga kaanu kwaara koyo si deeni* (life is agreeable because the leader does not scold us).

Niamey became the Chef-Lieu de Cercle du Djerma in 1903, and then lost it briefly to Dosso in 1904. In 1905, not only did Niamey regain its status as the Chef-Lieu de Cercle, it was chosen as the provisional capital of the Territoire Militaire du Niger, which then spread from Timbuktu and Gao (in today's Mali) all the way to N'Guigmi near Lake Chad. By 1905 Niamey's population had risen to 1,800 inhabitants, including its first few Hausa residents. These early Hausa migrant traders and laborers settled in the Zongo neighborhood. All major cities in West Africa have a Zongo, a foreigner's quarter that hosts migrant merchants in particular. During the first few years of colonization, migrants from Sudan, Senegal, Northern Nigeria, and Southern Niger settled in Zongo, and by 1906 its first chief, *Sarkin Zongo*, was turbaned. Salaman encouraged migration to the provisional capital through policies such as abolishing taxes and forced labor in the city, distributing free parcels of land, and the establishing major markets while imposing elevated taxes on markets in neighboring towns, and by 1911 the population of Niamey reached 3,000 persons.

Meanwhile debates raged among French colonial officers regarding the "final conquest" of West Africa, borders between military territories such as Mali and Niger, and the selection of permanent capitals. Colonel Venel's arguments won the day in Niger, and Zinder—an ancient city and the seat of an important sultanate situated 900 kilometers to the east—was made the Chef-Lieu du Territoire Militaire du Niger in 1911. It retained this status until 1922, when Niger became a French colony. Zinder then served as the capital of Niger until 1926.

In 1926 the French moved the capital of Niger from Zinder to Niamey for several reasons. First, the French had decided to deal primarily with the Zarma in the administration of the territory of Niger. Second, Zinder lacks an abundant water supply, whereas Niamey rests on the banks of the Niger River. Third, the French and British were still in conflict over territorial and economic issues, and Zinder was too close to Nigeria, by then heavily under British influence. At the same time Zinder was too far from Cotonou, the nearest seaport under French control.

Since 1900, Niamey has been defined by migration. That is, much of its growth has been due to migration. In fact through its last 110 years of history, first and second generation immigrants have constituted a substantial majority of the population. Most migrants up until about 1930 came from Western Niger. Subsequently Niamey gradually became a magnet for Nigeriens throughout the country. Some came to take jobs for the colonists or as traders. However, massive exodus of rural populations in the wake of drought and famine were central factors in Niamey's rapid growth (Gado 1997:35). These included horrific famines of 1901-1903, 1913-1915, 1931-1932, and 1954, all of which are named in local languages. Thus, Niamey has long served as a refuge, a last resort for survival, but also as a place to begin a new life.

The first major influxes to the settlement followed the establishment of Niamey as Niger's capital in 1926 when it had 3,142 inhabitants. That year a major fire ravaged the thatch dwellings that dominated the settlement that clung to the riverbank, and surviving residents were ordered to rebuild with mud bricks. Another major fire badly damaged the town in 1935. This time authorities relocated all neighborhoods—except for Gawaye and its fishermen—away from the river and to higher ground on the plateau to the north. The loss of life due to the two fires was counterbalanced by the influx of famine-refugee migrants in 1931-1932, and Niamey grew to 8,152 residents by 1940. France used Nigeriens and other West Africans for their own purposes in World War II, conscripting thousands of young men. Colonial policies shifted after 1945, and Nigeriens—now recognized as citizens—began shaping the city and their future in new ways by establishing political parties, electing Djibo Bakary as the first Nigerien mayor of Niamey in 1956, and gradually assuming more administrative responsibility. New neighborhoods—Boukouki, Lacouroussou, Balafon, Banizambou, Sabongari, Nouveau

Marché—were added, and Niamey expanded to include 33,816 citizens at the time of independence from France in 1960. This growth transformed Niamey from a village to a town, and set the stage for far more massive growth in the subsequent 50 years.

Postcolonial Niamey, 1960-1988

Niger's peaceful transition from colony to independent state in 1960 contributed to postcolonial Niamey's spectacular growth. Hamani Diori of the Parti Progressiste Nigérien (PPN) was chosen as Niger's first President. He led a repressive civilian regime constituting Niger's 1st République until 1974. While he was busy building a new nation and a new capital, Diori maintained close ties with France (that have continued in various strategic, financial, and cultural ways until the present). In an unusual twist reflecting the unpredictability of flows of culture in modernity, Presidents Diori of Niger, Habib Bourguiba of Tunisia, and Léopold Sédar Senghor of Senegal, acting together in 1960, were the first to propose the establishment of a formal institution to consolidate and promote international Francophonie cultural and linguistic identity, solidarity, dialogue, and cooperation among newly independent nations wishing to pursue continuing relations with France. Today, the Organisation Internationale de la Francophonie (OIF) includes 56 member nations, and Niger remains an important player.

The population grew from 33,816 inhabitants in 1960, to 56,997 in 1967, to 135,388 in 1975, to 242,873 in 1977, and to 399,846 in 1988 (Gado 1997:50). Furthermore, the percentage of people living in urban areas of Niger increased nearly three-fold from 6.22 percent to 15.35 percent from 1960-1988 (Motcho 1992:2). Niamey also underwent rapid geographic expansion and became much more densely populated. Niamey covered 1,367 hectares in 1970; 2,347 hectares in 1977; and 4,844 hectares in 1988 (Motcho 1992:3). Population densities in 1975 were estimated at 62 inhabitants per hectare; in 1983 at 73.5 inhabitants per hectare; and in 1988 at 82.2 inhabitants per hectare, including some central neighborhoods with as many as 400 inhabitants per hectare (Motcho 1992:3).

Several factors led to the exponential expansion of Niamey from 1960 to 1988. Niamey's new status as the capital of independent Niger opened up civil service jobs to all Nigeriens, though Zarma secured the top posts and continued to dominate Nigerien politics until 1991. By 1980, 14 percent of Niaméens, or roughly 42,000 people, were government workers (Hamidou 1980:92-3). Niamey was essentially the only place in Niger where French expatriates settled. Diplomatic missions were established, and massive international humanitarian and development aid sectors were established. Peaceful conditions prevailed. Merchants were encouraged to settle. As civil servants and traders established themselves, their families and wide arrays of dependents followed them to Niamey.

Many Nigerien farmers were unable to harvest anything and many pastoralists lost their entire herds due to drought that led to famine in 1969, 1972-74, and 1984-1985, forcing tens of thousands to leave their rural homes and go to Niamey and other West African cities. The famine of 1972-1974 was the key factor in the doubling of Niamey's population in just five years. Furthermore, the poor handling of the crisis led to the downfall of Hamani Diori, who was overthrown in a *coup d'état* led by Lieutenant Colonel Seyni Kountché in 1974. Some famine-refugee migrants returned home when conditions improved, but more opted to settle more or less permanently in Niamey.

Rural to urban migration is, of course, not unique to Niger. The capitalist world economy locates capital and commodities in cities embedded in nation-states—even on the periphery of the world-system—leading to the globalization of urbanization. By the late 1980s, migration accounted for 73.2 percent of Niamey's rate of population growth (M. Cohen 1989:69). Indeed, very few of the Hausa I met in 1988 in Niamey were born there. Most were seasonal and recently settled migrants who had come from small villages and towns across Southern Niger.

Hausa migrants played a central role in the rapid growth of Niamey from a small city of 30,000—of whom only 3,600, or 12 percent, were Hausa in 1960 (Hamidou 1980; Bernus 1969:35, Decalo 1989:165)—to a bustling West African capital of 400,000 in 1988 where Hausa were a slight majority. (Nevertheless, in 1988 I met several Hausa men who remembered a time in their lives, or their parents' lives, when they dared not go to Niamey for fear of being murdered by Zarma.) Hausa became a slight majority by about 1980, and have maintained that position up to the present as the city has grown to 1,222,066. This constitutes a highly unusual transformation given that Niamey rests some 150 kilometers west of the westernmost boundaries of "traditional Hausaland."[1]

The changing demographics of 20th century Niamey in turn influenced new residential patterns in general and in Hausa communities in particular. Waves of immigrants from across Niger settled wherever they could find affordable lodging in Niamey such that by as early as 1980 (and ever since) the city has been thoroughly residentially integrated by ethnicity. The Hausa production of locality in Niamey has not emphasized the cultural and moral distinctiveness of Hausa ethnicity, as is often the case in more distant Hausa diaspora communities (cf. Cohen 1969; Pellow 1999; Yamba 1995). This is due to their substantial numbers, the shared devotion to Islam that unites Nigeriens across ethnic boundaries, and Nigerien *brassage*.

Hausa have made Niamey "a home away from home," though most Hausa do not consider Niamey to be a "Hausa city." They take pride in their role in the growth of Niamey and value particular aspects of the quality of life there. In referring to Niamey, many Hausa simply say that they are "Thanking Allah that they have food, water, and decent clothing," and indicate that these basic necessities are not always available in their home villages. Many other Hausa express appreciation for the "cosmopolitan civilization" of Niamey. Finally, most Hausa deeply value the *kwancen hankali* ("peace") in Niamey, especially as they have become more aware of *tashin hankali* ("war and violence") in some West Africa cities through mass media or their own travels.

The period between the mid 1970s until late 1980s was a time of relative hope and prosperity. Uranium was discovered in the Sahara of Niger in 1957, and after commercial mining began in 1971 Niger quickly became one of the world's leading producers. Areva, a France-based multinational mining corporation, secured the lion's share of the profits, but enough remained for a modest uranium boom in Niger as a whole and in Niamey in particular. Much of the current skyline of Niamey was constructed during this period with uranium revenues.

Many rural migrants saw their standard of living rise modestly after settling in Niamey. As they established themselves in the late 1980s, they gave birth to the first major generation who would be reared in Niamey. But this period ended with uncertainty. Niger had to accept its first Structural Adjustment Program in 1985, jointly organized by the International Monetary Fund and the World Bank. Tensions emerged over the inequitable distribution of the uranium largesse, and then the global market for uranium plummeted. When Kountché died in 1987, Ali Saibou, his Chief of Staff, took over and embarked on nebulous plans for a transition to civilian rule.

Niamey, Globalization, and the Neoliberal World Order, 1988-2010

Niamey is the modern capital and nerve center of Niger, the center of the nation's economic, political, administrative, and cultural activities. Today, the city has about six times the population of Niger's second biggest cities, Maradi and Zinder, which have about 200,000 residents each. Niamey rests atop two plateaus reaching over 200 meters in altitude and is bisected by the Niger River. Only the Kennedy Bridge—named after U.S. President John F. Kennedy—spanned the river from 1970 until 2010 when a China-based firm completed construction of Le Deuxième Pont ("The Second Bridge"). Most activities are concentrated in and at least three-quarters of the population lives on the northeast bank, *rive gauche* ("left bank"), of a wide bend in the Niger River. The southwest bank, *rive droite* ("right bank"), is home to Université Abdou Moumouni and residential neighborhoods. The Communauté Urbaine de Niamey ("Urban Community of Niamey") is headed by a mayor and municipal council and includes five urban communes, divided into 44 districts and 99 *quartiers*—each with its own *Chef* and elected board.

Niamey is simultaneously the most and least representative place of Niger. Because it includes all ethnic groups of Niger, roughly in proportion to their overall national representation, Niamey is, in a sense, highly representative of Nigerien cultures. This same reality also makes

Niamey unique and has led to the development of distinct, hybridized, modern urban culture. Niamey also stands apart from the rest of the country due to its size and political influence. Furthermore, the city is far more acutely and directly affected by global trends, policies, and technologies than other places in Niger.

Niamey and Niger have been deeply implicated in regionalism and globalization for a very long time. The arrival of Islam one thousand years ago from North and West Africa, the rise of various powerful West African empires that ruled substantial territories, and the trans-Saharan and trans-Atlantic trades in people and goods followed by French conquest and colonial rule have linked Niger—for better and worse—to the modern world-system. The sweeping changes in Niamey over the past 22 years can only be understood in the context of contemporary globalization, involving the accelerating transnational movement of people, money, goods and technologies, mass media, and ideas. Specific global trends, policies, and technologies have played key roles in the four crucial changes that Niamey has experienced over the last two decades, namely, urban growth, deepening poverty, democratization, and information and communication revolutions. Nevertheless, Hausa of Niamey have negotiated and tried to make sense of the challenges of globalization in particular ways.

Tripling of the Population of Niamey

During my last day in Niamey in January 2010, Hassane reminisced on the particular roadside in the Abidjan neighborhood where he and streams of other migrants from Kuka have been meeting for conversation, work, and prayer for 30 years. As we sat in shade looking out at the bustling public square, rimmed by a dozen compounds, two small mosques, and several traders, and where youth playing football competed for access to the street with cars, motorcycles, and camels, Hassane reflected, "when I arrived in 1985 there were only two compounds here, and just there in the center of the square where the *jardin d'enfants* ("kindergarten") is now, the bush, trees, and cattle began." Today several kilometers of densely crowded neighborhoods lie between Abidjan and the northerly direction to which Hassane was pointing.

Niamey's population tripled from 400,000 in 1988 to 1.3 million in 2010. It grew to 500,000 in 1995, and to 700,000 by 1997 (Gado 1997:50). By 2005, Niamey had 859,000 residents (Hamidou and Ali 2005:96), and reached 1,222,066 in 2010 (République du Niger 2010:1). New neighborhoods regularly appear and Niamey's geographic footprint expanded five-fold from 1988 to 2010, from 4,844 hectares to 23,930 hectares, and became even more densely populated. Furthermore, the percentage of people living in urban areas of Niger rose from 15.35 percent in 1988 (Motcho 1992:2) to 20.4 percent in 2010 (République du Niger 2010:1). Niamey is poised for another massive growth spurt. In a report for the Ministère de la Population et de l'Action Sociale, Hamidou and Ali (2005:96) project that Niamey's population will rise to 2.1 million in 2020, to 3.7 million in 2030, before reaching 11.4 million in 2050.

Migration from throughout Niger remained a major factor in Niamey's growth during this time, just as it had in the past. In particular, Hausa migrants continued to view Niamey as a popular destination for temporary and long-term or permanent settlement, contributing to the maintenance of Hausa as a slight majority in the city. Internal growth, spurred by the world's highest fertility rates of 7.1 (République du Niger 2010:1), and the emergence of the first large generation born and reared in Niamey also contributed to its expansion.

Niaméens capitalized on this multi-ethnic "population bubble" to further intensify cultural and linguistic exchange and construction of cosmopolitan urban cultural formations. From 1988 to the present, Niamey remained, arguably, the safest capital city in West Africa and even today violent crime is rare. However, under-funded urban infrastructure has not kept pace with growth, and declining economic conditions increasingly thwart the ambitions of residents. While Niamey has expanded, increasing numbers of Nigeriens are migrating out of the country, typically using Niamey as a steppingstone. The vast majority of Niaméens of prime migratory age (15-45 years) want to leave the country, for a few years at least.

Deepening Poverty and Expanding Inequality: Structural Adjustment, Devaluation, Decentralization, and Inflation

While few Hausa migrants in Niamey were truly prospering in the late 1980s and early 1990s, almost all had improved their standard of living by coming to live and work in Niamey, and while most were cautiously optimistic many entertained high hopes for future success. In *Engaging Modernity: Muslim Women and the Politics of Agency in Postcolonial Niger*, Ousseina Alidou (2005:13) succinctly described what they could not see coming, "by the mid-1980s, the collapse of the uranium market, followed by the IMF's Structural Adjustment Programs (SAPs), and shortly after by the devaluation of the currency of francophone Africa, the CFA [by 100% in 1994], plunged the country into a devastating economic depression with severe sociopolitical and other consequences."

The five SAPs imposed on Niger by the IMF from the mid-1980s to the present have constituted the primary instruments of the assault of neoliberal economic globalization against Niger (Dearden 2012). While they have helped state balances of payments and perhaps contributed to macro-level growth earning Niger praise from the IMF, SAPs have had devastating consequences for the vast majority of Nigeriens, and the poorest have been the most adversely affected. SAPs have emphasized cuts in state spending for health, education, staple food subsidies, and other vital social services. After SAPs led to skyrocketing prices of Western biomedical pharmaceuticals and hospital admissions, many entrepreneurs have stepped in to provide less expensive mobile, often single dose, biomedical sales or resuscitated the popularity of traditional herbal healing. Furthermore, the proliferation of Chinese herbal medicine in the last four years offers another relatively inexpensive option for Niaméens. However, all of these practices, at times, involve dangerous side effects due to misapplications. Furthermore, SAPs eliminated scholarships and increased school fees, "leading to student and teacher strikes...and school closures over the years, juvenile delinquency, prostitution, and high unemployment rates" (Alidou 2005:13). SAPs also contributed to inflation, particularly in the cost of staple foods, adding to the suffering and decline in standards of living (see table 2.1).

Table 2.1 Inflation of Staple Foods and Rent in Niamey, 1994-2009

Product	*1994-95*	*2009-10*
Millet (100 kg)	9,500-10,000 CFA	20,000-22,000 CFA
Corn (100 kg)	7,000-7,500 CFA	18,500-20,000 CFA
Sorghum (100 kg)	7,000-7,500 CFA	15,000-17,000 CFA
Beans (1 tiya or bowl)	200-250 CFA	750-900 CFA
Peanut Oil (1 liter)	350-400 CFA	1,200 CFA
Palm Oil (1 liter)	225-250 CFA	550-600 CFA
Sugar (1 kg of cubes)	200-225 CFA	650-700 CFA
Sugar (1 kg of powder)	150-175 CFA	325-375 CFA
Milk (480 g can)	250-275 CFA	500 CFA
Milk (1 kg can)	425-450 CFA	1,000 CFA
Rice (1 kg of 2nd quality)	175-200 CFA	500-550 CFA
Baguette (1 loaf)	75 CFA	200 CFA
Rent (36 sq. meter apt.)	5,000 CFA/Month	15,000-20,000 CFA/Month

SAPs have pushed the privatization of state industries, leading to the selling of key nationalized sectors and mass layoffs of Nigerien workers. Meanwhile a small but influential and growing minority of Nigeriens was positioned to benefit from economic liberalization, leading to sharply expanding inequality between social classes and resentments about it—as is always the case with SAPs in particular and global capitalism in general. Indeed, the Global Gini Index (2010) rated Niger as one of the 20 most unequal countries of the world in terms of distribution of family income.

During most of the years of the last decade, Niger was rated at the very bottom of the United Nations Human Development index. The IMF deserves blame for many of Niger's woes. The withdrawal of state support for health, education, and employment in the world's least developed nation as required by SAPs constitutes a neocolonial attack and global crime against Nigeriens. But the IMF alone did not cause Niger's plight. A corrupt ruling elite and their merchant allies, the continuing power of the military, the meddling of France, predatory multinational mining corporations, and a difficult environment that has long been prone to drought and appears to be getting worse as a result of recent global heating have all played a part.

All of this defines what it means to be on the outer periphery of the neoliberal world order. In his innovative and influential new book, *Global Shadows: Africa in the Neoliberal World Order*, anthropologist James Ferguson (2006:14) contests conventional globalization theories and challenges the idea that globalization promotes economic, political, and cultural convergence between Africa and the rest of the world, arguing that "the networks of political and economic connection do indeed 'span the globe,' as is often claimed, but they do not cover it. Instead they hop over (rather than flowing through) the territories inhabited by the vast majority of the African population." "Where capital has been coming to Africa at all, it has largely been concentrated in spatially segregated, socially 'thin' mineral-extraction enclaves" (Ferguson 2006:38), such as the uranium mines of Niger. He emphasizes that (2006:21),

> "Globalization" has not brought a global consumer culture within the reach of most Africans, and still less has it imposed a homogenization of lifestyles with a global norm. Rather, it has brought an increasingly acute awareness of the semiotic and material goods of the global rich, even as economic pauperization and the loss of faith in the promises of development have made the chances of actually attaining such goods seem more remote than ever.

Globalization processes efficiently create "forms of exclusion, marginalization, and disconnection" (Ferguson 2006:41).

In sum, the middle-aged generation of Hausa, born primarily in rural Niger, had a brief taste of modestly improving conditions upon their arrival in Niamey in the mid 1980s before enduring downward social mobility ever since. Most of the current generation who were born in Niamey in the last 20 years has known only severe economic crisis and insecurity.

From Autocracy to Democracy and Freedom of Expression

In 1987 President Ali Saibou created the Mouvement National pour une Société de Développement (MNSD), and won Presidential elections in 1989 as the only candidate since opposition parties were banned. Nigeriens grew increasingly frustrated by Saibou's broken promises. Conflict between the government and Tuareg regarding the distribution of uranium revenues and environmental contamination ignited a rebellion in the north in 1990 that lasted until 1995. Meanwhile, students and union workers participated in a wave of strikes and demonstrations calling for democratic reforms and protesting against SAPs. Democratization occurred partly as a result of local initiative regarding local problems, and Saibou's willingness to step aside. However, it did not happen in a vacuum. It came in the wake of the fall of the Berlin Wall and the end of the so-called Cold War. Wealthy western democracies pushed democracy as a condition of aid and a wave of political transitions occurred around the world. In several Francophone African nations—Niger, Benin, Congo, Mali, Togo, and Côte d'Ivoire—the democratization process unfolded through the National Conference phenomenon.

Niger's National Conference, held in and broadcast live from Niamey in 1991, set the stage for Niger's unstable but gradual transition to a democratic, multiparty system of government; "among the many recommendations that emerged...the most salient were demands for political pluralism, the institution of a democratic government, and the decentralization of political power" (Alzouma 2009:488). In 1991, Saibou's government was suspended and an interim government under Amadou Cheifou was formed.

The first free multi-party elections were held in 1993, and Mahamane Ousmane of the MNSD was elected President. Rivalries within the coalition of nine political parties brought the government to a standstill. Colonel Ibrahim Baré Mainassara used this as justification for a military coup d'état in January 1996. In July 1996 Baré won highly fraudulent presidential elections. In April 1999, the chief of his own presidential guard, Major Daouda Mallam Wanke, staged a military coup that involved the assassination of Baré. Later that year, in July 1999,

Mamadou Tandja of the MNSD was elected president. Despite some heavy criticism, Tandja successfully ran for the presidency in 2004, and he was elected for another five-year term. In 2005, as part of Niger's fifth SAP, Tandja was pressured into imposing a 19% VAT on basic food products. The timing was disastrous, given the drought and locust invasions that led to a poor harvest in 2004 and contributed to famine in 2005. To make matters worse, Tandja publically denied the famine existed. Nigerien and international journalists who dared to cover the crisis and called it a "famine" were arrested and silenced. Many Nigeriens were outraged by his callousness, and argued that Tandja missed an important opportunity to explain the structural causes of recurring malnutrition and famine to the world. In a bitter irony, as a military officer Tandja aided Kountché's takeover in 1974 in response to Diori's inability to alleviate famine.

Tandja regained some popularity after overseeing Niamey's hosting of the 5th Jeux de la Francophonie in December 2005, and even more among some Nigeriens after negotiating a series of deals for expanded uranium and petroleum mining with an increased proportion of revenues staying in Niger, the construction of Niger's first refinery, and the building of a new bridge over the Niger River by a Chinese firm. But recurring disputes over access to the profits and jobs in the uranium industry and associated issues of governance sparked a new civil conflict between the state and two Tuareg groups as well as other Nigeriens in 2007 that lasted until 2009 but still simmers. By 2008, and within sight of the end of his mandate on December 22, 2009, Tandja began speaking of himself as the indispensable leader of Niger, who deserved to rewrite the Constitution to extend his term. Despite stiff opposition, Tandja stubbornly pressed forward in 2009, dismissing the National Assembly and the Supreme Court, and held a bogus referendum—boycotted by the opposition—that enabled him to stay on, in principle, for three additional years. On February 18, 2010, he was overthrown in a coup led by Squadron Commander Salou Djibo, who claimed to be rescuing Niger's democracy.

Niaméens have exuberantly seized novel opportunities for freedom of expression afforded by political liberalization. Prior to 1991, the Nigerien state exercised monopoly control over the media, providing one radio station, one newspaper, and one television station. Despite periodic repression, Nigeriens have enjoyed a relatively free media ever since the conclusion of the Conference Nationale. Most media production and access has been and remains based in Niamey. Later chapters will examine in more detail how the ways that Hausa and other Niaméens critically produce and consume mass media to make sense of the world and their place in it are crucial to their efforts to survive with dignity. Niaméens have gained unprecedented and accelerating access to local and global news, opinion, and entertainment. Meanwhile, democratization has allowed a disparate range of voices to publically articulate their interests, including Islamic groups, women, youth, "rebels," and others with grievances against the state or alternative visions of Niger.

Independent radio stations and newspapers emerged within months of the lifting of restrictions, and private television channels a few years later. Many have come and gone over the past 20 years, but some have been in operation for most of this period. Today Niaméens enjoy access to more than a dozen local private radio stations, a dozen independent newspapers, and five private television stations. (Many of these are now accessible on Nigerien websites.) State-sponsored media survive and remain very popular in all three markets. For example, *Le Sahel*, the daily state paper, has by far the largest readership in Niamey.

Furthermore, access to international radio, television, and video culture has expanded exponentially during the past two decades. Many Niaméens appreciate the daily Hausa language news programs broadcast by the British Broadcasting Corporation (BBC), Voice of America (VOA), Deutchewelle, and Radio France Internationale (RFI). Many Francophone Niaméens listen to RFI almost exclusively. Hausa men of Niamey over the age of 15 years typically listen to two hours of international radio daily, often getting news from multiple national perspectives (such as British, French, German, Nigerian). Indeed, they are on average far more critically informed from multiple perspectives about leading contemporary global news stories than Americans are. Wealthy Niaméens own satellite dishes enabling them to access scores of global channels. Niamey's markets now overflow with cassette tapes, videos, and DVDs, primarily of Islamic sermons, music of various styles from around the world, Bollywood, Hollywood, and Nollywood Hausa language films, and Asian martial arts films. In fact the rise of video culture has meant the extinction of Niamey's cinema culture. One by one all of Niamey's cinemas have closed operations in recent years.

Given Niger's poverty and 29% literacy rate "Radio is the most effective medium when it comes to overcoming spatial and illiteracy constraints in communication" (Alzouma 2009:490). Niaméens enjoy universal access to radio, including the two-thirds who are non-literate and the poorest of the poor, because many programs are broadcast in local languages, and radios are as cheap as $3 each, portable, and easily shared in groups. Luc Peter and Stephanie Barbey's 2007 documentary film, *Magic Radio*, explores Niger's vibrant radio culture. Their brief summary of it, "The FM Revolution in Niger: Radio's Impact on Capacity Development" (2007), written together with Ajay Tejasvi, begins by observing that "the radio is always on in Niger, constantly educating, entertaining, and helping people keep a check on power," and asserting that "the radio has become the main means of communication" (Peter, Barbey, and Tejasvi 2007:1). Private radio stations, most of which are based in Niamey, cover "a multitude of topics—politics and governance, marital and social councils, health and beauty tips, cooking recipes, public awareness campaigns, music and entertainment...[making them]...available to ordinary people through radio" (2007:1). They include issues and news that are censored or avoided by state media. Private and state radio have also been valuable to "capacity development" by broadcasting—in French and several local languages—educational programs, dispensing advice for farmers, traders, and consumers, and emerging as perhaps the most important source for acquiring knowledge about preventive health care, benefitting even those without access to primary health care.

Niaméens have used radios to promote civic engagement, to encourage transparent governance, to improve mutual understanding within and among communities, and to develop peer-to-peer learning and education of people of all ages. Islamic associations, youth, women, and other interest groups have seized the radio as a key medium for articulating their concerns and visions for social change. Different generations have experienced *La Révolution FM* in different ways. Many middle-aged and elderly Hausa of Niamey highly appreciate freedom of expression, but would be willing to sacrifice it for good jobs and economic security. Hausa youth of Niamey, born and reared in a time and place of vibrant free speech, cannot imagine relinquishing this right.

Information and Communication Revolutions: The Internet and Cell Phones

Twenty years ago Hausa had fairly limited access to global news, opinion, and popular culture, and much of the communication between dispersed Hausa was funneled through the physical migratory routes of men and transmitted orally in *hira* ("conversation") groups scattered across Niamey and the global Hausa diaspora. The arrival of the internet (in the 1990s) and cell phones (in 2001) in the midst of Niger's democracy era have further contributed to the exponential acceleration of global and local information and communication exchange, and "have made it possible to express previously repressed nationalist sentiments, forbidden languages, ethnic loyalties, and new identities free from the control exerted between the boundaries of the state" (Alzouma 2009:483). The Nigerien state has lost its monopoly over the media, but at various times and particularly in the past few years, has been able to restrict press and radio freedom through intimidation, arrests and imprisonments, and forced closures. However, it "has very limited technical capacity to exercise control over online activities" and "actors (particularly diasporic communities scattered around the world) who are disputing its hegemony and legitimacy," and expressing a wide range of opinion, including widespread support for Nigerien unity and peace (Alzouma 2009:493, 483).

In the late 1990s, *cybercafés* and Internet training institutes emerged and proliferated in Niamey, and by 2000, 5,000 Nigeriens were Internet users. In 2006, across the nation approximately 35,000 Nigeriens (ITU 2007, 2008 cited in Alzouma 2009:489) were using the Internet, primarily at 45 *cybercafés*, 30 of which were located in Niamey. By 2009, 80,000 Nigeriens were "netizens." Many more Nigeriens, disproportionately

Niaméens, have Internet access than these figures suggest. Alzouma (2009:490) emphasizes that these figures do not include the "thousands of Nigerien students [who] are studying outside their country, mainly in France, Nigeria, Algeria, Morocco but also in the USA, Canada, [China], and elsewhere. They are the main users of the internet in Niger." Internet access time is shared in *cybercafés* of Niamey whenever space is available. Non-literate Niaméens use proxies to send and receive e-mail. Finally, Alzouma (2009:489) argues that the impact of internet users is disproportionate to their numbers because they are "the most politically active, the most educated, is urbanised and occupies a central position when it comes to promoting and fostering change in society." Today, Hausa of Niamey use the Internet to gain unprecedented access to information and opinion, and use e-mail and Nigerien-made websites for building and solidifying transnational connections among the global Hausa and Nigerien diasporas.[2]

Mobile phone service was introduced in Niamey and other urban areas of Niger in October 2001, and has incrementally spread to offer coverage in most parts of the country with significant population concentrations. The popularity of cell phones rapidly superseded that of computers. The impact of this change cannot be overstated, "although landlines existed prior to 2001, Niger had the second lowest landline coverage in the world, with only 2 landlines per 1,000 people" (Aker 2008a:7). Numbers of cell phone subscribers have risen exponentially. In 2002 the number of cell phones surpassed the number of landlines (Aker 2008a:57). In 2004, 50,000 Nigeriens were subscribers (Aker 2008a:57). By 2006, 397,000 Nigeriens owned cell phones, nearly an eight-fold increase in just two years (Aker 2008a:57). By June 2007, 634,000 Nigeriens were cell phone subscribers. A year later, 709,000 Nigeriens owned mobile phones (Cellular-News 2008). Alzouma (2009:490), drawing from a National Statistical Institute analysis, reports that by 2009, more than 1,300,000 Nigeriens (or 20% of the population over the age of 15 years) used cell phones, while according to some estimates (Isbrandt 2009) as many as two million did.

Many more Nigeriens, particularly in Niamey, have gained access to cell phones than these gross national figures suggest. Nigeriens share cell phones just as they share other technologies, such as radios, televisions, and Internet time in *cybercafés*. In addition, entrepreneurs rent cell phones for short-term usage. Furthermore, Niaméens are four times as likely to own cell phones as other Nigeriens. By 2010, nearly half of Niaméens over 15 years of age owned cell phones. Nigeriens, particularly in cities, now also have access to more than 600 private *télécentres*—some of which are mobile.

Four companies currently operate in Niger: Celtel/Zain that controls 80 percent of the market, Telecel/Moov that controls 10 percent, SahelCom with 7 percent, and Orange with 3 percent (Cellular-News 2008). Celtel/Zain has developed the most visible marketing profile in Niamey. In late 2007, Celtel unfurled two ten meter wide by six story tall color banners on the side of the BDRN bank in downtown Niamey. No other advertisements in the city are bigger than standard-sized billboards. In addition to pictures of attractive young Nigerien men and women enjoying their cell phones, the banners display Celtel's standard slogans, "*Partager. Notre Monde.*" ("Take Part in Our World") and "*Toujours. Accessible.*" ("Always Accessible"). By January 2010, the Zain logo had replaced the state insignia on Niger's airport exit card, revealing its influence as well as the privatization of the state.

The global spread of the Internet and cell phones involves more than simple technological determinism or marketing power. In their new edited volume, *Mobile Phones: The New Talking Drums of Africa*, Brujin, Nyamnjoh, and Brinkman (2009:11) present case studies that show how cell phones are "(re-)shaping social realities in African societies, and how Africans and their societies are, in turn, shaping the technologies of communication." I follow their interest in the latter, that is, in the creative processes involved in the cultural and social appropriation of communication technology. "Technologies acquire different meanings in different contexts" (2009:12), and are used for different purposes in different contexts. Anthropologists call this "transculturation," the transformation of adopted cultural traits, resulting in new cultural forms.

Hausa in Niamey creatively employ cell phones in a variety of important ways: (1) to serve core values, (2) for local economic decision-making, (3) as important status symbols or the latest markers of modernity,

(4) to promote literacy, and (5) to strengthen and expand transnational connections and a sense of community in the global Hausa diaspora, and for securing remittances. The first four are highlighted here, and the latter is discussed in detail in the following chapter. These appropriations are separated for the sake of clarity. Many Hausa of Niamey use mobile phones for all of these purposes.

First, the preeminent value of sociability among Hausa is expressed through reciprocity and the crucial importance of regularly greeting and communicating with people in one's social network. Most phone calls placed in Niamey consist only of brief greetings that last less than one minute. Hausa in Niamey use cell phones to greet more people than they have the time to physically visit, particularly as the city has expanded. And since cell phones are shared, callers can speak with multiple people (family or conversation group friends) in one phone call. Hausa do not consider cell phone calls as a substitute for face-to-face encounters, but regard it as much better than no communication at all.

Some people can afford to make more calls and longer calls than others. Many underemployed and unemployed Hausa stretch their budgets to the limit to make as many calls as possible. Hausa of Niamey deeply appreciate their family and friends—whether nearby or in diaspora—who make the temporal and financial investment to place calls to them. This is considered preferable to text messaging or "flashing."[3] Though Hausa in Niamey are sometimes annoyed by those who only send text messages and by flashers, virtually all agree that this is far preferable to silence.

Second, several recent studies (Aker 2008a, 2008b; Hartill 2008; Worstall 2008) analyze the rapid and pervasive integration of cell phones to enhance the efficiency of decision-making behaviors of traders (especially of grains and staple foods) and consumers in Niger. Each concludes that the introduction of cell phones—which facilitate rapid flows of information across widely scattered areas—reduced price dispersion across markets benefiting both sellers and buyers. Aker (2008b:1) documents that "cell phones reduced traders' search costs by 50 percent" and that "by 2006 grain traders operating in cell phone markets searched over a greater number of markets, had more market contacts, and did more business in more markets as compared to their counterparts without cell phones." Meanwhile, cell phone use in Niger has reduced the cost of staple foods in Niger, benefiting consumers; "Between 2001 and 2006, cell phones were associated with a 3.5 percent reduction in average consumer grain prices" (Aker 2008b:2). Worstall's (2008) economic assessment of Niger concludes that, "mobile phones are therefore probably Pareto-improving: some have been made better off and none worse off, a highly desirable state of affairs."

Third, Hausa in Niamey value cell phones as status symbols. Ownership of phones is differentiating. Some people have them and some do not. Furthermore, some people own elaborate models with flip screens, video, color graphics, and other features, while most settle for very basic models. Owners—especially youth—like to be noticed so they conspicuously show off their phones even if they do not have credit in them by carrying them in their hands, constantly fidgeting with them, or by flashing on the screen often at night. In the last two years, models that include radios have appeared and grown in popularity. They give owners a purpose to always display them.

Cell phones are also used to symbolize close relationships. Women and girls expect to receive them as gifts from their husbands and boyfriends (and it is possible that this is the main way that they acquire them). Issaka, a 25-year-old bachelor, explained, "no girl in Niamey will seriously date you unless you give her a phone and constantly *chap chap* (add credit to her account)." Indeed, in Niamey—like elsewhere in the world as reported in *Human Nature* (Lycett and Dunbar 2000)—men who can afford to give away cell phones seem to enjoy advantages in attracting partners over those who do not have the means to do so.

Fourth, Hausa and other Nigeriens are using mobile phones as an adult literacy platform in informal and formal ways. Cell phone users must, at a minimum, know how to identify numbers to place calls. Using cell phones to acquire rudimentary literacy with guidance from friends and family is slow and tedious for adults, but the five-fold difference between expensive talking and cheap short message services (SMS) provides an immediate and powerful incentive for the illiterate poor to learn to text. Indeed, I know several men in their forties, who never learned the alphabet until they bought their first cell phones, that learned how to keep address books and read and compose short text greetings within two years. Recognizing their potential, public and private actors have established adult literacy training programs that use cell phones as the primary tools of instruction.[4]

Hausa of Niamey are eager to own cell phones despite the relatively exorbitant costs to purchase and use them, because they recognize their immense social and economic value. In December 2008 the prices for new, basic model phones made by major brands such as Nokia, Motorola, and Samsung began at about $55, while models produced in China could be found for about half this price. A year later, in December 2009, the price had been reduced by almost half, to about $35. Despite this deflation, $35 is still the average monthly income among Hausa of Niamey. A thriving market in used phones permits consumers to purchase functional phones for less than $10. Using a phone requires procuring recharge cards through which call time is paid for by loading a unique pin number each time one wants to add credit to an individual account. The system facilitates the sharing of cell phones because users can determine the precise cost of each call.[5] While cell phones are beyond the means of more than half of Hausa in Niamey, many people who can barely afford some of the basic necessities of everyday life make extraordinary efforts to acquire one. Many men paying $30 a month to rent apartments own $50 cell phones and spend 50 cents a day making phone calls.

Many Africans across the continent now own and use cell phones even though they are trapped in poverty. Hausa in Niamey are adapting mobile phones in multidimensional ways that are particular to their circumstances, ambitions, and needs. Cell phones have changed the lives of Hausa men in crucial ways through the manner in which they have been thoroughly integrated in everyday lived experience, including their quests to survive with dignity. Most Hausa males, especially the youth, now regard cell phones as necessities, and cannot bear to do without them since they provide new ways to stay connected with more people. It is not impossible to survive with dignity without a mobile phone, but it is even more challenging especially for a highly mobile people. They are simultaneously about conspicuous consumption, and about a desire to feel like equal participants in global techno-economic modernity. Hausa are harnessing cell phones to promote new forms of sociality and literacy education. Finally, Hausa of Niamey are using cell phones to strengthen their global diaspora—as will be seen in detail in the following chapter—fundamentally changing what it means to be physically separated from family and friends.

Postscript

Elhadj Issaka was born in Niamey in 1910 and lived there until he died in 2005. He saw it all. He remembered when it was an overgrown village, and recalled with only a hint of bitterness when French colonists conscripted him to help build its first roads without pay. Shortly after independence, he rose to prominence in Niamey's social scene by skillfully investing in rice paddies along the Niger River and served as a *Chef de Quartier* ("Neighborhood Chief"), highly respected for his skills in mediating disputes, until his death. He sent his sons and daughters to France, Canada, Morocco, and the U.S. for higher education and work. Most of them returned to establish successful professional careers in Niamey. He was amazed and impressed that I speak Hausa, as he had never met a white man who could, and preferred that I address him as "Daddy." Shortly before he died, he shared an important life lesson with me by using the popular Hausa proverb,*"Duniya mai halin d'an mangoro,"* that I have borrowed for the epigram of this chapter. This means, literally, "the world has the character of a small mango." Figuratively, it means, "Success is like eating a mango: Just when you have tasted sweetness, it slips out of your hands and into the sand," or more succinctly, " Life can surprise you if you don't take care." He explained to me that as a boy he never imagined the changes that would unfold during his life: "I saw Niamey grow from a bush settlement. I am proud to have played a small role in its transformation to a modern, cosmopolitan capital. We have seen some sweet times but many difficult times as well. Right now we are suffering, but this will pass, as it always does, God willing."

— 3 —

Niamey and the Global Hausa Diaspora

Tahiya ta hi zaman gida:
Moving is better than staying put

Revaluing Home in Transnational Migratory Circuits and Diasporic Processes

Despite the theoretical recognition of the connection between "here" and "there," the vast majority of research—on the Hausa and other African diasporas—considers how migrants establish new communities in diaspora whereas very little focuses on "original centers" and how home sites—in this case, Niamey—contribute to the formation of diasporas and are influenced by them and returning migrants. Drawing primarily from ethnographic research, this chapter aims to fill this gap by centering on social processes and people in Niamey as well as multiple diaspora outposts (Accra, Kumasi, Dakar, Saginaw and Ypsilanti, Michigan, New York City, and Amsterdam). The chapter concludes by summarizing the core characteristics of the "global Hausa diaspora," considering how it is one transnational community consisting of interpersonal connections and multiple communities that are often interlinked with other diasporas, and the skills that are needed to succeed in this diaspora.

To understand the importance of home sites, one must first understand historical trends in Hausa migration. For centuries Hausa have been famous for their skills in building long-distance trading networks. Most Hausa of Niger eke out a living through circular migration, focusing on raising millet, sorghum, and beans under difficult Sahelian conditions during three to four month rainy seasons, and on labor or trade in the informal economies of Niamey and dozens of other West African cities—many of which have long-standing disapora communities of Hausa settlers—during long dry seasons. During the past 50 years,

Hausa have creatively adapted to postcolonial conditions and global neoliberalism through accelerating rural exodus and long-term or permanent out-migration within West and North Africa and to more distant locations in Europe and North America. An impressive body of literature examines the culturally specific ways Nigerien and Nigerian Hausa experience and navigate transnational processes while establishing and maintaining communities in Ibadan, Nigeria (Cohen 1969), Accra, Ghana (Pellow 2008), Kumasi, Ghana (Schildkrout 1978), Lomé, Togo (Agier 1983), Abidjan, Côte d'Ivoire (Toure 1990), Chad (Works 1976), Morocco (Maghnia 2001), Tunisia (Jankowsky 2001), Libya (Yamba 1995), Sudan (Yamba 1995), Saudi Arabia (Yamba 1995), Paris (Thomas 2006), and New York (Stoller 2002; Youngstedt 2004a) among other places. Indeed, some evidence strongly suggests that there are at least as many Nigeriens living outside the country as within it (particularly if this includes first and second generation emigrants).

Social theorists have reached a consensus regarding a general definition of diasporas (cf. Clifford 1997:246-50, Cohen 1997, Manger and Assal 2006:12-15, Safran 1991:83-84, Sanjek 2003), that simultaneously recognizes that there are many different specific and often overlapping diasporas that are differentially constituted and experienced by impetus (e.g., trauma, trade, labor, or education), history, size (absolute and relative to host populations), class, and gender, among other social variables. The core characteristics of diasporas include: dispersal and scattering "from an original centre" (Safran 1991:83), memories and myths that often glorify the homeland, adaptations and "cultural flowering" (Cohen 1997) in tolerant host communities, difficult relationships with hosts, the development of transnational identities, and a commitment to continuing support of the homeland that serves as a basis for the "group's consciousness and solidarity" (Safran 1991:83) and inspires a return movement. Transnationalism rests at the core of the diasporic experience; "the empowering paradox of diaspora is that dwelling *here* assumes a solidarity and connection *there*" (Clifford 1997:269, emphasis in original). Thus, the dynamics of diasporas involve both roots and routes (including movements away from and back to home); that is, "unlike don't-look-back emigration, diaspora includes occasional, frequent or long-postponed returns home" (Sanjek 2003:324).

A male youth's completion of his first dry season migration away from his rural home to a city such as Niamey with a successful return home with gifts and stories before the rainy season functions as an auxiliary, preliminary rite of passage to adulthood among rural Nigerien Hausa males, for it demonstrates resolve, ambition, and the ability to secure cash in a capitalist economy, all of which are necessary to marry—or achieve manhood. Most Nigerien men (and women) are on the move or in transit (seasonally, circularly, intranationally, or internationally) most of time from the time they are about 15 years old until they are about 45. "The market is dead here so we must leave home to support our families, and ourselves" explained one young man whose view reflects the thoughts of millions of Nigeriens.

"*Neman kud'i*" ("seeking money") is almost universally the first explanation offered by Hausa for their decision to migrate. Migration is about improving life chances more than anything else. Many Hausa must leave home in order to survive. They have few choices, really, given their position as pools of "surplus labor" on the periphery of the global economy in a time of neoliberalism and structural adjustment. Getting out does not guarantee success. Many experience great hardships scrambling to make a living in the urban informal economies of "host countries" as undocumented workers.

Ethnographies of "home," however, are just as important as analyses of scattered diaspora communities because "separate places become effectively a single community 'through the continuous circulation of people, money, goods and information'" (Rouse 191:14 cited in Clifford 1997:246). The important roles played by Hausa communities in Niamey, Niger in the ongoing creation of the global Hausa diaspora involve four key, interrelated dynamics that characterize socioeconomic transnational connections and adaptations in Niamey. They include: (1) decision making processes about who should migrate and who should remain at home, (2) the feelings of those "left behind" in Niamey, (3) the ways by which the recent introduction and rapid integration of cell phones in Niger facilitates transnational connections and the sending and receiving of remittances, and (4) contemporary Nigerien Hausa appraisals of remittances and perceptions regarding the commoditization of social relationships.

Definitions and typologies of diaspora are useful for broad cross-cultural comparison, but they sometimes risk reifying and essentializing core concepts such as "original center" or "homeland" and obscure heterogeneous experiences. The locations and meanings of home are often contextual, contested, ambiguous, and nebulous. Among Nigerien Hausa, home means different things to different people in their "traveling culture" (Clifford 1997) in which migration is the norm and due to the fluidity of ethnic boundaries in Niger, diverse family histories of migration, the variability of individual career trajectories, and generation gaps. In Niamey, middle-aged and elderly Hausa who were born in rural Niger before settling Niamey often perceive of home (usually their villages and towns) very differently than the first large cohort of youth born and reared in Niamey—many of whom regard Niamey as home.

Clifford's comparative study emphasizes that travel away from home may be "negatively viewed as transience, superficiality, tourism, exile, and rootlessness...[or] positively conceived as exploration, research, escape, transforming encounter" (Clifford 1997:31). This dichotomous view is reflected in two, contrasting yet roughly equally popular Hausa proverbs. Hausa youth and young adults typically prefer "*tahiya ta hi zaman gida*" ("traveling is better than staying at home"). Hausa in their forties and older usually conclude "*zaman gida ta hi tahiya*" ("staying at home is better than traveling")—at least for themselves. Thus, staying at home may be negatively viewed as demonstrating lack of ambition, resignation, or cowardice. In other cases, staying at home may be viewed positively as evidence of commitment to family and community, reliability, or courage. For example, a man who is a successful trader in Niamey may be considered prudent for staying put, rather than lacking in ambition. In contrast, impoverished men may find international migration the most viable means to support their families.

The statistical data presented in this chapter were collected in December 2007-January 2008 through interviews consisting of five sets of questions about migration histories with 130 Nigerien Hausa, including 124 men and six women (see table 3.1 and table 3.2).[1] My longitudinal research enabled me to select a reasonably representative sample of Hausa men in Niamey with respect to age, length of time spent in Niamey, occupation,

Table 3.1 Ages and Number of Years in Niamey among Hausa Migrants of Niamey 2007-2008, N=130

Ages	*Number of Years in Niamey*
15-19: 22 (.17)	00-01: 54 (.42)
20-29: 69 (.53)	01-05: 27 (.21)
30-39: 26 (.20)	06-10: 20 (.15)
40-49: 9 (.07)	11-15: 4 (.03)
50-59: 4 (.03)	16-20: 9 (.07)
	21-25: 8 (.06)
	26-30: 1 (.01)
	46-50: 1 (.01)
	Born in Niamey: 6 (.05)

Table 3.2 Occupations of Hausa Migrants in Niamey 2007-2008, N=130

Services: 63 (.48)		*Traders: 41 (.32)*		*Unemployed; Students: 26 (.20)*	
Security Guards	12	Multiple item traders	21	Unemployed	15
Butchers	9	Single item traders	20	Students	11
Domestic workers	8				
Tailors	6				
Laborers, Cooks (5 each)	10				
Shoe shiners, Clothes washers (3 each)	6				
Electricians, Taxi drivers, Mechanics, Carpenters (2 each)	8				
Bike repairman, Painter, Tea seller, Grain grinder (1 each)	4				

and hometown. Thus, this discussion is highly gendered as it focuses on the experiences of men. Nevertheless, I found opportunities to informally discuss migration experiences with many Hausa women over the years.

I recognize that Nigerien Hausa women navigate complex migratory trajectories that illustrate contemporary global trends of the "feminization of migration"; that is, "women play a significant role in all regions and in most types of migration" (Castles and Miller 2008:12). Nigerien Hausa women migrate almost as often as men do within Niger. There are more women (611,173) living in Niamey than men (610,893), and in Niger as a whole there are essentially as many women (1,549,387) living in urban areas as men (1,555,187) (République du Niger 2010:1). However, Hausa women are far less likely to independently migrate internationally than men are. Many Hausa women experience being left behind by migratory husbands, whereas virtually no Hausa men experience being left behind by migratory wives. Women often function as the anchors of the Hausa communities of Niamey and as key actors in the transnational connections that define the global Hausa diaspora. Effectively serving as household heads to ensure social reproduction, many take on difficult burdens of extra work when their husbands fail to send remittances, while others assume responsibility for investing remittances.

The phrase "left behind in Niamey," used earlier, seems to imply that those left behind are insignificant "homebodies" out of touch with their family and friends in the global Hausa diaspora. On the contrary, people "left behind" in Niamey play a crucial role in generating the Hausa diaspora through preparing and sponsoring the migrations of family and friends. They are linked in financial and personal networks—now more tightly integrated than ever through the use of cell phones—that make them part of one transnational diasporic community. Furthermore, "left behind" is relative in other ways. First, most Hausa in Niamey are migrants themselves who hail from villages, towns, and cities across south central Niger. Second, the vast majority of Hausa in Niamey has previously migrated abroad, or intend to do so in the future, or both. Finally, Hausa of Niamey include involuntary and voluntary "homebodies"—and these conditions shift over time. Thus, there are few true "homebodies" in Niamey as most people's lives are defined by transience and liminality rather than permanence and completion. As Clifford (1997:37) explains, "with everyone more or less permanently in transit" (or at least thinking about migration), the question becomes "not so much 'Where are you from?' as 'Where are you between?'"

Even though Hausa men and women spend most of their lives in transnational and national migration circuits, very few forget about their *gida* ("home"), variously defined. About 80 percent of Nigerien Hausa are born in small, rural villages of south central Niger, and among these most regard their place of birth as home. Idrissa (2009:161) similarly emphasizes that, "While living in urban settlements like Niamey or Maradi, most Nigeriens who are not indigenous to the place will reflexively refer to their *terroir* ['traditional countryside'] as their first identity of origin—almost never to their ethnicity." Once they reach their mid-40s, most men and women hope to return home—however defined—and begin a gradual process of retirement. They are often exhausted from years of travel and come to revalue the peace and comforts of home. Those who have lived abroad for significant lengths of time in large urban areas typically spend a few years in Niamey before returning to their hometowns. However, increasing numbers of Hausa who were born in rural Niger are choosing to retire in Niamey. Most men seek to retire and eventually be buried in their home villages. For example, Nigerien and other West African immigrants in New York City have established formal associations—such as L'Association des Nigeriens de New York—from which family and friends can draw to transport bodies home for burial (Stoller 2002:167). Even those who were born in diaspora, say Accra, and have never even been to Niger, often identify their father's natal village in Niger as "home." However, as increasing numbers of Nigerien Hausa spend most of their years in Niamey—often with more family and friends there than at "home"—Niamey has become a "second home." Indeed many Hausa now find it acceptable or desirable to be buried in Niamey.

In sum, Niamey, as home, is a fruitful place from which to explore Hausa men's strategic migratory practices. Niamey is a popular destination for rural migrants. It is a place Hausa men yearn to leave and a place to which they yearn to return. Niamey is also a place where Hausa wait for those who have left. Moving may be better than staying put, but sometimes Hausa are stuck and are only able to imagine from afar what living elsewhere might be like. Moreover, there are different kinds of moving (rural-urban, international, circular) and different kinds of being stuck. Hausa may be stuck in Niamey due to poverty, and Hausa may be stuck in the U.S. or France due to their undocumented status and be unable to return home. Soulley, a 50-year old man who recently returned to Niamey after spending 20 years in Abidjan, expressed it this way: "If I can get what I want in Niger I have no business going to a foreign country because as a famous Hausa singer put, 'there is no place like home'."

Overlapping Migratory Patterns and Diasporic Formations

Nigerien Hausa migration is connected to, contributes to, and illustrates all of the core general trends to today's "age of migration," including "the globalization of migration...the acceleration of migration...the differentiation of migration...the feminization of migration...the growing politicization of migration...and the proliferation of migration transition" (Castles and Miller 2008:10-12).

Over the last 20 years, Nigerien Hausa have contributed to the "globalization of migration" by moving further distances from home. Until the late 1980s, almost all Nigeriens who left the continent were young Francophone men who went to France. By about 1990, Nigeriens began to perceive that France and other European countries were imposing increasingly restrictive immigration policies and growing increasingly racist and anti-Muslim. Migration to the U.S., and especially New York City, entered the Nigerien Hausa radar screen. Since then, some 30,000 Nigerien Hausa have established communities in North America, including New York City, Greensboro, Harrisburg, Columbus, Indianapolis, Ypsilanti, Laval and Montréal, Quebec. Residents of Niamey have adopted the abbreviation "Ny" for their city, establishing a parallel with "NY," and frequently explain, "We are the little New York." In recent years, growing numbers of Nigeriens have migrated to China in pursuit of education and jobs. Others speak of trips to Singapore, Dubai, and Sydney. More Nigerien Hausa move—primarily to West and North Africa countries—than ever before, representing the "acceleration of migration." The "differentiation of migration" can be seen in the increasing range of migrants (and prospective migrants) motivated by diverse goals. Migration is not as constrained by age, education, and gender as it was in the past. Old men and women, including non-literate ones, are ready, willing, and (sometimes) ready to go anywhere. The prevalence of migration among Hausa women, as already mentioned, demonstrates the "feminization of migration." The "growing politicization of migration," and ebbs and flows in immigration policies of African, European, and North American nations—and particularly tightening regulations after the terrorist attack in New York City—influence Nigerien decision making. The "proliferation of migration transition" occurs when traditional lands of emigration become lands of transit migration and immigration as well. In the last decade, hundreds of thousands of people from West and Central Africa have embarked on perilous journeys across Sahara, often following ancient caravan routes through Niger, seeking jobs in the Maghreb or Europe. Thousands have ended up staying in Niger either on their way to or on their way back from the north, often out of desperation but sometimes because they find opportunities to make a living.

The following discussion considers types and patterns of migration and movement to, within, out of, and back to Niamey. Many individuals over the course of their career trajectories participate in all of these forms.[2]

Niamey as a Destination for Rural Nigerien Migrants

Hausa migration, as seen in Chapter 2, has played a key role in the historical growth of Niamey as Hausa became a slight majority around 1980 and have retained that position ever since. Niamey has become a "second home" to many Hausa migrants and a "primary home" to a new generation of youth coming of age today. However, it is important to remember that Hausa communities in Niamey are diaspora communities by definition, even though Niamey is within Niger. The following dialogue illustrates this point. I have had many similar discussions over the years, particularly with middle-aged men. Typically the encounter begins with a stranger in a market or in a taxi whom I greet, and engage in brief conversation to negotiate prices or destinations. Then, as the encounter is coming to a close, my newfound acquaintance praises my ability to speak Hausa. (This is evidence of Hausa graciousness and not necessarily of my linguistic skills.)

Taximan: Where did you learn Hausa so well?
SMY: Here in Niamey.
Taximan: No, really? You must have learned it in Maradi or Dogondoutchi.
SMY: I've been there, but I really learned to speak Hausa in Niamey.
Taximan: But this is a Zarma city.
SMY: Almost everyone here speaks Hausa here, right? Even more than Zarma?
Taximan: Yes, I think that is true. See you later.
SMY: Arrive safely.

The taximan's assumption that I must have learned Hausa in Hausaland because Niamey is a "Zarma city," reflects the perception—particularly among the middle-aged—that Hausa are away from home in Niamey. Simultaneously his acknowledgment of the prevalence of Hausa speakers in Niamey points to the reality that in fact Hausa constitute the majority of Niamey's population, and almost everyone in Niamey speaks Hausa. Indeed, Hausa have built dense social networks and communities in Niamey, organized around family, hometown, occupational, congregational, and conversation group affiliations. Their connections, friendships, and marriages are not defined solely by Hausa ethnicity. Rather in Niamey their communities are interwoven with those of many other ethnic groups due to Nigerien *brassage*. Youth 15-25 years old who were born and reared in Niamey (or moved there as children) typically feel that Niamey is really home even if they have some symbolic attachment to their father's rural hometown. They do not ask me where I learned to speak Hausa.

Movement within the City

Hausa are constantly on the move within Niamey. Men typically cover 10-kilometer circuits on foot everyday in the city for work (or looking for work), prayer, and social networking. This is partly because they have time on their hands, as most are either unemployed or underemployed. But this is not the only reason. The daily rounds of Hausa men in Niamey are motivated by the quest for a vibrant social life of intelligent conversation and clever humor filled with a wide range of friends and acquaintances. Niamey is an "outdoor culture" particularly for men. Most men spend little time at home regardless of their marital status or employment status. Most jobs in the informal economy are outdoors. Most prayers are conducted in open-air mosques and in sidewalk gatherings that sometimes expand to block off roads. Most men participate daily in several street corner conversation groups that are scattered throughout the city.

Most Hausa women of Niamey also circulate daily throughout the city, though a minority is partially or fully secluded. Their places of work are often distant from home. Women make trips to markets nearly every day to purchase cooking supplies. Many Hausa women spend a great deal of time visiting family and friends, participating in naming and wedding ceremonies, and women-centered social networks and formal associations.

Monthly and annual movements and migrations from one domicile to another are due to two primary factors: the high cost of rent, and the circular migratory patterns of many Hausa who spend dry seasons in Niamey and the wet season farming in their villages. Most Niaméens are renters. A few have been renting the same apartment or compound for decades, but most move every few years both near and far within the city. Moves are almost always based solely on financial considerations. Many are constantly ready to move if they hear of better deals or their fortunes change for better or worse. Seasonal migrants that are not well connected in Niamey have to find new lodging every year. Other circular migrants find more stability in Niamey by forming groups (based on kinship, hometown connections, friendships) to share rent and make arrangements such that at least one man in the group resides in the lodging at all times during the wet season, so that those who go home to farm can easily relocate to Niamey after the harvest. Some of these rental relationships last a decade or more.

Niamey as a Central Staging Ground for International Migration

Decisions about who will leave the country take place across Niger. However, most of the practical planning for international migration occurs in Niamey rather than in rural villages, for it is in Niamey that Hausa find higher concentrations of people with international migration experiences and connections, ready access to official travel documents, and—for the well-to-do—Niger's only international airport. Nigerien Hausa have made Niamey a place where they can get urban diaspora experience with many of the comforts of home. Indeed, it is far more common for Hausa to spend a few years learning urban social skills in Niamey before migrating abroad than it is for Hausa to depart rural homes directly for foreign destinations. This exemplifies the global pattern whereby migrants typically first move from rural areas to cities in their home countries before embarking on secondary international migratory journeys (Castles and Miller 2008:4).

Niamey is a place that many people want to leave. Movement and transience define the ethos of Niamey where migration is a constant topic of conversation. It is a city of dreamers and dreams—both realized and frustrated. Niaméens recognize that leaving the country requires broad social networks and support as very few have the means to do so alone. Since people are constantly going and coming, Nigeriens must constantly nurture old relationships at a distance and cultivate new connections. That is to say, Hausa who are eager to emigrate must maintain a sense of solidarity and community in Niamey to have a reasonable chance of success.

Migratory dreams and aspirations are expressed in many ways. *Fada* ("formal conversation") groups are often named after desirable global destinations, and names such as Brooklyn, L.A., and Paris are spray painted on walls throughout Niamey. Men I met 20 years ago as newcomers in Niamey who are now in their forties and fifties regularly ask me to take them home with me to the U.S. Many are joking, but not all of them, including Salissou who explained, "I am serious. I will do any kind of work, even sweeping streets and emptying trashcans. And I won't cause any trouble for you or your family." Issaka, a 25-year old man who has grown up in Niamey, talks incessantly about his desire to move to the U.S., even though his father is destitute, he has no formal education, and speaks neither French nor English. He wears t-shirts with U.S. Embassy logos from around the world that he has purchased in Niamey's used clothing markets. His friends usually call him "Americain" rather than Issaka, and he has taught them to greet him with what he regards as cool African American handshakes. "I love you guys," he told his *hira* mates, "but if I get the chance to go to the U.S. I will never come back." However unrealistic, his identity is defined by this American dream.

Patterns of International Migration

For many years, Nigerien scholars and many well-informed citizens have been telling me that there are at least as many Nigeriens living outside the country as within it particularly if both first and second generation emigrants are counted. My recent research provides strong evidence that this may be the case. Among my sample of Hausa migrants in Niamey, 82 percent have at least one family member or friend who is living abroad. Moreover, among those 82 percent each have on average two family members and friends living abroad. This snapshot of the global Nigerien Hausa diaspora includes 71% of migrants in 12 West African countries, 12% in North Africa, 9% in Europe, 6% in North America, and 2% in Saudi Arabia (see table 3.3). This roughly matches World Bank (2006) data that list Côte d'Ivoire, Burkina Faso, Nigeria, Chad, Benin, Togo, France, Italy, Germany, and the United States as the top ten destination countries for Nigerien emigrants in 2005.

Furthermore, the ongoing economic crisis in Niger and the reported intentions of Hausa in my sample suggest that international migration will remain important. Two-thirds are planning to migrate abroad and they identify 90 destinations. Among these 90 destinations, 60% are in

Table 3.3 Locations of Family and Friends Abroad, N=225

West Africa 160 (.71)		*N. Africa 27 (.12)*		*Europe 20 (.09)*		*N.America 14 (.06)*		*M. East 4 (.02)*	
Nigeria	39	Libya	17	France	9	U.S.	13	S. Arabia	4
C. d'Ivoire	26	Algeria	6	Belgium	4	Canada	1		
Togo	23	Tunisia	2	England	1				
Benin	22	Morocco	1	Germany	1				
Ghana	19	Egypt	1	Switzerland	1				
B. Faso	8			Italy	1				
Mali	7			Netherlands	1				
Cameroon	6			Norway	1				
Senegal	6			"Europe"	1				
Gabon	2								
Guinea	1								
Congo	1								

West African nations; 18% are in European nations; 10% are in North African nations; 7% are in North America; and 5% are in the Middle East and Asia (see table 3.4). Seventy percent of the Hausa in the sample have previously migrated abroad. In addition, only one-third of respondents who have no current plans to migrate abroad have never left Niger. Put another way, only 15 of the 130 Hausa interviewed have never left the country.

Circular Migration Including Intranational and International Routes

Much of the migration to and from Niamey is circular including both seasonal rural-urban migration within Niger and international migration that keeps Nigeriens out of the country for months, years, or even decades at a time. This means that people are constantly leaving and returning to Niamey with infusions of diverse experiences, stories, skills, fashions, languages, and money. Migrants from Niamey influence the lives of family and friends in Niamey whether they return or not. Many are gone for indefinite lengths of time during which people must re-order social structures in order to adapt while anticipating long-awaited returns.

Table 3.4 Intended Migratory Destinations of Hausa of Niamey, N=91

West Africa 55 (.60)		*Europe 17 (.18)*		*N. Africa 9 (.10)*		*N.America 6 (.07)*		*M. East, Asia 5 (.05)*	
Ghana	13	"Europe"	5	Libya	7	U.S.	6	S. Arabia	2
C. d'Ivoire	9	France	4	Algeria	2			India	1
Togo	8	Belgium	3					Pakistan	1
Benin	7	England	3					"Asia"	1
Nigeria	6	Germany	1						
B. Faso	4	Switzerland	1						
Cameroon	4								
Mali	2								
Senegal	1								
C.A.R.	1								

Dynamics of Transnational Connections and Adaptations in Niamey

Selecting Migrants

In Niger, group considerations and assistance are almost always crucial to migration decisions. The further the destination the less likely that prospective migrants can handle costs and preparation independently. A few have the means to migrate on their own, but most Nigerien Hausa rely on extended family, *hira* "informal conversation" groups, or *fada* "formal conversation" groups to support their migration even if they are only moving a few hundred kilometers within the country or to a neighboring country. Others look to individual relationships with wealthy patrons for help with travel costs and expenses associated with resettlement.

Individual families and *hira* and *fada* conversation groups typically perceive that they can only afford to invest in one or two members' international migration and thus engage in careful and difficult decisions regarding who is considered worthy of sponsoring. Prospective Hausa migrants compete indirectly for this scarce resource. They do not appear simultaneously before a "jury" of their kin and peers listening to each other's appeals or trying to directly outdo their rivals. The process plays out during informal encounters that take place over months and years in which individuals seek to demonstrate valued qualities, establish positive reputations, and orally make their cases. In family palavers, many voices are heard but a man's father has the final say. In conversation groups, decisions are reached by democratic consensus except that those prepared to contribute more have more power. Men spend hours considering the qualities of those who have successfully secured migration sponsorship. Men who are friendly, hard working (particularly if they are perceived to have occupational skills that are portable to other urban areas), linguistically adept (in African languages, French, and, increasingly, English), cell phone owning, humble, devout Muslims with proven track records of supporting family and friends through migration to Niamey are generally regarded as the best candidates.

Migration sponsorship is perceived as a group investment, counterbalanced by the inherent duty of the emigrant to send remittances home. Individuals make contributions according to their means and the degree of trust that they have in would-be migrants. The amount given in support influences the amount expected in return. Not only are migrants obliged to repay the loans that allowed their travel, they are expected to regularly send remittances home for as long as they are away from home. Hausa do not think of this as interest in financial terms, but rather as social commitment that in turn enhances the prestige of the remitter.

Occasionally families and conversation groups choose individuals who have never stated desires to migrate abroad but who demonstrate the desired qualities of trustworthy migrants, highlighting the value of migration as a communal, adaptive strategy. These chosen ones sometimes resist, chafing at the burdens that international migration entails, including homesickness, separation from wives, and high expectations of generosity. However, they typically relent due to informal pressure, occasionally including hiring *marok'a* ("praise-singers") to publicly extol their virtues.

Feelings of Those "Left Behind" in Niamey

Hausa have made Niamey a home away from home, taking pride in their role in the growth of Niamey and valuing many aspects of the quality of life there—as highlighted earlier. However, Hausa migrants have experienced increasing difficulty in earning a decent living in Niamey over the past 20 years. Today only about ten percent of men have achieved their principal goals in Niamey. These goals typically include establishing oneself in an occupation that will become increasingly lucrative over time allowing one to live in some modest material comfort, marry before the age of 30, and regularly send money home. Many cite steady inflation and expensive rent, food, and taxes as the biggest drawbacks of Niamey, making it nearly impossible to get ahead. Furthermore, a significant minority suffers in dire poverty in Niamey lacking the resources to simply return home.

While enduring economic decline, the cost of bridewealth has risen at a rate faster than the overall inflation rate, leaving many frustrated 30 and 40 year old bachelors. The declining pool of eligible and financially stable young bachelors similarly discontents women. Many reluctantly accept marriages with much older men in polygynous marriages. Although many Hausa women in Niamey do not mind polygyny and some prefer it to monogamy, most first-time brides prefer to be the first brides of their husbands, and a substantial and growing minority strongly prefer monogamy.

In this context of economic decline, most Hausa men desire onward migration from Niamey to a foreign destination to try their luck for at least a few years. Men who desire to leave the country but who are unable to secure the resources to do so may be deeply frustrated particularly if their appeals for sponsorship have been rejected. While they retain hopes for future migration, they patiently wait for news and remittances from family and friends especially if they themselves have invested in the sponsorship of migrants.

Despite the "feminization of migration" among the Hausa, married women are more likely to be left behind by migrant husbands in Niamey than to be international migrants. Hausa custom—as is the case in most Nigerien cultures—expects that wives should reside in the homes of the parents of their husbands while their husbands are in diaspora even if they were not doing so before their husbands departed—and most do.

Women's experiences in this arrangement vary and are influenced by the interaction of personalities, the generosity of their husbands, the size of their in-laws' homes, the degree of privacy they are afforded, and the length of the time their husbands are away from home. Although Hausa women understand the necessity of their husbands' migrations given the lack of economic opportunities in Niger, they typically find this living situation to be very stressful as they are often expected to carry out expanded domestic labor in large extended families, may face rude in-laws, and must cope with separations from their husbands for years at a time. Some find this so intolerable that they move out despite their husbands' wishes (Stoller 1999). Stress associated with long-term absences of husbands is a common factor in divorce, as I learned through a number of cases.

Many women make other arrangements during the absences of their husbands. Some women simply refuse to live with parents of their husbands and insist on living alone or with their own families. Moreover, not all husbands have living parents. Women head about one in five households in Niamey (Youngstedt 2004c). In contrast to the possibility of enduring hardship, some women find advantages in being "left behind" as they come to appreciate their independence—in some cases in which they live with supportive and kind in-laws, and particularly if they are living alone with their children (Stoller 1999). They feel liberated from the domestic demands of their husbands and relish more opportunities to pursue their occupations and to socialize with family and friends. Furthermore, if their husbands are successful in diaspora and regularly send money home, they typically enjoy a higher standard of living than their counterparts who lack this resource. Women often have divided feelings about their husbands' returns in these situations. Some come to wish that their husbands would come home periodically just long enough so that they can have children.

Transnationalism, Cell Phones, and Remittances

Nigerien Hausa employ cell phones to strengthen and expand transnational connections and a sense of community in diaspora, and for securing remittances. The regular communication afforded by cell phones has changed the meaning and feeling of being "left behind" or away from home. Keeping in touch is important. It is expensive. It is commoditized. But it is worth it.

Hausa are making revolutionary changes to their far-flung diaspora by utilizing mobile phones to create new and unprecedented opportunities for communication across distances. Prior to the late 1990s, Hausa separated by migration communicated with each other primarily by proxy; that is, news and cash and gifts were given to individuals traveling back and forth through networks of communities dispersed across Africa and delivered in person. For a few years in the late 1990s and early 2000s, e-mail accessed at new, public *cybercafés* in Niamey became a popular means of communication and remittance negotiation with émigrés, particularly for the literate and relatively well off and their friends. Since 2001 and accelerating ever since, cell phones have been adopted as the primary technology facilitating symbolic and financial communication linking the Nigerien Hausa diaspora. Using cell phones as their main tool of time-space compression, the vast majority of Hausa migrants in Niamey today—including 85 percent of people in my sample—communicate regularly with their family members and friends abroad.

Hausa in Niamey use cell phones to communicate more frequently with international migrants than was feasible in the past. Cell phone owners can be contacted at any time at virtually any place. This constitutes both their primary advantage and their primary disadvantage, as anyone who owns one knows. Hausa consider the synchronic communication offered by cell phones as far more personalized and immediate than that afforded by other asynchronic channels, such as handwritten letters, e-mail messages, or couriers. Literacy is not required to place and receive cell phone calls. Those who are literate can save money by sending text messages rather than placing phone calls.

Most international calls received and placed by Hausa in Niamey are brief—two to five minutes—and consist primarily of greetings and family news updates. "Just a one to two minute call home every one to two months to let everyone know that things are fine is acceptable," according to Ousseini whose son is working in Paris. In addition, the question of money is always lurking in international conversations. Usually it is put off until just before the conclusion of the conversation. (In other cases, migrants are simply informing those in Niamey that they have sent or will send money.) Hausa in Niamey now use cell phones to communicate their specific needs with international migrants; such as, medicine for an ill child, a sheep for Tabaski, food to survive, and expenses for baptisms, marriages, and funerals. Migrants in diaspora find it more difficult to deny requests made during phone conversations than they do when requests are sent through letters, e-mail, or couriers. Abdoulrazack, a Hausa man who has been living in Ypsilanti, Michigan for more than decade, commented on this, "Years ago my family sent me letters. They are not literate, so they dictated letters to my cousin. Somehow I could ignore their pleas for money in these letters. I just sent money whenever I had a little extra. Now, when I hear my mother crying on the phone, I melt and run straight down to the Western Union outlet."

Cell phone communication exacerbates the pressure that many migrants feel to support family and friends left behind in Niamey. Many migrants rise to this challenge by purchasing cell phones as gifts for those in Niamey and expressing their strong desire to keep current with news at home. Many live frugally in diaspora in order to send as much money home as possible. In contrast, many Hausa in diaspora communities grow so weary of steady streams of phone calls from family and friends in Niger asking for money that they use two phone numbers—one that they share with people that are likely to ask for money and another that they share with people who are unlikely to ask for money. Another strategy entails purchasing calling cards and using public phones to call home so that one can remain in touch with home on one's own terms. Ousmane, working as a butcher in Dakar, explained, "I paid for my bus ticket to Dakar. I do not owe anyone anything. Besides, I earn a very modest living here. I would rather save money to visit home once a year or so and to give gifts in person so I know that the money is not squandered."

Cell phones have emerged as the primary media for securing the remittances upon which increasing numbers of people are virtually entirely dependent for everyday necessities, and for emergencies. Remittances are notoriously very difficult to measure. Many Nigerien Hausa prefer to send cash through proxies who return to Niamey, and this is not accounted for in official statistics. Many remittances are wired, primarily through Western Union, though Moneygram has emerged as a competitor in recent years. In the last couple of years, it has also become possible to wire money through cell phones to bank accounts. Some evidence indicates that remittances are increasing. According to World Bank (2009) data, Nigerien workers sent home remittances totaling $14 million in 2000, $66 million in 2005, and $78 million in 2007 and 2008. (It might not be coincidental that these increases parallel the accelerated adoption of cell phones.) Olivier de Sardan's (2007) analysis indicates that remittances from the Nigerien diaspora were likely more significant in mitigating Niger's famine in 2005 than state and international humanitarian assistance.

In my sample, 36 percent of respondents report having received remittances from family and friends abroad, and among them 61 percent indicated that they themselves received remittances whereas 39 percent indicated that it was sent to their parents to manage for their families. More than four in five received only money, while a few received gifts such as cell phones and clothes. The average remittance, on roughly an annual basis, was $270. To put this into perspective, the annual per capita income in Niger is about $300. This average remittance obscures inequality; that is, remittances ranged from $22 to $1,666. Sixty-one percent of men who indicated specific monetary figures, received between $22 and $166 (see table 3.5). Eighty-seven percent of those who received money reported that it made a significant difference in their lives, whereas only 13 percent complained that they did not receive enough to really help them.

Table 3.5 Types and Sizes of Reported Annual Monetary Remittances

Types of Remittances, N=38		*Sizes of Reported Annual Monetary Remittances, N=28*	
Money only	31 (.82)	10,000-30,000 FCFA	6 (.21)
Cell phones and clothes	4 (.11)	31,000-60,000 FCFA	8 (.29)
Money and gifts	3 (.08)	61,000-90,000 FCFA	3 (.11)
		91,000-120,000 FCFA	6 (.21)
		121,000-150,000 FCFA	1 (.04)
		300,000 FCFA	1 (.04)
		400,000 FCFA	1 (.04)
		500,000 FCFA	1 (.04)
		750,000 FCFA	1 (.04)

Migration and Remittances: The Good, The Bad, and The Ugly

Migration is a core adaptive strategy and a means of survival for Hausa, involving establishing and maintaining transnational diasporic connections, that is designed to lead to improved opportunities for individual migrants and infusions of remittances to family and friends in Niamey and across Niger. The social performance of migration is differentiating. Its success rests on synergy between individuals and groups. Some migrants succeed whereas others fail, including some who are never heard from again. This can be due to particular circumstances, and the personal qualities and skills of individual migrants as well as good and bad choices made by groups about whom to sponsor. Much is at stake. Not only are the reputations of individual migrants on the line, more importantly the reputations, investments, and finances of families and communities in Niamey are at risk. In a context of economic scarcity, contestations over remittances are more becoming more frequent and have influenced the perception that social relationships are increasingly commoditized in Niamey. The older generation laments this shift. The younger generation, particularly those who were born or reared in Niamey, is more likely to see an individualistic, cash-oriented economy as a simple fact of life.

Lively discussions and heated debates regarding remittances have become a staple theme in Hausa street corner conversation groups and family meetings in Niamey in the last decade, due to the increasing importance of remittances in social reproduction and survival.[3] Almost all people who received cash remittances praise and humbly thank the donors. Indeed, those who fulfilled the cultural expectation to support family and friends will receive hero's welcomes upon returning to Niger. But the situation is complicated as jealousy can creep into relationships for a number of reasons. For example, some men who are generous with remittances are otherwise regarded as immoral or unlikable for any number of reasons. As one man poignantly observed, "Now respect can be purchased with remittances. My brother in Greensboro, North Carolina just sent home $500. Many people in the family cannot stop praising him even though they know he drinks whiskey everyday and has not prayed for years."

While they suffer in dire poverty, many Hausa in Niamey are upset with their relatives and friends abroad. Many Hausa of Niamey claim that their comrades in diaspora are growing ever more selfish. I do not have evidence to support the claim the migrants are sending less money home, but I think that this perception reflects a declining economic climate in Niamey and the global economic recession. That is, Niaméens need remittances now more than ever. Almost two-thirds of respondents with family or friends abroad report that they have not received any remittances, including 14% who have received no news at all from their migrant compatriots. Commenting on this, many Hausa simply say, "Today it's every man for himself." In Niamey's street corner conversation groups and family discussions, Hausa spend more time and energy complaining about irresponsible international migrants—expressing especially deep exasperation regarding those who never even bother to call or send an occasional e-mail message—than they do praising generous family or friends in diaspora. For example, neither his family nor his friends have heard from Ousmane who left Niamey for New York City more than a decade ago shortly after his father died. His mother, Hadija, expresses her sadness about this almost daily in comments such as, "We do not need money from him; we just want to know that he is alright."

His brother, Alou, says that the family would be satisfied to receive even a one-minute phone call during holidays. His friend Djibrilla concluded that, "His mother or other family could have died and he would not even know it. It is very strange, he must really hate Niger to behave like this."

Many Hausa in Niamey fail—due to lack of knowledge or frustration—to recognize the difficulties faced by their migrant brethren and sisters in diaspora communities that typically rest precariously on the margins of the global economy, despite their own, often difficult, experiences abroad. Economic conditions in the nations where Nigerien Hausa have been and currently are most likely to migrate—Nigeria, Côte d'Ivoire, Togo, Benin, Ghana, and Libya—are only marginally better than in Niger. Most Hausa in diaspora desperately yearn to send money but cannot as they are barely making ends meet. Hausa of Niamey often have grossly inflated expectations of those who manage to make it to Europe or North America. In a comment that echoed dozens of others, a man severely criticized his own brother who has been living in New York City for six years without sending any remittances, "Any Hausa in New York who is not fully supporting at least fifteen people in Niger is either lying and living the high life or incredibly foolish and lazy."

Contestations regarding exactly whom should receive remittances and on what they should be spent have also intensified. Sons sometimes resent and resist their fathers' demands to turn over remittances to them to manage for their families. Wives left behind by their migrant husbands typically reside with their husbands' parents, as mentioned earlier. In many cases this relationship is severely strained by jealousy and competition for gifts, in a context in which loyalty to affinal and consanguineal relationships is measured monetarily. Wives and parents-in-law trade accusations and counter-accusations of hoarding or squandering the remittances sent home by husbands or sons (Stoller 2002). Migrant men face difficult and uncomfortable questions from each.

Hausa in Niamey prefer to control how they will spend remittances, and resent international migrants who try to assert control. This is especially true among those who helped to sponsor international migrants. Most migrants who send money home expect or ask for it to be spent on everyday necessities such as food, rent, and medicine; while a few send home cell phones (or "top-up" cell phone accounts) or clothes rather than money. Today, they increasingly resist homebodies' requests for money to support "luxuries"—such as purchasing sheep for Tabaski, or hosting expensive naming and wedding ceremonies. Their stance on "rational" investment parallels one of the core messages articulated by the Izala reformist movement. Though only a minority of *'yan Izala* are international migrants, the similar financial strategy favored by migrants and *'yan Izala* represents a common solution to a common problem—severe poverty.

The Global Hausa Diaspora

Historian Benedict Anderson (1991:6) has famously argued that, "all communities larger than primordial villages of face-to-face contact (and perhaps even these) are imagined. Communities are to be distinguished, not be their falsity/genuineness, but by the styles in which they are imagined." Generated by historical and pervasive ongoing migration, the global Hausa diaspora is held together by long-distance communication and circulations of people and money as well as a broad sense of ethnolinguistic and Muslim solidarity forming one imagined transnational community. Hausa people are here, there, and everywhere. One Hausa story makes this point with humor, "When American astronauts landed on the moon they were greeted by Hausa traders." I have concentrated on Niger where 7.5 million Hausa reside. Another 30 million or more Hausa live in Northern Nigeria. All told, there may be as many Hausa living away from Niger and Nigeria as within these countries. Many Hausa—wherever they are—take pride in the emergence of Hausa as a global language as reflected in the fact that many of the world's leading radio stations report international news daily in Hausa, including, BBC, VOA, Deutsche Welle, RFI, and Radio Beijing.

Hausa individuals experience and participate in this global diaspora in extremely variable ways. The Hausa diaspora consists of multiple home sites in both Francophone Niger and Anglophone Nigeria that mean different things to different people. Furthermore, some diaspora communities are decades and centuries old (Kumasi, Abidjan, Paris, Mecca) whereas others (Shanghai, Columbus, Ohio) are very new. Some Hausa of Niamey effectively participate in very small segments or communities of the broader diaspora, such as maintaining a dyadic relationship with a family member abroad. Many Hausa of Niamey maintain connections with multiple, even dozens, of family and friends living across Africa, Europe, and North America.

The global Hausa diaspora, held together by interpersonal connections and multiple communities, is interlinked with and overlaps other diasporas. Ethnicity is very fluid in Niger where it is one of many sources of affiliation and identity construction. Hausa often downplay ethnicity in diaspora by participating, for example, in pan-Nigerien networks and associations (Association des Étudiants et Residents Nigériens aux USA and L'Association des Nigériens de New York), rather than ethnic specific organizations. In addition to cell phones, Nigerien websites also play an increasingly significant role in facilitating transnational connections and identities. The most popular websites today, nigerdiaspora.info and tamtaminfo.com, are not ethnic-specific. They offer access to Nigerien newspapers, radio stations, independent reporting, and discussion boards. Furthermore, in the U.S., Nigerien Hausa often feel a close sense of solidarity with and affiliate more with fellow Muslim, Francophone West Africans than they do with Anglophone Nigerian Hausa. In sum, many Nigerien Hausa at home and abroad feel they belong to and participate in (local and global) Muslim, Nigerien, worldwide "Black," and Francophone communities in addition to the global Hausa diaspora.

Arrays of skills are needed to succeed in this diaspora. Hausa must cultivate strong interpersonal communication skills in order to build and maintain local, regional, and global social networks. Men and women who are linguistically adept, that is proficient in multiple Nigerien languages and French as well as being able to learn new languages quickly, are best positioned for success. Hausa who make use of cell phones and the Internet feel more personally connected to home and can access the widest range of contacts and information about work opportunities. Finally, Hausa must be resilient and tough while balancing personal initiative and group obligations in order to survive with dignity.

In summary, Niamey serves as an integral node and symbolic home of the increasingly dispersed Nigerien Hausa diaspora. Understandings of traveling cultures are necessarily incomplete if they fail to pay attention to home sites and concepts of home. For it is at home that global processes generate the conditions that motivate migration, it is at home that people launch their migratory careers, and home is inexorably changed by those who are away whether or not they remain in contact and whether or not they return. Hausa in Niamey make calculated investments in the sponsorship of migrants expecting to receive remittances in return. While many are disappointed by the inability or unwillingness of their migrant family and friends to come through for them, others have become almost entirely dependent on remittances for their survival. A few others have seen their standards of living rise significantly due to the generosity of their migrant comrades. Hausa have rapidly deployed cell phones since their introduction in 2001 for maintaining and building personal and economic relationships and facilitating multilocal community connections, including the sending and receiving of remittances. Migrants now feel much more pressure to send money home when they can easily be contacted in a very personal way than before the spread of cell phones. Conflicts over remittances are becoming more common with so much at stake. Many middle-aged and elderly Hausa bemoan that struggles over remittances symbolize the divisive nature of money and broader disturbing trends in the commoditization of social relationships.

— 4 —

Striving for Survival and Meaning in Hausa Communities of Niamey

Zaman duniya sai hank'uri:
Only with patience can one make it in the world

Careers and Communities: Work, Family, Islam, Social Networking

This chapter addresses the specific ways that Hausa make a living, establish communities, and create meaning in unique ways on the ground in Niamey through work, family, Islam, and social networks. These social elements are intertwined in career pursuits, and converge in informal street corner *hira* ("conversation") groups—the most important institution of public culture in Niamey. This absolutely crucial institution has been almost completely neglected by other scholars. Most Hausa men in Niamey spend most of their waking hours in *hira* groups. They use these groups to navigate their lives as migrants and to negotiate and fashion their own conceptions of modernity. More than any other aspect of Hausa social organization, *hira* groups bring together, in a concentrated fashion, circulating people and circulating ideas and thus offer a prime localized entry into the global reality of modernity.

The final part of the chapter turns to an exploration of the emergence and proliferation in the last decade of formal men's *fada* ("conversation") and women's *foyandi* ("conversation") groups. These types of groups evolved from older *fada* and *foyandi* practices as well as *hira*. Though they often share much in practice, in contrast with informal *hira*, *fada* and *foyandi* groups are more formally structured with specific community agendas, official names, elected officers, and membership dues that are paid on a sliding scale relative to one's means. Some groups transform themselves into officially registered NGOs, typically focusing on neighborhood development in Niamey or hometown improvement.

Drawing from anthropologist Walter Goldschmidt's seminal work, *The Human Career: The Self in the Symbolic World* (1990), I consider Hausa careers as constituted by individuals' productive, reproductive, religious, and social networking activities performed in the context of community values, social institutions, and economic conditions. From this perspective, Hausa individuals are seen as motivated actors, striving to attain material and physical well being, and perhaps even more importantly, self-esteem. Prestige striving is the primary strategy for achieving, maintaining, and enhancing self-esteem. Through the lifelong trajectory of their career pursuits, Hausa individuals establish a sense of symbolic self. The sense of self is continuously shaped and reshaped by communities as the individual develops patterns of attachment and identification with ideologies, key social units, and patterns of collaboration. Examination of the careers of individuals facilitates appreciation of the depth of lived experience and its satisfactions and frustrations. Thus, I begin with a case study of Youssoufou Garba, a man that I have known throughout the course of my research in Niamey. His unique experiences offer a person-centered entry into the matrix of work, family, Islam, and *hira* that define Hausa careers and communities in Niamey.

Youssoufou Garba's Career Trajectory

Youssoufou Garba, now 55, fondly remembers his youthful days spent with family in the 1960s and 1970s in Niamey. He recalled, "We could make our own football team, given that I had ten brothers and two sisters, and we dominated neighborhood football games!" The Garba siblings had great expectations; they felt invincible. Their father spent his career working for the Nigerien civil service—moving the family to Niamey in 1965 for his last assignment—and their mother led women's Islamic studies circles. Youssoufou explained, "Our parents emphasized that we needed three things to succeed in life: we must be good Muslims, we must get modern education, and we must always respect others and be polite to all people, especially our elders." All but one of the Garba siblings heeded their parents' advice, and most established successful professional careers.

After three years of post high school training, Youssoufou secured a plum job as an engineer in the Ministry of Mines. Through participating in circles of young professionals, he met a beautiful, educated, and sophisticated woman from Côte d'Ivoire. They fell in love, married, moved into a modern concrete apartment complex, and not long after had a daughter. Life was good, but it didn't last. Youssoufou was nearly killed in an industrial accident, requiring nine months to recuperate, including three months in a hospital followed by six at his parents' village where they had retired. His wife had waited patiently for him, but her patience ran out after Youssoufou returned to Niamey and was not re-hired despite a solid nine-year work record and medical clearance. She decided to return to Côte d'Ivoire and wanted to take their daughter with her. Youssoufou reluctantly agreed, expecting that the situation would be only temporary. He thought that surely he would get a new job and summon her to return. That was 1987. Yousoufou never secured another steady job in his chosen profession, and has barely scratched out a living through occasional odd jobs, such as working on cars or wiring houses, that he gets through friends over the past 23 years. His wife never returned, and he has seen his daughter only a handful of times.

If not for family, Youssoufou would likely be destitute. His parents decided that he and his youngest brother, Abdou, could live in their modest *banco* ("mud brick") compound in Niamey. Many times over the years Youssoufou has had to turn to his brothers and cousins when he was flat broke or for medical care, particularly for his nearly annual debilitating bouts with malaria. A younger brother and a younger cousin along with a younger *hira* group friend have been the most consistently helpful.

Youssoufou remarried in 2002. He met Zeinabou through buying meals from her at a street corner stall in the neighborhood. Her first husband died young. Her second husband, with whom she had two daughters, converted to Christianity shortly after their marriage. Zeinabou was not pleased but grew to tolerate this development as well as her husband's insistence that his daughters be given Christian names (Josephine and Mary) and be reared as Christians. However, she could not bear his constant pressure to convert her, and divorced him on these grounds. Zeinabou stayed in her widowed mother's compound—densely crowded with extended family—in the neighborhood for about a year before marrying Youssoufou. Her mother was willing to accept a very modest bridewealth given that Zeinabou was in her forties, had married twice previously and had two children, and had never been to school. She liked Youssoufou as he treated her politely, and respected him for his education and his reputation in the neighborhood as a good, devout man. Furthermore, she liked the idea that her daughter would be just a five-minute walk away. Zeinabou hoped to bring her daughters into Youssoufou's compound, but he refused, invoking Muslim law that stipulates that he does not bear responsibility for them as well as practical arguments—his compound is small and Zeinabou could visit her daughters daily. After their parents' divorce, Josephine kept her name but stopped going to church, while Mary, to her mother's delight, converted to Islam and changed her name to Mariama, a conventional Nigerien Muslim name.

Abdou, now 40, is the wayward son. Among the Garba siblings, he is the only one who dropped out of school, quit performing his daily prayers, never held a job, and never married. As a young adult, he once stole his father's ox, sold it in the market, and disappeared for two weeks' of partying with his friends. Abdou regularly insults Zeinabou and her cooking even though she often provides him his only square meal of the day. Youssoufou and his family find his character to be unbearable, and Youssoufou has considered evicting him many times over the years, but asks, "What can I do, he is still my brother?"

Zeinabou has continued selling cooked food, generating most of the couple's meager income. Despite Youssoufou's predicament, she urges him to take a second wife. He appreciates this, but cannot act on it. After three miscarriages, one of Zeinabou's elder sisters "gave" them her two-year old son. Youssoufou and Zeinabou, especially, were pleased to have Ali and immediately began treating him affectionately as their own son, bought him clothes, and paid for a traditional circumcision in their home. After two years, Ali felt at home in his new family even though he still had memories of his parents. One day, without notice, Ali's parents paid a visit, announced that they wanted Ali back, and took him.

Youssoufou took this stoically, but Zeinabou fell into a deep funk. She began complaining about Abdou's rude behavior and insisting that her daughters move in with her, and Youssoufou kept refusing. Then, one day eight years into their marriage, Zeinabou simply did not come home after work. When she reappeared three days later, she declared that she wanted a divorce. Youssoufou was upset because he felt that he had done nothing wrong, but he kept his cool. He visited Zeinabou's mother to respectfully discuss what had happened and was able to convince her that Zeinabou was in the wrong. But Zeinabou stubbornly returned to live with her mother and they divorced.

A few months later, Youssoufou married Hassana, the daughter of a friend in the neighborhood. The exact circumstances are murky as the arrangements were made so quickly that Youssoufou did not even inform his family. He simply explained that he could not face being single and eating street food again. Within months Youssoufou grew weary of Hassana's constant demands for gifts that he could not provide. Meanwhile, unbeknownst to Youssoufou, his mother arrived in Niamey to try to convince Zeinabou to reunite with him. Days after divorcing Hassana, Zeinabou, accompanied by her mother and Youssoufou's mother, asked to remarry Youssoufou. He agreed and they are back together and remarried after six months of separation, almost as if nothing had ever happened.

Zeinabou's income is not sufficient to offset the decline in family assistance that Youssoufou has experienced since marrying her. Two years into their (first) marriage, they could no longer afford to pay their electricity bill, and they have used kerosene lanterns and flashlights ever since. He understands that he cannot be a top priority now that he is married, that his siblings have their own children to support, and that most of his siblings regularly send money home to their retired parents allowing them to live comfortably and to regularly visit Niamey. He is, however, deeply upset that some of his younger brothers and cousins who are financially comfortable no longer come to visit him.

Youssoufou remains upbeat and always ready to laugh, shoot the breeze, or engage in serious discussion despite all of the tribulations he has faced and his steadily declining standard of living. He attributes this primarily to his deep Muslim faith. The fact that he still likes to get up each morning is also due to his love for Zeinabou, the personal satisfaction he derives from being embedded in wide circles of extended family and conversation group friends who enjoy his company and respect his intelligence, and the sense that he is an informed citizen of the world. When he is not praying or visiting with family and friends, he spends several hours daily listening to RFI international news reports.

Making A Living

Youssoufou Garba's life history is unique; however, it reflects broader patterns and illustrates the central theme of the book. Youssoufou lost his prestigious high paying job and as a result has endured pauperization and declining health but nevertheless finds joy and purpose in his life: he is surviving with dignity. This is the most striking quality of his experience. Youssoufou's inability to find work despite his education and experience exemplifies the bleak economic climate of Niamey. (It also represents squandered human capital in a country least able to afford it.) Hard work is highly valued and respected in Hausa culture, but many men and women suffer unemployment and underemployment. This tension between a prized work ethic and idleness is one of the defining features of life in Niamey. Nevertheless, many Hausa prefer to think of the glass as half full.

Last year, for example, a *hira* group in which I have been participating for more than a decade broached this topic. Ibrahim began by asking me, "Do you have time to just hang out with friends for conversation in the U.S. like we do here?" I responded, "No, unfortunately we do not. This is one of the main things I really appreciate about Niamey." "I did not think so," Ibrahim said. Aliyou chimed in; "I had a friend who lived in New York. He said that all he did was work, work, work, and with no time for socializing he was miserable." Ousmane, who could see his point, explained, "Yes, I understand, I could not live without lots of daily conversation," and most in the group readily agreed. But Issaka, affectionately known to his *hira* mates as "Americain" due to his long-stated dream of going to the U.S., dissented, "I would miss you guys, but I am ready to get on the next plane to spend the rest of my life working at whatever job I can get even if I don't have time for conversation." Lamine concluded the conversation, "Well, yes, I would probably do the same if I had the chance, but I am really happy that we are here together every day." Later in the day while reading I was struck by the words of feminist South African novelist Zukiswa Wanner, "It's better to cry in a limousine than to laugh in a taxi" (2009:142), indicating that wealth is preferable to poverty even if it means exchanging solitary misery for the joy of good company. The following day I quoted Wanner's words to the group and asked them to respond. The lively discussion that ensued was roughly equally split between those who saw wisdom in her perspective and those who would resist sacrificing a vibrant social life for material prosperity.

Most Hausa struggle to make a living in Niamey. Virtually all Hausa migrants in Niamey in the late 1980s had extensive experience in farming typically having spent the first 15-20 years of their lives working on their father's farms. Many of today's generation of youth coming of age in Niamey have never even been to a farm. A series of Structural Adjustment Programs over the past 25 years have gutted the public sector leaving very few stable civil service jobs and leading to an ever-increasing expansion of the informal economy in which more than 90 percent of Niaméens work. Anthropologist Donna Perry (1997:235) has argued that the growth of the informal sector is the result of global, not national, processes in the neoliberal moment. Most Hausa work independently or work for piece-rates or daily-rates for cash. Those who work with others typically work with family or with hometown friends. About one-half work in the service sector in jobs requiring various levels of skill, particularly as security guards, butchers and cooks, tea and coffee vendors, mechanics, tailors, and taxi drivers. More than one-third work as traders, ranging from a few wealthy merchants who have large shops to the majority who sell only one item (such as fruit or kola nuts) or a handful of items (typically cigarettes, candy, snacks, cell phone top-up cards) on foot or from small portable tables. Most of the remainder makes a living in artisanal professions (particularly as leather workers), as manual laborers (especially as water carriers and porters), as traditional healers, or as beggars. Seasonal migrants are generally restricted to micro-commerce or manual labor, whereas settled migrants pursue occupations in all facets of Niamey's economy, including a tiny minority with lucrative jobs in banking, medicine, civil service, and other professions.

Most Hausa have tried a series of occupations in Niamey. For example, the following middle-aged men's fluid work histories are roughly typical. Hassane has worked as a butcher, sold animal fodder, cooked for a wealthy family, sold tin cans he collected, and sold fruit before starting his current table trading business. Bouhari currently records music and sells DVDs. Previously he worked in a bakery, worked for a Nigerian shoe company, sold spare car parts to tourists, and sold tea and coffee from a small table on the roadside. After finishing his studies at the Islamic University in Say, Abdou preached and traded hardware goods on a small scale from a stall at the Petit Marché. He is now focused on importing spare parts for refrigerators and air conditioners, and plans to begin importing tire tubes as well. Innousa has cooked macaroni, worked as a day laborer in rice paddies, worked as a motorcycle mechanic, and has worked independently in small-scale trade. He now occasionally finds work as a day laborer for a wholesale construction firm unloading and stacking goods, and sells tapestries consigned to him by a wealthy merchant at the Grand Marché. Ganga has sold fried cakes for his mother, assisted his father with carpentry, served as a tailor's apprentice for a Malian man, and sold artwork for a Guinean man outside of the Musée Nationale. He is currently enrolled in a technical school studying computers.

Family Norms and Manipulations

Family is central in Hausa social life. Family life is structured by rules that define complex rights and obligations, but Hausa creatively work around them in many circumstances. Hausa kinship is bilateral, emphasizing fluid lateral connections (often on the male side due to patrilocality) not unilineal connections beyond three generations. Consanguineal ties take precedence over affinal ties. One's first loyalty is to one's blood kin. Marriage and parenthood define adulthood and are considered obligatory in Muslim Hausa culture. Marriage is virilocal or patrilocal; that is, married couples reside near or with husbands' parents if possible. In any case wives move into the homes of their husbands. Any children they bear will follow the same pattern; sons will stay at home or nearby and daughters will move in with their husbands' families. Men may have up to four wives as defined by Islam, but in practice most married men are married monogamously. Most Hausa have many full siblings and half siblings, and dozens of cousins, aunts, and uncles. Fostering is very common, particularly among siblings. The *gida* ("compound" or "household")—ideally led by a senior male who directs the labor of other members and makes the key financial decisions regarding pooled family resources—is a primary unit of everyday social organization, and "the core of the co-residential unit is a group of males linked by ties of kinship traced through males" (M. G. Smith 1954:21). The *gida* also includes wives and unmarried daughters, and often some extended family and non-kin as well. The broader extended family rarely acts as corporate group. Hausa seldom see a substantial portion of their complete extended family at the same time and place. The two main exceptions are naming ceremonies and weddings. Smaller segments of family visit one another in succession, with some overlap, during Muslim festivals and to offer condolences after funerals.

Husbands and fathers are obligated to feed, house, and clothe their wives and children. Co-wives expect to be treated equally by their husbands. Husbands and fathers are obligated to teach their wives (if necessary) and children the rudiments of Islam, and if they have the financial resources they are expected to send their wives and children to study with *malamai* ("Islamic teacher-scholars"). In return, husbands and fathers expect obedience, respect, loyalty, and domestic labor (cooking and cleaning) from their wives and children. Wives and mothers have the right to retain their own incomes. Mothers do the bulk of work guiding their daughters from birth to marriage, and take primary responsibility for rearing young boys. Mothers and fathers typically share responsibility for instructing and nurturing sons after they are about six years of age. Children are expected to defer to the authority of their parents (especially their fathers) in most important matters, such as decisions about migration, remittances, and marriage. Strict age hierarchies should be maintained. Younger brothers and sisters should show great respect for elder brothers and sisters (even if only one year separates them), and elder brothers and sisters should help younger brothers and sisters if they are able, especially if they are away from home, such as in Niamey. Children should assist their parents in retirement. Sons inherit twice the share of females, and all full children of parents are entitled to a share of inheritance structured by this underlying principle. Finally, the overarching principles of family solidarity and reciprocity crosscut these specific rules. That is, one should help family members in need whenever one is able in accordance with one's means, or as Youssoufou put it, "You can never forget your family."

Hausa manipulate and bend these norms and rules to serve particular interests at particular times. This is nothing new in Hausa culture; generations of scholars have emphasized the fragility and tensions of Hausa family life (e.g., Alidou 2005, Hill 1972, M.G. Smith, 1954, Wall 1988, Yahaya 1973, Yusuf 1974). More than 50 years ago, M. G. Smith (1954:26) reported that "divorce occurs on average two to three times during a woman's life" among Muslim Hausa of Northern Nigeria, with jealousy among co-wives being an important factor. However, in Niamey today family life is strained by a variety of social dynamics that pose unprecedented challenges to its integrity. In broad terms, the "traditional" Hausa family is adapted to rural farming more so than urban labor and trade. Hausa are constantly coming to and going from Niamey, as seen in the previous chapter, so family are often separated by great distances for months or years at a time. This can cause marital tension, in particular, even when migrants are sending remittances. And ever-looming poverty, in a cash oriented urban economy, requires creative and flexible use of family resources to ensure survival.

Youssoufou's family career illustrates this flexibility. His marital history is defined by particular contours, but he is not alone. Due to financial constraints, marriage is increasingly difficult to achieve, and marriages are unstable. Divorce is common and so is remarriage. The majority of middle-aged Hausa men and women in Niamey that I have encountered over the last two decades have divorced at least once. Contrary to stereotype, women are often very assertive. Zeinabou has twice demanded divorce. Youssoufou considers himself to be the symbolic head of the *gida*, but in effect he has accepted Zeinabou as its co-head in practice.

She is the primary breadwinner and one of the main sources of financial support for Youssoufou and Abdou, while also supporting her daughters. While this is not the norm, it is not that unusual either. Roughly one in five households in Niamey are headed by women as a result of the frequency of divorce, long-term absences of migrant husbands, widowhood, and the increasing assertiveness of women. On rare occasions when he has a little extra money, Youssoufou shares some of it with Josephine and Mariama of his own volition recognizing Zeinabou's importance. Furthermore, Youssoufou would be far worse off if his parents had not turned over their compound in Niamey to him and Abdou. His brothers and sisters who all live in more comfortable accommodations chose not to contest this "living inheritance." In other families, particularly those with fewer resources than the Garba family, this is contested. Many other families in Niamey also make creative and practical decisions irrespective of inheritance law or tradition. For example, in Chapter 6, I will consider a case wherein a married daughter with children effectively inherited her parents' compound, with the consent of her two single brothers who continued to occupy small quarters within the compound. Finally, Youssoufou has relied financially on younger relatives and friends not older ones. These relationships were forged over years of interaction and through mutual interests and respect. While this is somewhat irregular relative to the age principle, some young migrants who find good jobs in places like New York City, Paris, and Greensboro, North Carolina support a dozen or more family members each in Niamey.

Hausa of Niamey find family to be a source of emotional and financial support as well as a difficult burden depending on particular circumstances. Perceptions are typically linked to the life cycle as children depend on parents, then parents support children and others, and the elderly in retirement depend on their children. But poverty can make one a burden, as Youssoufou has been to his family. In turn, Youssoufou helps his unemployed brother, Abdou. However, Youssoufou's younger brother, cousin, and friend do not perceive of Youssoufou as a unreasonable burden, just as millions of Nigerien Muslim Hausa do not perceive of their family members as unreasonable burdens. They think of generosity with family as a core element of what it means to be a good

Muslim. The sense that "*Duniya me halin d'an mangoro*" ("Life can surprise you if you don't take care") may also motivate generosity. Roles can be reversed in an instant.

Islam: Faith, Community, and Social Capital

Islam plays a central role in Hausa communities of Niamey. Similar to the Mawri Hausa of Dogodoutchi studied by Masquelier (2009:2),

> Although few Muslims [in Niamey] formally follow the Sufi path (*darika*), many are loosely identified as *'yan darika* (members of a Sufi order) partly because they ostensibly adhere to practices [such as "*zikiri* (recitation of the names of God)...the use of Qur'anic amulets...the celebration of the Prophet's birthday...the redistributive ethos"] that—in the absence of a clearly defined sense of collective Sufi identity—are loosely defined as Sufi but also, and more important, because they oppose Izala reformism.

Hausa of Niamey, however, typically say, "we are simply *Musulmai*" ("Muslims"), rather than "we are *'yan darika*." Most Niaméens identify themselves as traditional Muslims, even the minority who rarely or never pray or engage in other pious acts. The vast majority of adults over the age of 30 years and most youths diligently perform the five daily prayers, observe the fast during Ramadan, act charitably toward the poor, and follow core dietary rules such as avoiding pork and alcohol. Islam transcends ethno-linguistic boundaries and plays a central role in Nigerien *brassage*. It provides a deep sense of community solidarity in Niamey, despite some recent conflicts between competing sects. While some Hausa men pray consistently in one place, one of the striking qualities of everyday social life in Niamey is that most men pray with whomever they happen to be near during the call to prayer. Many men circulate daily throughout Niamey for work or to meet with family and friends, and thus pray at 20 or more spots during the week. Most Hausa women pray in the privacy of their homes.

Establishing and projecting a Muslim reputation is virtually essential to career success in Niamey. Masquelier (2009:17), citing the vast anthropological literature on the topic, explains that Islam "often becomes a way to face the present, a source of symbolic capital that can bring about economic and social advancement." Niaméens strongly prefer working, marrying, and establishing friendships with Muslims. Indeed, Youssoufou's family and friends would be far less likely to support him and his chances of finding a wife would have been very slim if he were not regarded as an upright Muslim. Non-Muslims find themselves excluded from professional opportunities, family life, and community honor. Their marginalization typically unfolds in subtle ways. Family and friends rarely ostracize them completely (though rejecting Islam constitutes grounds for divorce), and they are not physically abused. Muslim Hausa of Niamey do not emphasize their "blasphemy" or "sin," though some preachers do. Rather, non-Muslim Nigeriens—more than anything else—are regarded as completely lacking common sense and therefore as untrustworthy. (Muslim Hausa of Niamey do not usually make the same blanket assessment of people living in non-Muslim countries.)

In this context, it pays—materially and symbolically—to be regarded as a "good Muslim" in Niamey. Therefore, some Hausa strive to project a Muslim persona even if they have little or no faith. This can be achieved by the simple act of performing prayers, especially in the context of Niamey's public, outdoor culture where most men pray in outdoor mosques near their places of work, home, or favorite conversation groups. A man or woman who does not join fellow market traders or conversation partners in prayer is immediately noticed.

Among several visits with migrants to their home villages, two directly revealed the contextual nature of religious performance and identity. In each case I travelled with men who diligently perform Muslim prayers, observe the Ramadan fast, and wear traditional Muslim Hausa identifying attire in Niamey to their home villages in the Arewa region north of Dogondoutchi. Neither men performed Muslim prayers during weeklong visits. Instead they help organize and participated in *Bori* spirit possession ceremonies. *Bori*, the traditional local religion of the Hausa, has been under public assault for centuries by Muslim Hausa who regard it as blasphemous. Many Muslim Hausa regard the mixing of Islam and

Bori as even more objectionable than participating in *Bori* alone. As our bush taxis were approaching Niamey during our returns, the men dug their prayers mats out of their travel bags. They headed straight for a mosque as soon as we arrived.

Hausa men who participate in both Islamic and *Bori* rituals do not see this as contradictory, but rather as an integrated strategy for pursuing prosperity and health. However, they are painfully aware that virtually all Muslim Hausa vehemently reject their perspective, and hence are very secretive about it. Thus, establishing public reputations as "good Muslims" is part of the survival "toolkit" Hausa men dig into when necessary. To be rejected by family, friends, and neighbors is an unacceptable indignity for most Hausa men. Maintaining a Muslim persona is vital to efforts to survive with dignity.

In sum, most Hausa of Niamey draw strength and dignity from Islam. Western and other forms of modernity have not displaced Islam in Niamey. Islam is not seen merely as compatible with modernity, rather Islam is integral to Nigerien Hausa articulations of modernity. Through Islam, Hausa find purpose in life and hope for eternal reward. Islam serves as a potent "culturally constituted defense mechanism" for Hausa of Niamey. Islam explains and helps Hausa cope with misfortune. Submission to Allah and acceptance of fate promote humility and, above all else, patience. For Muslim Hausa, only small children and those lacking common sense are impatient because impatience implies contestation of Allah's will. The Hausa people's unsurpassed capacities to exhibit and (most of the time) actually be patient are simply yet profoundly expressed in what is probably the most popular proverb of Niamey, used as this chapter's epigram, *Zaman duniya sai hank'uri* ("Only with patience can one make it in the world"). With enough patience Hausa in Niamey can endure anything; they can survive with dignity.

Hausa of Niamey strive to establish wide, effective, and flexible social networks through work, family and friends, and Islam. What one knows and does operates in synergy with who one knows. These core career pursuits—material and symbolic—coalesce in *hira* ("informal conversation") groups. That is, *hira* groups involve family and friends who work, hang out, and pray together.

Hira ("Informal Conversation") Groups as Material and Symbolic Adaptations

Migrant Hausa men draw upon their street side *hira* ("informal conversation") groups in order to orient their lives, practically and symbolically, in Niamey, Niger. Counteracting the extraordinarily difficult material conditions they face in their diaspora communities, Hausa cherish the vibrant sociability, dignity, leisure, and intellectual stimulation of daily *hira* participation. Their appreciation of the power of language and verbal art to transform social experience is expressed in the popular proverb, *magana jari ce* ("speech is wealth"). This chapter views the public culture of *hira* groups as a key space for creative reflection, engagement, and response to the intrusions of globalization. Drawing upon these groups in an active way is not simply a way of managing the modern, it is in effect one crucial way that Hausa men create their own modernities, however provisional, contested, or ambivalent. Five interrelated dynamics highlight the centrality of *hira* groups in their contemporary lives.

First, Hausa men use *hira* groups and Islamic prayers to structure their sense of time, and to reflect on and adjust to other modern concepts of time. On any given day, most Hausa men in Niamey have little or no money-earning work. Their most common jobs, such as selling fruit or hot tea and coffee from a small table, lend themselves well to *hira*. These are men with time on their hands. Indeed, most men spend most of their waking hours in *hira* groups!

Second, men use *hira* groups to negotiate—in a practical sense—the urban and modern terrain of Niamey as well as its interconnections with other areas of Niger and the wider Hausa diaspora. The first order of business for migrants upon arrival in Niamey is to find their hometown *hira* group or groups: to secure or at least get informed advice about lodging and jobs; to "learn the ropes" about life in Niamey; and to integrate themselves in the communication networks linking Niamey and "home." Migrants seeking work need wide and effective social networks, especially since many jobs are temporary. For most, long-term success depends on having links to settled migrants and especially wealthy traders who are willing to establish patron-client relationships. The best way to establish and maintain effective social networks is through regular, skilled performance in several *hira* groups.

Third, men use *hira* groups to mediate the intrusions of other understandings of modernity in a space where they can retain some sense of autonomy and self-respect in the face of proliferating visions of modernity by insisting upon certain traditional values (articulate speech, leisure, male social interaction that is appropriate within Islam) that are undervalued in Western culture. As a "traditional" institution, *hira* groups continue to address central Hausa concerns in the production of urban space in Niamey, most notably, the desire for a vibrant social life emphasizing vibrant conversation and acceptance of the dignity and worth of all men. Through participating in dense networks of *hira* groups, at least one of which is frequented by friends and kin from home, migrants are creating homes away from homes.

Fourth, men use *hira* groups as a safe arena of debate and definition of their own not-so-traditional modernity, from appropriating pop culture to testing various ways of thinking about what is and is not permitted within Islam, to reflecting upon Niger's place in the global economy by discussing radio, television, and videos. Cultural debates draw from an expanding reservoir of symbolic resources: each other's increasingly varied migratory career histories, the multiculturalism of Niamey, and the proliferation of global and local mass media.

Fifth, men retain *hira* groups actively as a space of social distinction, an arena of performance through which men of relatively modest means can nevertheless make a mark in the male Hausa social world. This pursuit of prestige, based on verbal skills, knowledge of the world, and character, is heightened in Niamey where job opportunities are so limited. Simply put, for many unemployed and underemployed migrants, *hira* groups offer the best, and sometimes the only realistic way to achieve distinction. Furthermore, even men who do not earn special distinction gain personal fulfillment by association with prestigious, charismatic individuals.

The broader goal of this chapter (and the discussion that follows in the next chapter) is to contribute to a nuanced understanding of globalization and modernity by centering on how real people—situated on the outer periphery of modern global economy—in their everyday lives experience, mediate, resist, and create alternative modernities in a globalizing world. Hausa understandings of modernity, like those of other people around the world, are marked by hybridization, creolization, and local appropriation of global symbolic resources, not global homogenization or westernization. Through focusing on *hira* groups, it is apparent that the mundane, the quotidian, is actually a supremely important space for adaptation and innovation. Examining *hira* groups simultaneously reveals the local faces of global processes and the global character of local events.[1]

Globalization and modernity are neither uniform processes nor are they experienced uniformly by Hausa men and women. This part of the chapter offers a highly gendered view of the world expressed through a gendered institution; that is, I focus on male *hira* groups. Hausa in Niamey are rigidly segregated by gender. Women with few exceptions are excluded from men's *hira*, and play a relatively limited social role in the public culture of Hausa communities in Niamey. Though Hausa women in Niamey have less time and freedom to pursue *hira* than Hausa men, they relish their own *hira* groups, which meet in private spaces, and use them as important resources for orienting their lives in Niamey. Gender places Hausa differently in an already highly variegated global cultural economy.

My discussion of *hira* groups is structured as follows. First, I consider *hira* performance in the context of Hausa oral artistry. Second, I offer a detailed overview of the structure, rhythm, and purposes of *hira* groups, including a "thick description" of a specific set of *hira* groups. Third, I summarize several new concerns discussed in *hira* groups today, such as poverty, religion, and mass media. Finally, I conclude by reviewing the reasons why *hira* groups are of supreme importance in the lives of male Hausa migrants in Niamey, and by asserting that Hausa men use *hira* groups to establish a comfortable position in and unique understandings of global modernity.

Hausa Oral Artistry and *Hira* Performance

A nuanced interpretation of the central role that *hira* groups play in the construction of modernities among labor migrants in Niamey requires appreciation of the power of words and the extraordinarily rich and vibrant "traditions" of verbal art among the Hausa. Interpreting the famous proverb *magana jari ce* ("speech is wealth"), Cooper (1999:87) demonstrates that "oral performance can be a form of capital ... that oral performance can be thought of as a transaction involving wealth." Hunter and Oumarou (1998) argue that Hausa self-conscious awareness of the power of language is reflected in a vast repertoire of metalanguage as well as several proverbs expressing the volatility of this power, and "the potential of language for irrevocably altering a situation, for causing an imbalance, for causing trouble ... language must not be used frivolously." *Hira* group participants recognize the danger of *hululu* ("idle chatter") that "can turn into gossip or even lies" (Hunter and Oumarou 1998:161). A man with communicative competence displays the ability to use and interpret language in socially and culturally appropriate ways; he knows what to say and when and how to say it.

Hira participants are both listeners and performers. Numerous proverbs highlight the importance of listening. Skillful *hira* performance entails balancing these roles in a context of fluid, negotiated, and sometimes conflicting informal rules of conversation. For example, *hira* groups fluctuate between aggressive, rapid, turn taking involving multiple simultaneous conversations on the one hand; and periods of silence which can last for several minutes on the other. The value of the latter is expressed in the classic adage *kurum ma magana ce* ("silence is also language"). Indeed, Hunter and Oumarou (1998:162) document that "silence is the theme of several proverbs, touted as appropriate behaviour or endowed with its own communicative impact."

Furniss' (1996) comprehensive presentation of the literary culture of the Hausa of Northern Nigeria, offers detailed analyses of all the major genres, including: proverbs, riddles, oral and written poetry and song, praise-singing, theater, and fictive and non-fictive stories. He does not, however, interpret these genres as distinct entities. Central to his thesis is the view that genres operate as "parallel domains of discourse" which require "attentiveness to the migration and overlap of textual materials between media of communication" and to "the interaction of genres operating within particular social and ideological contexts" (Furniss

1996:1). This perspective is supported by cross-cultural evidence on verbal performance that reveals that "pursuit of a particular interactive focus (teaching, exhorting, befriending, confronting, etc.) generally involves negotiated changes of genre in which features of one genre are embedded within a token of another" (Bauman and Briggs 1990:64).

Hira group participants draw on their experiences as performers and consumers of multiple verbal genres. Indeed, conversation groups, as "speech events," involve a remarkable synergy of Hausa genres, informal and formal talk, which highlight the overall importance of verbal wit and the vitality of verbal expression among the Hausa. Among the diversity of genres and the uses for which they are employed by Hausa, Furniss (1996:8) concludes that "two very different voices [are] represented: the laughing, whimsical, satirical voice of popular humour; and the serious, didactic, moral representation of upright, honourable behaviour. These counterpoint voices recur again and again across many genre boundaries and on a wide variety of subjects." These juxtaposing channels similarly mark much of *hira* performance.

Recognizing the broader context of Hausa verbal art, this chapter views the public culture of *hira* groups as a highly strategic site for the investigation of the ways by which globalization and the media affect, and are interpreted by, Hausa migrants in their diaspora communities in Niamey. My discussion is grounded in the theoretical insights and empirical evidence of the sociolinguistic literature on oral performance that highlights the "heterogeneous and dynamic character of language use and the central place it occupies in the social construction of reality" (Bauman and Briggs 1990:60). Through the collective construction of the world around them, *hira* group participants demonstrate the power of "verbal art to transform, not simply reflect, social life" (Bauman and Briggs 1990:69). Social interaction in *hira* "requires an integrated analysis of action, mutual [and contested] knowledge, and social context" (Goodwin and Heritage 1990:284). This approach emphasizes that "intersubjective understandings are actively achieved as the outcome of concrete interactive processes" that create "mutual understandings [that] are highly contingent and revisable" (Goodwin and Heritage 1990:286. As focal arenas of public cultural debate, *hira* groups interactively interpret and evaluate the world to creatively produce unique understandings of modernity.

The Structure, Rhythm, and Purposes of *Hira*

I first sat in *hira* groups for extended periods of time during ethnographic research in small, rural, Hausa villages numbering three hundred to one thousand people in south central Niger during the farming seasons of 1988 and 1989. Evenings were devoted to *hira* groups meeting in *zauruka* ("compound entrance rooms") or on dirt paths in the center of town. Relaxed, informal discussions focused on local matters such as farming conditions, village gossip, and joking. Men also enjoyed telling stories of adventure and discovery, of their migrations to Niamey and beyond. They were asked many questions: How much does it cost to get to Niamey? How can I find people from our village once I get there? Who will help me find work and a place to stay? I also had my first taste of *hira* in Niamey in 1988. Since then my research has focused on the *hira* groups of Hausa migrants in Niamey. After communicating my goals as an ethnographer, I spent countless hours hanging out in conversation groups, listening, participating to the best of my ability, and then later reconstructing the highlights and central themes of *hira* sessions. I reasoned that tape recording would be too invasive to the flow of *hira*.

Conversation groups meet at roadsides all day throughout Niamey. At any point when active, they typically consist of about ten participants, with a core group of about six men around the same age and usually from the same hometown. However, the composition of groups fluctuates on an hourly, daily, and seasonal basis. Groups can swell to include two-dozen men. Most conversation groups in Niamey are integrated ethnically to a greater or lesser extent. The vast majority of the men in the *hira* groups in which I participated identify as Hausa, including those in eight groups that I have studied intensively (for at least three years and as many as 20) and dozens of other groups that I have visited sporadically.

While I became affiliated with most of these groups by pure chance (e.g., by stopping to buy a soft drink) or through connections who introduced me to their favorite groups, I purposefully chose groups representing all of the major regions and Hausa subgroups of Niger, meeting in diverse neighborhoods scattered throughout Niamey, and consisting of men working in typical occupations (Sabo 1996): small-scale trading; service jobs, such as tea and coffee preparation and selling; manual labor, such as water carrying; and trades involving varying levels of skill, such as tailoring, repairing, butchering, and leather working.[2]

The focus of my research is on *hira* as it occurs within particular *hira* groups that have an enduring social existence. However, *hira* can refer to any conversation between any two people at any time. Olofson (1975), who studied Funtua, a Hausa city in Northern Nigeria, offers the only sustained discussion of *hira* in the ethnographic literature.[3] Olofson (1975:149) defines *hira* "as voluntary, relaxed, effortless, and pleasurable conversation, an activity which it has been said the Hausa man abroad misses most about his home and language." Socially, he found that a precondition for both *hira* and *harka* ["life," "movement," "social interaction," "business transaction"] is "*jituwa* 'harmony'. . .between interactants who are on good terms with each other and who share mutual pleasures." In Niamey, I also found that *hira* groups can only establish an enduring existence if their core participants share and appreciate friendship, lighthearted interaction, and the simple willingness to pass the time together shooting the breeze. Roughly speaking, then, *hira* groups are the practice of friends getting together for long informal conversations.

In Niamey, Hausa men's love of *hira* is expressed in the comments of two migrants. Moussa, a settled migrant from Zinder, never lets a day go by without several hours of *hira*:

> All types of *hira* are equally good. All types are good depending on the context. Some days it's religion, others life in the world, sometimes we discuss thieves, or religion, or the life in Niamey. Each type is great; none is better than the next. Today my friends and I are discussing religion, tomorrow something else, the next day marriage. We talk about everything. Sometimes we stay by my front door until midnight or more. My friends come to see me and I go to see them. We don't have a special place. I also talk with my neighbors every day.

Aliou, a dry season migrant from a hamlet about two hundred kilometers east of Niamey who relishes *hira*, explains, "*hira* is the best thing about life in Niamey. We must have *hira* every day or we could not be happy. You see that I never leave my table trading business from the time I wake up until I go to sleep, and people are always here discussing, laughing, and arguing."

Hausa use *hira* to make life bearable when faced with poverty, loneliness, and despair. Similarly Olofson (1975:152) argues, "To Hausa, *hira* is in many senses the stuff of life, whether rural or urban in setting, and the more of it, the better."

Public, institutionalized, street side *hira* groups value highly the art of conversation, pure "sociability" (Simmel 1949), democracy and the equal status of most regular participants, and discuss the broadest range of topics. However, hierarchies among speakers exist in all groups. Older men, Islamic leaders, and expert conversationalists enjoy freedom to initiate topics and their views may sometimes silence others. They are always offered the best seats, typically requiring that other men must take places on mats.

Hira is not merely a matter of fun and games or "killing time." It is serious, for much is at stake. Participation is not truly voluntary. While a man has a great deal of freedom to choose his *hira* partners, topics, times, and level of participation, every "normal" man must regularly participate in *hira*. A man who avoids *hira* groups is regarded as an outcast, as *rashin hankali* ("lacking sense"), or possibly a *mahaucaci* ("crazy man"). Such a man, it is said, is bound to feel not only unhappy, but is cut off from social networks, information, and connections which are absolutely essential for any chance at material success in Niamey. Though instrumental concerns cannot ensure the durability of *hira* groups, they are crucial nonetheless. *Hira* is about building community, building social networks, and creating long-lasting bonds. While most men turn to family first when they have no money, many *hira* mates are seriously united and willing to make difficult personal sacrifices to provide food, shelter, and substantial loans to others in need.

Furthermore *hira* involves difficult verbal work and skill in considering many complex, intellectual, personal, and controversial topics. Men are aware that their oral skills and identities are constantly being evaluated by others, and that they are "on stage." *Hira* groups function as "informal encounters" (Goldschmidt 1990:147). Despite the requirement of fun-loving camaraderie, *hira* is differentiating in terms of prestige. Special individuals who are appreciated for their story telling prowess, abilities to coin new phrases, or skills in delivering smart quips that impress their friends, enliven *hira* groups.

Hira performance can expose a man to multiple threats and challenges to his reputation, hence "one pervasive strategy in everyday life, and hence also in dialogues, is the optimal display of one's social self for other participants" (van Jijk 1985:4). Kirk-Greene (1974) argues that the concept of *mutumin kirki* ("good man") in Hausa involves the demonstration of a wide range of personal qualities and values, including: *gaskiya* ("truth"), *amana* ("trust"), *karamci* ("generosity"), *hank'uri* ("patience"), *hankali* ("common sense"), *kunya* ("shame," "modesty"), *ladabi* ("good manners"), *mutunci* ("humanity"), *hikima* ("Islamic wisdom"), and *adalci* ("Islamic scruples"). In practice, *hira* performance and recognition of a particular *mutumin kirki* operate reciprocally: "All of these qualities (as well as their opposites) have reflexes in language as is evident in . . . verbal art performances. These are the qualities that build *hali*, character, and they are the qualities that endow a theory of ideal language behavior" (Hunter and Oumarou 1998:168-69).

Most groups include dry season migrants and settled migrants. Most men have a favorite group, but visit two to four others daily. Some men spend many hours each day traveling throughout the city from one group to another, joining dozens of groups, each for a short period, thus mirroring social organization in Hausaland. "A significant part of the social texture of a Hausa town," according to Olofson, "consists of a dense network of *hira* groups in a compact social space" (1975:149-50).

Many *hira* groups have been meeting, at exactly the same spots, for more than a decade, particularly if they meet at the business site or outside the home of a settled migrant who shares the same hometown as many of the participants. (Seven of the eight groups that are the focus of my study fit this description.) Some groups break apart or lose their meeting place when key participants leave Niamey, when members argue, or when men become interested in other *hira* groups.

Many groups have ongoing conversations twelve to eighteen hours a day. Most have irregular hours but are active daily. There is little or no formality in terms of the means whereby groups assemble or dissolve for the day. Most men come and go as they please or as necessary to meet other obligations.

A *wurin hira* ("place of conversation") is anywhere that people meet regularly for conversation. In Niamey conversation groups gather by the sides of streets. Many say that the busier the street the better it is for conversation, as this offers opportunities to experience and comment on the bustling activities of the city—social interaction, motor and pedestrian traffic, trading either from established stalls or on foot, the diverse practices of many ethnic groups, and street football games. Men typically sit side by side in lines facing the street, and several conversations may occur simultaneously. While *hira* groups value the vitality of street life, they really have nowhere else to meet. Most migrants live in cramped quarters—typical single migrants rent nine square meter apartments.

Hira groups typically meet at the business sites of small-scale traders or tea and coffee sellers. The trader usually provides an open-air thatched shelter for shade, chairs, benches, or mats, a radio, and more and more commonly, a television and DVD player. Only a few *hira* groups are named, and it is highly prestigious for a man to have a *hira* group named in his honor.

Due to the general lack of time constraints, the diverse makeup of participants, the complex demands of living in a diaspora community, and rapidly expanding symbolic resources (especially mass media) conversation groups in Niamey consider a much wider of range of topics than their rural counterparts. Even so, most discussions focus on what people can see in the streets in front of them or on personal matters: relating an incident, amusing or disturbing, that happened to one of the friends; considering an important decision such as onward migration; and explaining the difficulty one is experiencing, for example, in finding work, in preparing for marriage, in being separated from one's wife or family.

Migrant Hausa men in Niamey consider a kaleidoscopic range of topics in *hira* groups. *Hira* is fluid; there are no agendas. It is impossible to predict the topics a *hira* group will open with on any day, what will cause agreement or arguments, and where it will all end. Sometimes men will revisit a particular topic that they feel needs more examination when they meet the next day.

While there is tremendous variation across groups and individuals, the following topics are the most popular in the groups I studied: world and national news, particularly news about politics, diplomacy, war, technology, international celebrities, religion, and football; individual migration histories, which are compared and contrasted; life in Niamey in particular and Niger in general, especially jobs, lodging, and various social problems; the character and personality quirks of (usually) absent *hira* partners or other people from the neighborhood. While many participants enjoy abstract discussions of Islam, most conversations focus on applying Islamic teaching and values to particular, everyday events, people, and situations. A mélange of other topics such as the weather, prices of particular commodities, and hometowns are also commonly discussed. Over the past two decades, rapidly expanding access to mass media is increasingly informing opinion and debate about these topics as will be explored below. But first, I want to discuss one particular set of *hira* groups.

Kuka *Hira* Groups in Niamey

Kuka is home to 1,000 mostly Kourfeyawa Hausa farmers who grow millet, sorghum, and beans just north of Dogondoutchi, about 300 kilometers east of Niamey. For 30 years the center of the Kuka migrant community in Niamey has gathered in a deeply rutted, slightly sloping, dusty, unpaved public square, about the size of a football field. Streets from all four corners bring a steady stream of auto, motorcycle, bicycle, livestock, and pedestrian traffic through this urban space. Surrounding the square lie six large, rectangular, mud colored, brick compounds, and two small mosques. Windowless mud and cement walls, many in a state of disrepair, face the square, offering privacy to two large relatively prosperous families (one Hausa and one Zarma), and four large, struggling families (one Hausa and three Zarma). In the early 1990s the state constructed a *jardin d'enfants* ("kindergarten") that occupies about a third of the square. For years, children and goats came to pick through a mound of trash that accumulated adjacent to the *jardin*'s walls due to Niamey's highly erratic garbage collection infrastructure, until El Hadji Sani—the leader of the Kuka contingent in Niamey—organized young men to keep it clean. In the largest open space, though also the most sloped, young men from Kuka and the neighborhood play competitive football games during most evenings. Barefooted or wearing flip-flops, teams of six to a side with Kuka men on each kick a partially deflated half-sized ball toward goals consisting of two cinder blocks, all the while wary of the traffic which crisscrosses their street pitch.

Since the 1980s, at any time of day between sunrise and midnight, roughly forty men, three-quarters of them from Kuka, meet in four to five interlinked *hira* groups dispersed around the square. (This set of *hira* groups is one of the eight I have studied intensively.) The first group of about six young regulars operated a motorcycle repair service in a shed on one side of the school from 1980 to 2000 with busy days but many days of little work. The shed remains and has drawn a new crowd of men from Kuka who constructed a small open-air mosque delineated by cinder blocks adjacent to it ten years ago. Today this group consists primarily of elderly men, including a traditional healer who sees clients here throughout the day, though many of the now middle-aged mechanics stop by regularly. The second group of eight or so men meets along a street corner where they specialize in making *kilishi* ("jerky"). Men pause to greet them while they are working, but avoid staying for long due to swarms of flies. The butchers circulate among the other Kuka-based groups when they are not working.

The third *hira* group of this set meets at El Hadji Sani's compound, which occupies two-thirds of one side of the square. Drawing from his wealth derived from farming as a young man and his reputation as a *malam* ("Islamic teacher-scholar"), El Hadji Sani, a Bakourfaye (singular of Kourfeyawa) Hausa, in the late 1970s, was one of the first men from Kuka to settle in Niamey. Now about seventy years old, he has long been a leading figure in this diaspora community. In his large compound, he established a small mosque and Qur'anic school with the assistance of a visiting mission from Saudi Arabia. This Arab connection enhanced his prestige and endows the mosque and school (and in a sense, the Kuka community writ large) with a special aura of sacred, learned legitimacy. For many years, his compound hosted one of Niamey's first air conditioner and refrigerator repair shops, managed by his two eldest sons and employing two Yoruba men and about six apprentice repairmen from Kuka. He also offers two guest rooms large enough to accommodate about ten migrants from Kuka, who stay with him for free.

El Hadji's mosque and reputation connect him to *malamai* from Kano and Katsina—old centers of Islamic learning in Northern Nigeria—several of whom periodically visit him for days or weeks at a time. His business is also transnational as he relies on kin in Nigeria to provide spare parts unavailable in Niger, and kin in Accra, Ghana who operate a similar shop.

El Hadji spends his days at his thatch-covered mosque discussing the Qur'an with other *malamai* and his age mates from Kuka and the neighborhood, and instructing children and youths. During lulls, young men come seeking to establish patron-client relationships with him, asking him for loans, advice, job connections, food, and a place to stay.

El Hadji permits Hassane, now 49 and also a Bakourfaye Hausa, to operate a table trading business just next to his mosque and repair shop, a prime spot. Since 1984 this fourth group of the interlinked set has been the most dynamic and popular *hira* group in the Kuka community of Niamey owing to Hassane's reputation as a skilled conversationalist and all around *mutumin kirki* ("good man"). From atop several rickety wood tables covered by a small thatch hangar, Hassane sells a typical range of products: soap, salt, sugar, candies, cigarettes, kola nuts, pens, notebooks, batteries, and fresh fruit. He also sells ice cold Coca-Cola, Fanta, and Sprite from a small refrigerator, a leftover form El Hadji's repair shop, which distinguishes his business from that of most other table-traders in Niamey. The pace of work is slow, and customers seldom wait in line. Most make very small-scale purchases such as single cigarettes, leaving most of the day open for *hira*.

Hassane has collected three small wooden benches, several metal chairs, a couple of metal frame chairs with nylon cord backs and seats for honored guests, and a few woven mats, all of which face the center of the square. Hassane's radio cassette player is on for hours each day. Much of the time it provides background noise, but at times men carefully listen to, and then discuss the news and football games (local, national, and global), Islamic preaching (both Nigerien and Nigerian *malamai*), music (Nigerien, African, reggae, Indian film, and global pop).

After receiving his father's permission, Hassane began seasonal migrations to Niamey from Kuka in 1980 when he was seventeen years old. He came seeking money, to escape the poverty of his father, and to improve his standing at home. In his first four dry seasons in Niamey, he pursued a series of occupations including butchering, selling bundles of fodder, domestic work, collecting and selling tin cans, and selling guavas on foot. During this time, he struggled to pay rent on a thatch home in a very poor neighborhood and could only afford to eat *koko*, a sorghum-based gruel. Then, after securing loans and gifts from relatives and friends in Kuka and Niamey, he started his table trading business in 1984, which has remained in the exact same spot in the square ever since (though he replaced his table with a corrugated tin shed in 2002). He operated it during dry seasons for the next seven years.

Soon after entering this occupation, Hassane saved enough money to marry a poor woman from Kuka. For the first five years of their marriage, and even after they had two children, Hassane left his wife and children in Kuka and spent the long dry seasons in Niamey because he could not afford to provide for them in Niamey. In 1990, Hassane solidified his relationship with El Hadji. Their Kuka connection together with Hassane's growing reputation as a good, humble, hard working, devout, responsible Muslim husband and father led El Hadji to offer Hassane and his family a small rent-free room in his compound. Freed from the burden of rent, Hassane moved his family to Niamey to further pursue trading as a settled migrant. For the next 15 years, he made only brief visits home. Hassane's business continued to grow, though he never earned more than the equivalent of about two dollars a day in profits. In 1999 he decided to marry a second wife, a young Zarma woman from the square. Since the woman was recently orphaned, with no known relatives, Hassane did not have to provide bridewealth. He described this as a "humanitarian act of charity" that had been coordinated by a *malam* who he met at his table. A year later, after his second wife give birth, Hassane decided to move to his own small apartment with his co-wives and their three children in a poor neighborhood about a thirty-minute walk from the square.

Hassane experienced joy and hardship during the next decade. His family grew to include nine children. However, their growing needs together with difficulty of keeping up with rent forced him to liquidate much of his stock of merchandise and discontinue table trading. In the past several years, aside from occasional odd jobs, he works only on Thursday nights selling milk and honey and other wholesome refreshments to crowds of about 500 who attend public Izala preaching sessions outside of El Hadji's mosque. Three years ago, another *malam* in the neighborhood who frequents Hassane's *hira* group decided to pay Hassane's rent. He explained that this was a good investment as he sees Hassane as a role model in the community.

To Hassane's great satisfaction, countless relatives, friends, and neighbors regard him as a friendly and engaging conversationalist. Hassane is patient, thoughtful with his words, intelligent, and quick to smile and crack jokes though generally quite serious. Virtually every migrant from Kuka stops by to chat at what is known as *wurin* Hassane ("Hassane's place"). At any given moment, roughly ten men, with a core group of six friends from Kuka, make up this hira group. But membership is fluid; men come and go all day long, some stay for minutes while others stay for hours. Some men return home to farm each rainy season, while others see Niamey as a steppingstone for onward migration to Hausa diaspora communities outside of Niger. El Hadji's younger visitors, *malamai* and traders from Nigeria and Ghana, usually spend most of their time at Hassane's table. Migrants, both seasonal and settled, from other towns in Niger are also active participants. Hassane has learned to speak Zarma fluently, winning him many friends in and around the square and helping his trade. He enjoys using rudimentary French with the occasional civil servant who stops by for a soft drink.

Over the past decade Hassane's *hira* group has consisted of a regular cast of characters. Innousa is a single fifty-three year old Bakourfaye Hausa jack-of-all-trades from Kuka who has migrated to Niamey for dry seasons each of the past 30 years. Omar is a 40-year-old Zarma man whose family moved to Niamey from a neighboring village when he was an infant. He finds occasional work as a laborer on construction crews. Cheifou, a man about 40 years old, has migrated to Niamey from Maradi during dry seasons for 20 years. During his first three years, he studied in a technical school to become a customs agent for Niger. Though he gained his credentials, he never was hired and has had to fall back on the small-scale job that paid for his education—mobile fruit and kola nut selling from a large tray balanced atop his head.

Forty-three year old Harouna is El Hadji's eldest son and the manager of and most skilled mechanic in the refrigerator and air conditioner repair shop. His legs are emaciated due to childhood polio but this does not interfere with his work. He has an infectious laugh and a deep knowledge of Islam. He settled with his father in Niamey in 1978. By the late 1990s the business prospered, enabling him to marry and move out of his father's compound with his wife and baby, establish his own repair shop on a busy paved boulevard about a kilometer from the square, and upgrade from a three-wheeled, hand-pedal-powered wheelchair to a motorized wheelchair custom designed by the Kuka contingent at the shed and capable of keeping pace with most city traffic.

Salisou, also in his early forties, is a Ba'are (singular of Arewa) Hausa from Kuka who has migrated seasonally to Niamey during most dry seasons since 1988, usually staying in El Hadji's guest room. In his first years in Niamey he worked as a "boy" (a term used by Nigerien Hausa for a domestic worker), for various wealthy families. Since then his primary job has been selling lemons and oranges either from a basket on his head or at small stall in the Petit Marché. Some years, he joins a friend from Kuka working in small gold mines in Burkina Faso and Mali.

Namaje is a Bakourfaye from Kuka in his late forties who has migrated to Niamey during the dry season for more than two decades. He has never been able to afford to bring his wife and three children with him. He sells deep-fried yams on most days immediately next to Hassane's table. During parts of three dry seasons he plied this trade in Zaria, Nigeria.

Ali is a 47-year-old Ba'marade (singular of Maradawa) Hausa from Maradi who settled in Niamey 23 years ago. He has worked in casinos during most of his time in the city, and his regular salary exceeds that of most men in the group. He lived on the square in a thatch dwelling during his initial years in Niamey, but now resides in a comfortable two-bedroom apartment with his wife and three children in a distant neighborhood. The group appreciates that he goes out of his way to join them, and his humility and piety that overshadow his profession.

Emerging Concerns among Hira Groups Today

The most important or emerging concerns discussed in *hira* groups today include poverty and Niger's place in the global economy and cultural globalization processes; and religious debates and conflicts regarding Muslim identity and what is and what is not permitted in Islam. Exponentially accelerating access to and consumption of local and global mass media forms (cassettes, radios, television, film, and video) increasingly fuel discussion of these and other issues. I begin by outlining revealing encounters in Hassane's group to illustrate how these themes and resources are often intertwined.

In 1991, Malam Ali of Katsina, Nigeria came to visit El Hadji Sani for several weeks to discuss Islamic theology. Hassane and his friends accorded him much deference and listened intently to his instructions and Islamic interpretations of everyday matters. Malam Ali argued that football is sinful as it distracts people from fulfilling their religious duties. He claimed that Muslims should only participate in the sports the Prophet Muhammad pursued—swimming, horseback riding, and sword fighting. Hassane and company scoffed, but really did not know how to respond. Many men simply said, "Football is fun."

One day, Hassane and his compatriots began their street football game about thirty minutes before the first evening prayer. During the call to prayers, friends on the sidelines hollered that it was time to quit playing. Hassane's teammates and opponents resisted, desiring to finish the hotly contested match. Hassane and other players were clearly torn, but they chose to continue playing. By the time they were finished, friends and neighbors had long since completed their prayers. Hassane and most of the competitors quietly made their way over to El Hadji's open-air mosque to perform their ablutions and prayers. Hassane was clearly embarrassed. As he returned to his table, Malam Ali scolded him, "See what football does!" Hassane never let this happen again. He did not stop playing football, but he never lets it interfere with prayers.

Malam Ali returned for a short visit in 1998—during the World Cup. For three weeks, Télé Sahel, the national television service, devoted virtually its entire programming to the World Cup. Like many *hira* groups throughout the city, Hassane's group used an extension cord to bring a borrowed television set onto the street. Malam Ali again admonished them. But this time Hassane had an answer. The national team of Saudi Arabia had qualified for the tournament, and cameras captured their enthusiastic fans. Hassane asserted that, "If the center of the Islamic world enjoys football, then we can too." This argument frustrated Malam Ali, who retorted, "You guys will never learn," before leaving the group to rejoin El Hadji's Islamic discussions. As this episode indicates, being a *malam* is prestigious in most contexts, but social roles, "are not given or defined a priori but dynamically enacted and negotiated during the ongoing encounter" (van Dijk 1985:5). Indeed, the strong undercurrent of distrust of *malamai* is a topic that I will address in the next chapter. This example also illustrates the way in which exposure to mass media leads to global awareness (Abdou 1984, Sabo 1996), and how that can sometimes undermine the authority of local leaders.

When Hassane and his age mates first arrived in Niamey in the 1980s, they were content with their own pickup games on the street. By the early 1990s, they were listening to African Cup of Nations (CAN) games on the radio and were attending games between Nigerien clubs games at the National Stadium as well as games pitting the national team against West African teams. (The national team occasionally held its own against superior squads due in large measure to the clever tactic of scheduling games during the hottest part of the day.) Today they are watching games on television as well, and in general they are knowledgeable fans about football all over the world. The men of Hassane's group, like men in general in Niamey, take great pleasure in worldwide football, which makes them feel, in a sense, like global citizens. On the other hand, exposure to mass media is also contributing to the formation of an inferiority complex and self-deprecatory attitudes. By watching the World Cup and European soccer, the men are more aware than ever of the inferiority of Nigerien football and are now rather embarrassed by it. Namaje captured the mood of some men in the group when he declared, "Our teams look foolish in comparison to the rest of the world." He did not stop there, adding "We are poor because we are stupid, and even our women are ugly."[4] This led to a flurry of debate. No consensus was reached, but the important point is that the men were forced to engage with the perspective of a respected and well-liked friend.

Grinding poverty is a fact of life for many migrants in Niamey. Hausa are famous for their stoic resolve in the face of overwhelming difficulty. "*Zaman duniya sai hank'uri*," figuratively meaning "only through patience can one survive in the world," is the most commonly exchanged proverb among Hausa migrants in Niamey, as highlighted earlier.[5] Clearly the patience of many individuals is, nevertheless, being severely tested, and this is also reflected in the discourse of *hira* groups. One of the most common greetings among the Hausa is "*Ina gajiya*?" (How's the tiredness?"). Historically, there was only one possible answer, "*Ba gajiya*" ("There is no tiredness"). Today, however, many are responding to this once entirely formulaic greeting with the statement, "*Akwai gajiya*" ("There is tiredness").

During my research in the late 1980s and early 1990s, I rarely heard complaints about poverty and hunger and inequality. By 1998 and ever since, these issues have been staple topics of debate and discussion in *hira* groups. Many men assert that they have virtually no control over economic conditions by citing radio news reports. Some engage in pointed criticism of SAPs and currency devaluation. As one man shouted, "The IMF is just an instrument of neo-colonial oppression designed to keep us poor!" Others blame the continuing influence of France for their problems; or point to corrupt past or current national regimes. These explanations are not new. What is new is a growing, internalized sense of hopelessness and defeat by the world capitalist system. By 1998, for the first time, I began hearing men in *hira* groups make comments such as "We Nigeriens are lazy, we do not want to work and would rather sit around sipping tea and chewing kola nuts all day" or "People in the first world are always working, moving forward, inventing new technology such as the Internet, whereas third world people only want to eat and sleep." Men have continued to make these sorts of comments to the present.

Self-deprecation is also expressed in changing views about thievery in Niamey, a subject that arouses particularly intense emotions even though its incidence is actually quite rare. Honesty is a central Hausa value, and few, if any, crimes or behaviors arouse more anger among them. Stories about thieves spread rapidly among *hira* groups, and most agree that even petty thieves should be brutally beaten. Fifteen years ago Hausa migrants claimed that Niamey's thieves were not Hausa, and not Muslims, but rather migrants from cities in Benin, Togo, or southern Nigeria. By the 2000s, Hausa men in several *hira* groups agreed that thieves come from everywhere, including the smallest Muslim Hausa villages of Niger. These reactions, I suggest, largely reflect the dire straits faced by many migrants. Worsening conditions caused by the IMF and global neoliberalism are causing people to vent their despair on others (i.e., thieves), but also leading them to look upon the thieves as people who themselves are trying to cope with worsening conditions.

The intensifying sense of internal moral decay, reflected in attitudes about thieves, finds its most poignant articulations in stories and discussions about wealth and inequality. On several occasions, I heard men cite the proverb, *Da arziki da hassada tare suke kwana* ("Envy is the bedfellow of wealth"), to open their conversation on these issues. The poor majority deeply distrusts wealth, particularly if it is not shared and appears to be accumulated mysteriously in a sea of mass poverty. *Hira* groups consisting of poor men rile against greed, corruption, and ostentatious, conspicuous consumption. When two obese men passed a *hira* group I was sitting with in 2009, one of the participants joked, "Those guys cannot last more than three hours without eating during Ramadan," leading to uproarious laughter. Finally, in the last few years, stories about how men attain wealth through nefarious, occult means have been shared with increasing frequency—a topic that I will consider in detail in the following chapter.

Hira group partners typically pray together either as self-contained units or more commonly by joining others at nearby mosques. Some men perform almost all of their prayers in the company of their favorite group. This communal act is a central part of their solidarity. Meanwhile, the rise of Islamist movements over the past 20 years has led to lively and heated debates about the proper practice of Islam. (I will discuss this in more detail in the following chapter.) Core contested topics include: bridewealth, prayer times and postures, wife seclusion, women's and men's clothing, gender mixing, and imported and local popular culture. Discussions are usually polite but forceful. However tensions are occasionally potent enough to tear families apart and cause horrific arguments that lead to the dissolution of *hira* groups.

Hira groups draw increasingly on foreign and local mass media to inform their discussions. Audiocassette recordings of sermons delivered in Hausa by famous *malamai* of Northern Nigeria, and of Qur'anic recitations from Saudi Arabia are especially popular in *hira* groups of Niamey. Local Muslim productions also draw *hira* audiences. Men in several *hira* groups over the last few years report that they prefer televised preaching (especially the Télé Sahel program *Ask the Malam* hosted by one of Niamey's leading scholars) to attending their neighborhood preaching. They explained that they enjoy the freedom to vicariously participate in dialogue with the *malam* and exchange running commentary with their *hira* mates gathered around television sets (as opposed to remaining respectfully silent during live preaching).

According to Rabiou, a migrant from Maradi, "The BBC's world report in Hausa has virtually become a sixth prayer time." Rabiou's insightful observation captures wonderfully the whole spirit of Hausa modernity. Here modernity is about a different kind of temporal ritual, a new apprehension of time that feeds into the already established temporal patterns of Islamic practice and connection. It is about being connected to both Allah and the secular global world, exemplifying both Appadurai's (1996) notion of diasporic space and Giddens' (1994:xi) understanding of modernity as "the transmutation of time and space." Many Hausa migrants are proud of the recognition of Hausa as a global language, as discussed earlier. In addition to the enormously popular

BBC program, many *hira* groups are avid followers of the Hausa language programs of the VOA, Deutcshe Welle, and RFI.

Drawing from these stations and local ones, men in *hira* groups are remarkably well informed and engage in lengthy discussions and debates of global headline news of the day: the "war on terrorism," the Israeli-Palestinian conflict, wars in Africa, HIV/AIDS, the global recession, North Korea's stance on nuclear weapons, the earthquake in Haiti, and deadly conflict between Muslims and Christians in Nigeria. Hausa perspectives are typically, though not always, decidedly pro-Muslim and articulate a sense that Muslims are under global assault. They strongly argue for peace and social justice. For example, many *hira* groups tried to make sense of the violence that erupted in Jos, Nigeria in January 2010 and left hundreds dead. Many groups concluded that the root of this conflict is competition for good farmland, not religion. They did not blame Christians for the conflict any more than they blamed Muslims. "What happened in Jos could never happen here," was a common refrain. Another man explained, "We are all human beings. We Muslims and Christians in Niger can live together in the same compound and the same neighborhood without any problems. It does not matter. Nigeria is a very bad country." His view reflects widespread opinion in Niamey that Nigerians are the problem.

Many *hira* groups, despite the admiration of American affluence, criticize Western mass media in ways which affirm their own identities. In a typical gathering during a Télé Sahel evening broadcast in the mid-1990s, migrants watched *Dallas* and *L.A. Heat* reruns and crotch grabbing Michael Jackson and Madonna music videos with rapt attention. When the broadcast concluded, the friends commented that most Americans must be fabulously wealthy, greedy, dishonest, adulterous, and lewd. As one observer put it, "Americans may have almost everything, but at least we have morals!" On many occasions in *hira* groups in the 1990s I heard men admonish boys for fighting by shouting, "Use common sense, don't act like Rambo!" During the last decade, Niamey's youth have been particularly attracted to African American hip hop culture—and their own creative re-workings of it—opening much discussion. I have heard many young men's *hira* groups insist that they admire

African American rap and clothing styles but that they are not violent, lecherous gangsters as they perceive many African Americans to be.

By the late 1990s and to the present, men in *hira* groups have strongly preferred watching and discussing Mexican and Brazilian television serials, Hindi films, and Hausa video-films, rather than Hollywood action movies. Drawing from these sources, they are applying their social imaginations to mass media in ways which emphasize shared problems and cultural similarities rather than difference.[6] In 2000, *Marimar*, a Mexican serial, was the most popular program on television. *Marimar* depicts a budding love affair between a rich boy and poor girl whose relationship is opposed by the snobbish rich boy's family. While most popular among women, men also said they identified closely with the girl's plight—both her desire for love and her work as a servant.

Larkin (1997) explains the great appeal of Indian films among Hausa audiences in Northern Nigeria. Despite vast differences between Hindu Indian culture and Muslim Hausa culture, he "was struck by the common refrain that Indian culture was 'just like' Hausa culture" (1997:412). What became clear was that their commonalities involve parallel postcolonial struggles between traditional moral values and the profound changes of modernity, between arranged marriages and love marriages, the pull of family as opposed to individualism, traditional clothing versus western attire, and conflicts between innocent commoners and corrupt bureaucrats. Audiences were more emotionally involved with the Indian film screenings I have attended in Niamey than with any other films, rising from their seats to dance along with the actors and shouting with delight. Many *hira* groups now gather regularly to watch and discuss videocassette or DVD recordings of Indian films.

Hausa video films produced in Northern Nigeria first appeared in Niamey in significant numbers in the late 1990s, and have since flooded the market. Many men in *hira* groups express great pride in these, and explain that they directly address their own urban experiences and conflicts, much more so than other imported media. Most of the Hausa video-films available in Niamey have a clear didactic, moral message: Avoid sinful and destructive behavior (drinking, drugs, violence, gambling, adultery, corruption); those who are lured by these activities may become wealthy or happy in the short run, but are ruined in the long run. *Hira* groups, increasingly centering their discussions on Hausa video-films, cite these scenarios as warnings.

The Centrality of *Hira* in Lived Experience: A Brief Summary

Hira groups are of supreme importance in the lives of male Hausa migrants in Niamey. In the context of globalization, they serve as a public space to comment interactively on contemporary life, consider the outside world, and share ideas about how to make sense of and respond to the forces of modernity. *Hira* provides men with a sense of dignity and self-respect, valuable connections for navigating the economic and social logistics of living in diaspora, and crucial resources for mediating changing and competing worlds of meaning. Interestingly, Nigerien Hausa seldom use the term modernity directly, although they often allude to their own "lack of modernity" (Masquelier 2000:84) in discussing their poverty. Modernity, however, is neither simply an abstract thing that happens to them nor something that has excluded them. While men in *hira* groups sometimes express a sense of inferiority when considering what it means to be modern and what may be the place of Hausa society within that modernity, they are in fact, actively engaging in complex discussions to develop rich understandings of modernity, however provisional, contested, and ambivalent. Hausa men's "alternative modernities" (Gaonkar 1999) or "parallel modernities" (Larkin 1997) consist of series of unresolved, ongoing debates. Hausa subjectivities are much more than "primarily or initially emanations of or reactions to the Western secular subject" (Cooper 1999:100). In the cosmopolitan setting of Niamey, their views of the world—including their marginalization in the current economic crisis in Niger and differing interpretations of Islam—are analyzed in highly skilled oral performance that draws from heterogeneous resources, including mass media.

In describing their popular *juju* music, Yoruba proclaim, "Our tradition is a very modern tradition" (Waterman 1997). The Hausa could say the same thing about their *hira*. In their difficult lives in Niamey, they rely on their traditional institution, which has evolved over the centuries to address the concerns of migrants living in diaspora communities, to adapt to changing physical and symbolic worlds. Hausa men use *hira* groups to structure their own sense of time and to mediate the intrusions of other understandings of modernity in a space where they can retain some sense of autonomy and self respect in the face of proliferating visions of modernity by insisting on certain traditional values, such as articulate speech, leisure, and communal affirmation. The concept that "time is money," so central to Western modernities, does not explain the value of *hira* groups for those who participate in them. Hausa men's fluid, glacial pace of *hira* time is integral to their efforts to achieve a sense of comfort in modernity.

Fada ("Men's Formal Conversation") Groups: Solidarity and Community Development

Fada Harlem's Monthly Meeting

Through a friend's invitation I joined Fada Harlem, a *fada* group consisting of men in their twenties and thirties primarily from fairly wealthy families, on a Saturday in 2008 for their monthly meeting in the courtyard of a young bachelor's compound in the Nouveau Marché neighborhood. They chose the name "Harlem" to reflect one of the primary purposes of their association: To help one another get to Harlem or anywhere in the U.S. The group had helped purchase the airline tickets in the previous two years for three of its members who are now working in Harlem. Their remittances contributed a substantial share of the group's budget.

The men began with three hours of Scrabble playing, in French, and multiple rounds of strong tea. They joked about who had paid attention in school and who was the smartest. Some shared the gist of recent phone conversations with their friends in Harlem. Men alternated between French, Hausa, and Zarma in casual conversations and the official meeting that ensued. Finally, Moctar, the President, called the meeting to order. He distributed typed agendas to the 14 men in attendance that were seated in a circle on white plastic chairs rented for the occasion. Membership dues were the first item on the agenda. The men took turns delivering 15,000 FCFA ($33) each to Abdou, the Treasurer, who duly recorded them in a ledger. Abdou then announced that Abdoulhakeem, one of the friends in Harlem, had just sent 45,000 FCFA ($100) that he had saved through his work delivering pizzas.

The next item concerned debate about how the group should spend the 45,000 FCFA that the group had allotted for the month. Mamadou urged the group to allocate the funds to help pay for his plane ticket to New York. He presented a photocopy of his visa and an e-mail message from a friend offering him a place to stay to bolster his case that the money would be well spent. When Mamadou had finished, Seyni took the floor and reminded the group that his wedding ceremony was looming the following Saturday and that he had run out of money for a DJ and soft drinks that he wanted to make it a special occasion. He suggested that he should receive the money since several others of the group had received this assistance for their weddings. The group considered their choice for about an hour, but was unable to reach a consensus. To breach the impasse, Moctar suggested a compromise, "Let's spend the money on Seyni's wedding since this is such a momentous event. Harlem will still be there next month. We can put Mamadou's request at the top of the agenda for next month." Mamadou accepted, closing discussion of the matter.

The last item on the agenda was a radio station's request to interview Fada Harlem members regarding their position on President Mamadou Tandja's plans to re-write the Constitution so as to remain in office beyond his second five-year term. This led to lively dialogue. Most men expressed opposition to Tandja's plans, but were wary about sharing their views in public. As one man put it, "We could get in a lot of trouble. The government could seize our bank account." Three men volunteered for the task, but the group agreed that they should convene with Moctar and then present their strategy to the whole group before actually doing the interview. Abdou concluded, "We have to find clever ways of saying that we are pro-democracy without saying that we anti-Tandja. We should praise Tandja for his service to the nation, even if we have reservations about him." To close the meeting, Moctar thanked everyone for attending, encouraged the group to attend Seyni's wedding, and announced the date of the next meeting.

Fada Harlem is somewhat unusual in that its members are more Francophone and more wealthy than most. Nevertheless, I chose Fada Harlem as an example because it illustrates several key dynamics that set *fada* apart from *hira*, including its naming, formality, and engagement with radio. My discussion of *fada* draws from my attendance at several official *fada* meetings of three different groups and a dozen very informal gatherings that did not involve agendas, as well as several interviews with both men who belong to *fada* groups and those who do not. In addition, I rely heavily on a lengthy interview with Cheifou Idrissa (2010)—a Nigerien applied sociologist employed by Centre de Recherche Action par la Médiation Sociale, a Niamey-based NGO. Despite the proliferation of *fada* groups in Niamey and elsewhere, the scholarly literature makes only passing references to them.

The Transformation of an Institution

The centuries-old Hausa term, "*fada*," usually translated as "royal court," traditionally refers to meetings convened by a local *sarki* ("emir" or "king") or *mai gari* ("village head") and his advisors. *Fada* groups address community concerns, and offer consultations to and mediate disputes among their constituents. Some of these continue to function, but many were undermined by colonialism. Similar institutions exist among many ethnic groups of Niger.

Nigeriens are transforming this institution to address contemporary concerns in Niamey, creating new visions of local sustainable development. While voluntary associations have long played an important role in Africa, new configurations are increasingly important as documented in *Associational Life in African Cities: Popular Responses to the Urban Crisis* (Tostensen, Tvedten, and Vaa 2001) and *African Voices African Visions* (Adesida and Oteh 2001). The new model of *fada* builds on the traditional patterns of *fada*, and draws inspiration from ever-popular, ubiquitous *hira* groups. In fact, many *fada* groups emphasize free flowing discussion and entertainment, making them virtually indistinguishable from *hira* groups. However, many *fada* groups across Niamey today represent a radically new phenomenon in many ways. Unlike *hira* groups, they participate in community radio programs, name themselves and use formal governance structures, and are explicitly oriented by neighborhood or community concerns. In contrast with traditional *fada* groups, they consist of peers.

Nigerien sociologist Cheifou Idrissa (2010) explains that,

> The history of *fada* in Niamey began in the 1990s when democratization opened our spirits and led to protests in the street and even more so to strikes by teachers, students, and workers. The young students would never be found at home again; rather they would strike and lengthen their days by gathering for tea and card playing. One can know more today about the growth of *fada* for while the strikes have mostly stopped, the young graduates from the university and professional schools are condemned to unemployment.

These new *fada* groups emerged in tandem with the proliferation of private radio stations especially in the mid to late 1990s, including Amfani, Horizon, Radio et Musique, Sarauniya, Souda, Tambara, and Ténéré. *Fada* group leaders and members as well as radio journalists recognize that private radio stations provided the spark for the transformation of *fada*, and assert that *fada* would not be what it is today without radio. While a unique relationship between *fada* and radio pertains in Niger, the multiplicity and localization of radio across Africa plays a special role in development and political transformation; "no other medium of communication matches radio in terms of audience, political power or cultural influence" (Fardon and Furniss 2000:242).

Fada groups are consumers of radio programs, but have also played an active role in radio programs for more than a decade, and in the past few years, on private television programs as well. In contrast, *hira* groups only consume radio programming (though they do so quite actively). Radio journalists regularly air interviews with *fada* groups leaders and broadcast *fada* group proceedings, reaching wide audiences and promoting the credibility, seriousness of purpose, and vibrancy of *fada* as well as inspiring new recruits. Many listeners in Niamey now regard these programs highly, as offering some of the most reliable, current information on the pressing issues and problems in their neighborhoods and the city at large. For example, young men and women representing *fada* groups discuss HIV/AIDS prevention in specific detail, hoping that their youthful audience will be receptive to this information when presented by their peers in local languages.

The Structure, Nomenclature, Governance, and Composition of *Fada* Groups

One in five male youth and adults in Niamey now belong to a *fada* group, even though the *fada* movement is only about 15 years old. Earlier I made the distinction between informal *hira* and formal *fada* groups. In this case, I point out that *fada* groups consist of both informal and formal associations, or to be precise, *fada* groups exist on a continuum of formality. Informal *fada* groups, as mentioned briefly above, are virtually indistinguishable from *hira* groups. In many cases, the only difference is that informal *fada* groups are usually named whereas *hira* groups are rarely named. Informal *fada* groups consist primarily of youth and young men aged 13 to 35 years who are underemployed or unemployed. One young *fada* group participant, reflecting widespread views, simply stated, "If one has work, one does not have time for *fada*. *Fada* is for the young who do not have work. If one is still in school, one leaves *fada* to study at home." Idrissa (2010) emphasizes that, "These *fada* are not organized, they have no objectives."

Formal *fada* groups, in contrast, typically consist of middle aged and elderly men who have more financial resources to invest in *fada*. Many of these groups were founded by youths as very informal associations and built more formal structures over several years. According to Idrissa (2010), "They are organized differently than the *fada* of the young. They have an office, bank account, and relations with development projects, NGOs, and the mayor's office. They intervene in many sectors of local socioeconomic life."

Middle aged and elderly men and women typically distrust the *fada* groups of youth, despite some important exceptions that will be discussed later. Hassane's (of *hira* group fame) judgment that youth's *fada* is simply *zaman banza* ("stupid idleness"), especially if it involves men hanging out with women, represents the norm. He distinguishes this from the "true" *fada* of *manya-manya* ("the rich") that has a serious purpose. Idrissa (2010) similarly emphasizes that, "This [a youth *fada* group] is a place to learn about the life of the group, but it is also a place to learn about bad practices: smoking cigarettes, taking drugs, sexual delinquency (the prostitution of the young) which exposes them to STDs such as AIDS." Some youth do not care what elders think of their *fada*, but others do and struggle to overcome these stereotypes.

Most *fada* groups have a core membership of a dozen people, consisting primarily of age mates, but some groups have 40-60 people on their official membership rolls. Most people belong to only one *fada* group, unlike *hira*. *Fada* groups—depending on their resources—meet at street sides, in the courtyards of bachelors' compounds, or in thatched hangars specially constructed for *fada*. *Fada* group members do not work during meetings, in contrast to *hira* groups that often meet at the work places of members, for example, tea and coffee stands. Many informal groups meet casually on a daily basis for conversation and tea. Formal groups typically hold several-hour-long official meetings at least once a month. Some formal groups meet informally between official meetings.

Fada groups, regardless of their structure, usually mark their meeting spaces with signage, typically by spray painting the name of their group on public walls. These markings are typically rather crude, with uneven lettering and sloping lines. However, a few groups display professionally painted wooden plaques or canvas banners. I became aware of the existence of *fada* in Niamey in 1998 when for the first time the word "*fada*," followed by a diverse assortment of names, was written all over the city. I suggest that this is due to the fact that by 1998 private radio stations had had just enough time to establish themselves. Today *fada* tagging is the most ubiquitous public writing in Niamey. Not all of it refers to existing *fada* groups, as I also learned that anyone with a can of spray paint can leave his mark.

The eclectic nomenclature of *fada* is structured by the age of participants. Furthermore, *fada* groups consisting of younger members are far more likely to spray paint their names than *fada* groups consisting of older members. I recorded 50 names over three visits from 1998 to

Table 4.1 Representative Youth *Fada* Group Names Recorded from 1998-2003

Whimsical	*Global Icons and Cities*	*Hometowns and Neighborhoods*	*Radio Stations*	*Local Personalities*
Les Petits Qui Conduisent Un AvionSans Volant[a]	Bob Marley	Tahoua	Tambara	Sikkassi[b]
Goro ("Kola Nut")	Bin Laden	Zongo	Ténéré	
	Michael Jordan	Nouveau Marché		
	MC Hammer			
	Tupac Shakur			
	L.A.			
	Paris			

[a] "Fada of the Youths Who Fly an Airplane without Steering"
[b] This is the name of a popular young Zarma rapper who sings primarily about youth issues.

2003, and another 25 names in 2009-2010. From 1998 to 2003, names of informal, youth dominated groups included: whimsical names, names identifying hometowns of core members or neighborhoods in Niamey, names linking the group with their favorite radio station, names honoring local personalities, and, most commonly, names featuring global icons and global cities. This pattern remained more or less intact to the present. However, by 2009-2010 a new set of American, English hip-hop inflected names was preferred by the majority of informal groups. In contrast, from 1998 to 2010, formal *fada* groups were consistently named, in Hausa and French, after key local cultural values. (See tables 4.1, 4.2, and 4.3 for classifications of representative names.)

Typically there are direct associations between names of groups and their spirit or agenda. For example, Fada Les Amerikens and Fada Cash $ Money consist of young men who prefer rap to other musical forms and members who aspire to travel to the U.S. Fada Taimako ("Help") serves as rotating credit association for its 54 middle-aged members who meet monthly, and pay $4 per month dues. In contrast, Fada bin Laden is not a nascent terrorist cell; it focuses on tutoring primary school children in

Table 4.2 Representative Youth *Fada* Group Names Recorded from 2009-2010

Whimsical	*Global Icons and Cities*	*Hometowns and Neighborhoods*	*Radio Stations*	*Local Personalities*
Love	Cash $ Money	Maradi	Radio et Musique	Metafor[a]
Sha Shayi ("Drink Tea")	Zidane	Abidjan	Amfani	
Tazarché ("Continuation")[b]	Obama	Lazaret		
Super Gang	Les Amerikens			
Best Boys	Les Sodja Boys			
Great Boys	Vive Rasta People			
Boss	Bamako			
	Washington			
	Harlem			

[a] This is the name of a successful hip-hop group.

[b] The term "tazarché" was popularly used to refer to President Mamadou Tandja's efforts in 2009 to remain in office despite Constitutional term limits. Ironically this group was anti-tazarché.

Table 4.3 Representative Adult Fada Group Names Recorded from 1998-2003 and 2009-2010

Key Cultural Values: 1998-2003	*Key Cultural Values: 2009-10*
Sa'a ("Propitious Time," "Good Luck")	Roua ("Water")
Sai Hank'uri ("Through Patience Only")	Taimako ("Help")
Islamiquey	Haske ("Light," "Quick Intellect")
Kwancen Hankali ("Peace")	La Montagne

French and mathematics. Fada Michael Jordan members prefer football to basketball, and regularly clean their neighborhood's streets.

Fada group names illustrate different worldviews, most strikingly, the localist orientation of adults and the increasingly globalist perspectives and aspirations of youth. In his recent ethnography, *Street Dreams and Hip Hop Barbershops: Global Fantasy in Urban Tanzania*, anthropologist

Brad Weiss (2009) examines barbershops that function as key meeting spaces for Tanzanian youth in much the same way that Nigerien youth rely on *hira* and *fada* groups. Young Tanzanian barbers similarly choose names—and paint them on signs—that refer, in English, to hip hop culture and distant places perceived to offer more opportunities, never to local places. Typical names such as "Brooklyn Barber's Shop," "Boyz II Men," "Paris Cuts," and "Cape Town Barbers" reveal that their "horizon is firmly elsewhere. It is as though in naming and publicizing the places they regularly occupy, Arusha's barbers display and proclaim their own absence from the world they aspire to inhabit" (Weiss 2009:75). The names of *fada* groups among Niamey's youth are also increasingly in English and reveal a similar fascination with global hip-hop. Furthermore, names like Les Amerikens, Cash $ Money, and Super Gang illustrate tensions between global inclusion and exclusion. Niaméen youth are not delusional, they realize that they have almost no chance of becoming rich Americans nor do they aspire to be violent hoodlums. Such names remind them that they are poor Nigeriens. Nevertheless the appropriation and "glocalization" of these names is empowering, revealing that youth do have hope and ambition. They believe that they can become "Great Boys" in Niamey. Indeed, in contrast with the urban youth in Weiss' study, Niamey youth also refer to local politics, places, radio, and personalities in naming their *fada* groups. After all, while Niamey's youth have vivid global imaginations, *fada* is all about trying to make life better on the ground in Niamey.

Fada groups also differ significantly from *hira* groups with respect to governance and the composition of membership. Most groups—even informal ones that have neither agenda-driven meetings nor require membership dues—feature officers, including a president or general secretary, vice president, secretary, and treasurer. Some formal groups hold official elections. In many other groups, leaders emerge through valued qualities such as long-term experience with and deep knowledge of their members and reputations for checking up on absent members who may be ill and in need of assistance. Additional credentials include honesty, wisdom, empathy, humility, creative problem solving skills, and community orientation. Wealth is not a requirement, but in practice some men attain leadership through providing comfortable, quiet meeting spaces in their own compounds. Leaders do not coerce members, rather they seek to build consensus through persuasion and charisma. In many groups, individuals frequently rotate through leadership roles.

Fada groups rely on the good will, friendship, and solidarity of their members. Any youth or adult can join a *fada* group. While groups are typically associated with particular neighborhoods, membership is a matter of affinity not territory. Some groups include members from several neighborhoods. Many groups collect membership dues on a sliding scale. Cash-strapped men and women are welcome to participate even if they cannot make financial contributions, so long as they are willing to share productive ideas and offer their labor in communal projects. *Fada* groups are decidedly democratic and inclusive. Poor members are free to express their opinions and to disagree with rich members. *Fada* groups are information-centered communication cells emphasizing the open exchange of opinion and perspective with rhetorical panache. In these respects, *fada* groups are somewhat similar to *hira* groups, but are very different from the gerontocratic, aristocratic structure of traditional *fada* groups.

Today's *fada* groups are typically more multiethnic than *hira* groups and traditional *fada* groups. Many consist of Hausa, Zarma, Fulani, Kanuri, and Tuareg participants. This new development is the result of conscious and deliberate choices made by urban youth for whom ethnic differences and boundaries often have little salience. Some groups creatively play on complex joking relationships between specific ethnic groups and within segments of particular ethnic groups. I encountered several young men's *fada* groups that explicitly shared the opinion that ethnic division has no place in building contemporary Niger, arguing that it represents a colonial, archaic mentality held primarily by the elderly. (Their oppositional perspective is fascinating even though they may overstate the ethnic chauvinism of previous generations.)

A small but growing number of *fada* groups now welcome and include girls and women as members. This is a radical departure from thoroughly gender segregated *hira* groups and traditional *fada*. Some residents of Niamey, particularly the elderly, find this alarming especially if gender integrated meetings take place in private spaces after dark. Many youth in Niamey see this as a refreshing approach to integrated community development, recognizing that addressing women's needs is crucial to improving the lives of women and children.

Agendas and Purposes

Fada groups are community-oriented, emphasizing solving the problems of groups. They share this orientation with traditional *fada* groups, while this differentiates them from *hira* groups that are primarily concerned with solving the problems of individuals. Their activities range from very informal, solidarity-building events to ambitious, highly organized local development projects.

Many *fada* groups establish formal agendas of topics, and, if possible, broadcast their meeting times, places, and agendas on popular private radio stations. Social problems are the most popular topics, including: the scarcity of jobs and the rising cost of living, the erosion of public health care and education due to neoliberal constraints and state mismanagement, and the putrid garbage heaps on city streets picked through by desperate children. Furthermore, unlike autonomous *hira* groups and traditional *fada* groups, the new *fada* groups invite fellow *fada* groups to discuss particular topics jointly, and for social events. Youthful *fada* groups challenge other *fada* groups by invitation to football matches. While competitive on the field, games usually conclude with friendly conversation and the sharing of kola nuts, tea, and dinner. Host *fada* groups expect to be reciprocated by their guests. Some *fada* groups host mixed gender evening dance parties, particularly in bachelor's compounds, sometimes offering live music, soft drinks, and beer.

Many *fada* groups function primarily as rotating credit associations. Dues-paying members can count on assistance from their groups when they need extra money due to job loss, for costly medical treatment, or for expenses and preparations associated with naming ceremonies, weddings, and funerals. In addition, *fada* groups help sponsor members' migrations with loans or gifts and advice about connections in diaspora communities. This strategy is regarded as a group investment, not merely as helping an individual. Groups carefully consider the character of prospective migrants, particularly their histories of helping others, as well as their linguistic and cultural competence. Migrants are expected to send remittances to their extended families and to the *fada* groups who facilitated their efforts. One unnamed *fada* group that I studied closely, consisting of wealthy young men and women, helped sponsor the journeys of eight of its members to New York City from 1999-2003. All but one of these individuals has paid back their loans and then some.

Many *fada* groups—including youthful ones—are establishing positive reputations through local development initiatives. "Their principal activities," according to Idrissa (2010) and my observations, "are cleaning neighborhoods, big mosques, and cemeteries." In recent years, young men have been providing security through their *fada* street gatherings that last all night long, particularly in Niamey's oldest, most densely populated neighborhoods. Many residents recognize their contribution to public order by voluntarily providing them with tea, kola nuts, cigarettes, rice, and beans to fuel their discussions and keep them alert. They rarely pursue intruders or suspected criminals, because their ubiquitous presence on the streets of nocturnal Niamey is usually a sufficient deterrent (Gopfert 2009:10-13). Captured thieves are severely beaten and occasionally killed. As one man explained, "a thief being chased by a night watch patrol will run to the police for protection." *Fada* groups engage in a wide range of other beneficial activities. Some offer free tutoring services. One group works to help find respectable jobs for single mothers. Another spread the word and offered descriptions of a man who allegedly had been abusing children in a particular neighborhood. Residents claim that this helped to put an end to this sordid situation

A small but growing number of well organized, deeply committed *fada* groups with sufficient financial resources are carefully planning and successfully implementing ambitious development projects. Some recreate themselves as official, non-profit NGOs. For example, Organisation Non Gouvernementale Discipline, Aide et Développement (D.A.D.-Gomni) was established in 1995 as a gender-integrated *fada* group, and still operates as such in many respects. Gomni is a Zarma word meaning kindness. Since it became a licensed NGO in 1997 it has been led by a staff of 15 men and women volunteers and operated with a small office, computer, telephone, and bank account. Gomni's President is a Zarma man, and its six-person Executive Board consists of Zarma and Hausa individuals, including women serving as its Deputy General Secretary and Deputy Chief Treasurer. It does not consider ethnicity in rendering services. Donations from its mostly middle class board members and their connections in the business community of Niamey provide most of its operating budget. This is supplemented by regular remittances sent by a member working in New York City whose migration was sponsored by the group with their personal funds. Gomni has also received a small grant from an international NGO and is constantly seeking international NGO partners. Gomni's (2009) multi-pronged agenda for "supporting local initiatives and building local capacities with a view to sustainable development" involves poverty reduction, environmental, health, and education programs in and near Niamey. Gomni boasts a long list of accomplishments. Its poverty reduction work has included microcredit loans to 100 women gardeners and entrepreneurs, the creation of 30 grain banks, and the distribution of six tons of rice to 95 needy families. Gomni (2009) believes that "To protect the environment is to protect humankind." Toward this end, it operates a small nursery for tree seedlings, which are distributed free of charge to anyone who is willing to plant and tend them to combat desertification. This has led to the recuperation of 431 hectares of degraded land. Health projects have focused on malaria and HIV/AIDS education, the sales of mosquito nets at wholesale prices, and distribution of free malaria prophylactics. (Public health information, including pamphlets and posters, was donated by the Nigerien state and by the United Nations.) Gomni (2009) sponsors awareness-raising campaigns against the forced marriage of girls and for their education, asserting that, "Educating a girl is educating a whole nation." It has created 17 literacy centers, and distributed free pens and notebooks to hundreds of primary school students, especially girls. (See table 4.4 for a summary of core general differences between *hira* and *fada*.)

Table 4.4 Core Generalized Differences between *Hira* and *Fada*

Hira	*Fada*
Everyone involved	20% of male youth and adults involved
Radio consumers	Radio consumers and participants Co-evolution of radio and *fada* Interviews and live broadcasts of *fada*
At least one man works during meetings	No one works during meetings
Unnamed	Named groups, marked with signs
Acephalous	Leadership, governance structure
Some ethnic segregation	Little ethnic segregation
Gender segregation	Some gender integration
Informal, fluid	Formal, agendas
Autonomous groups	Some links between groups Discuss issues of mutual concern Football games Dance parties
Individual problem solving Migrant sponsorship Job and housing leads	Group problem solving Migrant sponsorship Street, mosque sweeping Night watch Rites of passage Tutoring Development projects

Foyandi ("Women's Formal Conversation") Groups: Solidarity and Community Development

Women's *foyandi* groups have emerged as an important counterpart to male-dominated *fada* groups. *Foyandi* groups consist entirely of women, unlike *fada* groups that sometimes include women. I did not attend any *foyandi* gatherings, and the scholarly literature addresses *foyandi* only in passing (e.g., Alidou 2005:18). Instead, I rely on comments offered by linguist Ousseina Alidou (2010), interviews with two women about their *foyandi* experiences, informal discussions with men regarding their take on *foyandi*, and Nigerien journalists' accounts (African Press 2007, Maazou 2009, Soumana 2010).

Journalist Souleymane Saddi Maazou (2009:1) reports that *foyandi* groups initially formed immediately after independence in 1960 to support women traders with capital, and to share the joys on naming and wedding ceremonies, though I think they are probably much older than this. Sociologist Djaharou Moussa argues that their transformation and proliferation is the result of the advent of democracy (Maazou 2009:2). *Foyandi* is a Zarma term, translated by Alidou (2005:18) as women's "friendship gatherings." All women of Niamey, regardless of ethnic background, use this word (Alidou 2010). Hundreds of *foyandi* groups operate today in Niamey as rotating credit associations. A teacher interviewed by Maazou (2009:2) explained, "We are structured so that all can join. The monthly premiums range from 5,000 to 60,000 FCFA [$11 to $133]. The women choose their club based on their income." I think these estimates are inflated and reflect the class position of the teacher. Rekia, a 50-year old food stand owner-operator who I interviewed, pays only 2,000 FCFA ($4) per month to belong to her *foyandi* group. Each month random drawings among those who have never received money are conducted to determine which woman will receive money for the month.

Foyandi involves associations of women who gather to spend the day together as friends to talk, laugh, feast, and combine business with pleasure (Soumana 2010). Women participate in *foyandi* groups as a crucial venue for building women's solidarity and initiative. They share neighborhood news, health concerns, childrearing strategies, and tips for dealing with men. In addition, women engage in friendly rivalries during *foyandi* meetings, competing to determine who is the best cook and who has the most beautiful clothes and hairstyles (African Press 2007:1). *Foyandi* simultaneously serve as an important institutionalized means of coping with current economic conditions, allowing women a measure of independence and to make important financial contributions to family resources. Women use *foyandi* funds for three main purposes.

First, they can rely on the emotional and financial support of *foyandi* groups for childbirth, weddings, funerals, and family emergencies.

Women call on their *foyandi* partners to cook and clean for their own events or those of their families. Second, women also use the funds to support their businesses, particularly restaurants, gardens, and shops featuring cloth and shoes. For example, the monthly recipient of funds at the *foyandi* meeting Maazou attended used her 300,000 FCFA ($666) to buy a refrigerator to sell fruit juice. Zeinabou spent the 15,000 FCFA ($33) she earned through her *foyandi* on new pots, allowing her to sell more food. Third, women spend their *foyandi* money on the education of their children, especially their daughters. Fatima described the importance of this to me,

> My husband, like most men in Niamey, claimed that he could only afford to pay for the post-high school education of our sons. I want my daughter to be independent because women can no longer count on men in Niamey. I want her to have a chance in the modern economy. Therefore, I used my *foyandi* money to pay for my daughter to attend a computer training institute.

The structure of women's *foyandi* groups is very similar to that of men's *fada* groups. *Foyandi* groups typically consist of 10 to 40 members. They are not ethnic-based associations. Some are grouped by occupation. For example, Zeinabou's group consists of fellow cooks.

Most women who are involved belong to only one group. Officers, usually a President, Vice President, and Treasurer, govern *foyandi* groups. Official meetings are held once a month to collect dues and disperse funds, but many groups meet much more often depending on the particular timing of ceremonials. In contrast with *fada*, *foyandi* groups are not named, as far as I know.

Men of Niamey have mixed feelings about women's *foyandi*. Youssoufou explained his feelings about *foyandi* to me,

> I do not mind if Zeinabou occasionally goes to *foyandi*. It is good for her to support her friends, and they have helped her in turn. But this is third weekend in a row that she was gone all day on both Saturday and Sunday. When she returns home, she says that she is too tired to

cook for me and goes straight to bed. That makes six days I had to buy street food and risk getting sick. She is so stubborn.

Youssoufou is not alone in his assessment. Many men are pressured to provide membership dues, but worry that their girlfriends and wives spend it on hair salons, cosmetics, and clothes. Abdoulsalam Adam, a famous male singer, satirically criticizes the "legendary financial greed" created by *foyandi* in a popular song (Soumana 2010). In contrast, Maazou (2009:2) indicates that, "Despite some deviations, many men see in these groups a framework of solidarity in a society increasingly dominated by individualism. 'Sharing the joys and sorrows strengthens sociability,' is welcomed by El Hadji Zakari, 'women can fight poverty'."

Postscript

This chapter has analyzed how Hausa in Niamey engage with work, family, religion, and social networks through *hira* and *fada* to adapt to challenging economic conditions and find joy and purpose. I have highlighted the crucial role of *hira* groups in bringing many of these key social concerns together in one informal, everyday context. *Fada* and *foyandi* groups, like the multitude of voluntary associations that have emerged in African cities in recent years (Tostensen, Tvedten, and Vaa 2001), respond to mounting poverty and inadequate infrastructure and services with innovative approaches. Their multi-ethnic, democratic, progressive governance oriented by community concerns and (in the case of *fada*) imaginative harnessing of the potential of radio, offers creative visions for building decentralized, grassroots civil society in Niger.

Niamey cityscape juxtaposing tradition and modernity.

An entrance to the Petit Marché.

A table trader.

A table trader.

Young men selling winter jackets on foot.

Praise-singers in action.

A man selling beef jerky.

A Qur'anic teacher.

A man with his son and friends.

An elderly woman.

A family gathering.

Friends taking a break.

A man resting.

A father-son reunion in Niamey.

A street corner conversation group.

Billboard advertising hip hop competitions.

— 5 —

Multiple Articulations of Modernity

Duniya a bi ta a sannu-sannu:
World affairs should be followed with caution

Until recently, many anthropologists and other social scientists overlooked the distinction between "cultural modernity" and "economic modernity" in their rush to valorize local, alternative, and parallel cultural modernities in Africa and elsewhere in the "Global South." This cultural relativist stance has yielded rich ethnographic explorations of the "local expressive forms through which modernity is being negotiated or appropriated" or created, but it often sidelined "the impact of Western-dominated power structures" and ignored "the inequalities that differential access to [economic] modernity may imply" (Geschiere, Meyer, and Pels 2008:1). In his influential recent volume, *Global Shadows: Africa in the Neoliberal World Order*, Ferguson (2006:259)

> maintains that Africans in a variety of social and geographical locations increasingly seek to make claims of membership within a global community, claims that contest the marginalization that has so far been the principal fruit of "globalization" for Africa...[contending]... that such claims demand new understandings of the global, centered less on transnational flows and images of unfettered connection than on the social relations that selectively constitute global society [and selectively exclude most Africans].

Hausa efforts to understand the world and their place in it constitute one of their most important strategies for surviving with dignity. *Surviving with Dignity* examines both cultural and economic globalization and modernity, following recent pleas in cutting-edge Africanist scholarship (cf. Alidou 2005; Ferguson 2006; Geschiere, Meyer, and Pels 2008; Weiss 2009). Hausa emphasize the difference between cultural modernity and economic modernity in ways that overlap with but also differ from anthropological constructs.

This chapter, guided by contemporary social theory, begins with a broad overview of Hausa experiences of globalization and modernity that leads to a discussion of the various central articulations of modernity that have currency among Hausa of Niamey today, including what I roughly label as Africanist–Traditionalist, Muslimist–Islamist, and Francophone-ist–Globalist. Each, in different ways, involves Hausa claims to global citizenship in both cultural and economic dimensions. Then, the dynamic interplay between these disparate visions of modernity are exemplified through examining how people draw on them to interpret and act upon everyday matters of great contemporary concern, namely, discussion and debate about money and the recent rise of stories and rumors of occult economies.

Experiencing Globalization and Modernity in Niamey

Hausa life worlds can only be understood in the historical context of contemporary globalization. Life in Niamey—while unique in many respects—does not unfold in a vacuum. Globalization and modernities are inextricably linked. "Globalization" involves an array of macro-level forces and flows that connect, to varying degrees, people all over the world. "Modernities" refers to the ways that people reflect and act upon globalization processes in their quest to make sense of the world and their place in it. This discussion begins with a brief review of key dimensions of globalization that are profoundly consequential for Hausa communities of Niamey. Then, it focuses on "modernity at large" (Appadurai 1996) as a prelude to exploring multiple articulations of modernity among Hausa of Niamey.

Contemporary globalization, in broad terms, involves the accelerating transnational movement of money and finance, people, goods and technologies, mass media, and ideologies. These interconnected processes affect all people, though in vastly divergent ways (Appadurai 1990; Cooper 1999; Beynon and Dunkerley 2000). Indeed, Appadurai (1990) argues that neither economic convergence nor cultural homogeneity is possible because these five major factors of globalization operate in "disjuncture." Worldwide political-economic models, institutions, structures, and systems that influence lives all over the planet, such as the neoliberal capitalist economy, international trade, the IMF and the World Bank, the United Nations, and the interstate system, also drive globalization.

Globalization paradoxically involves dynamics of connection and disconnection. Global connection transpires primarily through cultural forms. Global disconnection is most acutely devastating in the economic realm. People everywhere are implicated in global capitalism that is increasingly dominated by multinational corporations backed by neoliberal policies, enforced by global institutions that accelerate inequality among and within states. Multinational corporations and their shareholders are positioned to realize enormous power and profits. Most people who live in peripheral nations in Africa and elsewhere experience increasing poverty and debt.

Each of the four monumental changes in Niamey over the last two decades is indelibly linked to globalization: urbanization is a worldwide pattern; neoliberal capitalism—now the world's dominant economic system—has exacerbated global economic inequality; the 1990s saw a wave of interconnected democracy movements around the globe; and the Internet and cell phones are of course inventions that have swept the planet in the last decade. These dimensions of globalization work in interaction. For example, deepening poverty as well as access to global mass media inspires accelerating migration to Niamey and the broader Hausa diaspora that is increasingly closely connected by cell phones. The global circulation of Nigerien people also leads to the circulation of remittances (both money and goods) and ideas.

Modernity is a slippery and polysemic concept—theoretically, analytically, and empirically. The terms "modern" and "modernity" continue to be confused with "modernization theory" that posits that "traditional societies" can simply progress to modernity through the transfer of

Western political models and industrial technologies. "Even if grand narratives of modernization and development have lost credibility, among Africans as well as those who study Africa, notions of being or becoming modern continue to wield extraordinary power in everyday African life" (Geschiere, Meyer, and Pels 2008:1), as they represent the promise of a better future life, in cultural terms and even more importantly, in economic terms. Many Africans, including the Hausa of Niamey, feel that they have made important strides toward achieving "cultural modernity," but most feel excluded from "economic modernity" or a sense of economic security and prosperity and access to global consumer goods, health care, and running water. Furthermore, many Hausa of Niamey—perhaps the majority—regard "economic modernity" as the most important marker of modernity. This is what some Hausa mean when they say, "We are not yet modern." Geschiere, Meyer, and Pels (2008:1) argue that Africans' conceptions of unilinear progress from tradition to modernity must be recognized, even if this simple model has been discredited by academics. That is, scholars must remain "conscious of the teleological force of the notion of modernization...[but]...resist its power to draw us into meta-narratives that should be critically investigated instead of reproduced (Geschiere, Meyer, and Pels 2008:1).

Following Gaonkar (1999:13) I regard modernity as describing the ways particular people in particular places around the world encounter, experience, and develop an "attitude of questioning" contemporary globalization processes. Even more simply, "'modernity' seems to refer to a basic sense of living in a new time" (Geschiere, Meyer, and Pels 2008:1). Thus modernities are plural and evolving; "Everywhere, at every national/cultural site, modernity is not one but many; modernity is not new, but old and familiar; modernity is incomplete and necessarily so" (Gaonkar 1999:18). Similarly, Bastian (2001:89) poses the question, "Can people's experience of being modern ever be homogenous, when their histories, societies, and basic cosmological understandings are not the same?" Social theory also emphasizes that contemporary transportation, information, and communication technologies create "a new consciousness of 'globalization'" (Geschiere, Meyer and Pels 2008:1); "Modernity is precisely the transmutation of time and space" (Giddens 1994:xi).

"Modernity" and "cosmopolitanism" are essentially synonymous, and thus I sometimes use these terms interchangeably. In his introduction to the influential volume, Cosmopolitanism, a special issue of the journal *Public Culture*, Pollock (2000) argues that cosmopolitanism consists of complex ways that people think and act beyond the local in this historical moment defined by globalization, nationalism, and multiculturalism. Cosmopolitanism in Niamey plays out in myriad instances of "ways of living at home abroad or abroad at home—ways of inhabiting multiple places at once, of being different beings simultaneously" (Pollock 2000:587). In Niamey, as elsewhere, "cosmopolitanism is not a circle created by a culture diffused by the center, but instead, that centers are everywhere and circumferences nowhere" (Pollock et al. 2000:587-88).

Thinking, in the abstract, of "modernity at large" (Appadurai 1996), facilitates an appreciation of the global character of local events as well as the local faces of global processes. Appadurai (1996:3) interprets this general process by taking "media and migration as its two major and interconnected diacritics and explores their joint effect on the work of the imagination as a constitutive feature of modern subjectivity." Mass migrations are not new in Hausa history. However, today, when accelerating mass migrations are "juxtaposed with the rapid flow of mass-mediated images . . . we have a new order of instability in the production of modern subjectivities" (Appadurai 1996:4).

Diasporic public cultures and spaces emerge in the context of globalization and modernity. Media and mass migration compel and impel "the work of the imagination" in public culture, conceived of as "a space of contestation in which individuals and groups seek to annex the global into their own practices of the modern" (Appadurai 1996:4). Friedland and Borden (1994) concur that connections between the global and the local are the essence of modernity. Thus, the term "public culture" refers to a "zone of cultural debate" (Appadurai and Breckenridge 1995:5) that operates in a public space. *Hira* groups, the radio, and mosques are core arenas of public culture among Hausa communities of Niamey, as described earlier. Indeed, in my view, culture is defined primarily by exchange, dialogue, contestation, and conflict, rather than by concord and unity.

While the parameters of modernity can be outlined, "the clarity promised by defining modernity is illusory" because modernity is "a historical phenomenon that is still evolving" and is characterized by "contradictions and ambivalences" not by "internal balance, clarity, and closure " (Geschiere, Meyer, and Pels 2008:2). This, however, does not preclude the study of modernities. Ethnography of the lived experiences of real people in real places offers nuanced insights into understanding modernities. I pursue a "relational" approach to modernities in two dimensions (Geschiere, Meyer, and Pels 2008:2). First, parallel and alternative modernities emerge in relationship to each other. Second, I regard modernity as nearly entirely open, and not pre-given or foreclosed by the definition of any particular society or discourse. This perspective blurs and can even eliminate the distinction between "tradition" and "modernity" that the term "modernity" implies. In the social realities of everyday life in modernity, "often 'tradition' turns out to be modern, or 'development' contributes to making people more backward" (Geschiere, Meyer, and Pels 2008:5). For example, anthropologists Comaroff and Comaroff (1999) and Gescheire (1997) have interpreted ritual and witchcraft practices and beliefs as thoroughly modern ways that some Africans are engaging with globalization. Similarly, Alidou (2005:5) argues that Nigerien "women have taken advantage of the malleability of 'tradition' (including the religious and the secular) to craft their modernity." Indeed, in many ways Hausa of Niamey insist that tradition has a valid place in modernity.

Alternative Modernities in Niamey

The central articulations of modernity that have currency among Hausa of Niamey today include what I label as "Africanist–Traditionalist," "Muslimist–Islamist," and "Francophone-ist–Globalist." These very rough labels are used only as a starting point. Each refers to a wide range of thought and action. Each has gendered, age, and class-based varieties and nuances. These alternative modernities take form through intermingling, that is, in relationship to each other and to other modernities at large in the world. These relationships are defined by negotiation, accommodation, and contestation. In many social contexts in Niamey (and elsewhere in Niger), these worldviews compete with each other for power and the right to control the interpretation of culture, morality, and the truth (cf. Alidou 2005:5, Idrissa 2009, Masquelier 2001, 2009). Meanwhile, many Hausa of Niamey, particularly the young (as will be highlighted in the following chapter), draw from all of these visions of modernity in their reflections, behavior, identity constructions, and understanding of the contemporary world. Indeed, Niamey is filled with Francophone, Muslim, Nigerien, Hausa men and women. With incredible dexterity, they negotiate, appropriate, experiment with, and perform (trans-locally, trans-nationally, trans-culturally, and trans-linguistically) all of these alternative modernities. The three multidimensional alternative modernities are presented separately for organizational clarity, while, at various points in the discussion, exploring the relationships and links between and among them to emphasize the complexity of the ways that they are inextricably linked in the everyday lives of Hausa men.

Place matters, even in a migratory diasporic culture, as emphasized throughout the text. Contestations, divisions, and accommodations between the particular core alternative modernities at play are intensified and take particularly complex cosmopolitan forms in Niamey. Even in recognizing urban specificity, Niamey is not necessarily "more modern" than rural Niger in some simple hierarchy—even though many Nigeriens look at it this way. Most Nigeriens are "rurban"—to borrow Idrissa's (2009:206) clever neologism—people who maintain rural and urban connections through pervasive circular migration, trade, remittances, and communication. However, as Idrissa (2009:192) emphasizes in his survey of the social landscape of Niger, Francophone and Islamist ideas and organizations have very little influence or presence in wide swaths of rural Niger. Niamey is a place where time and space are compressed in unique ways. Only in Niamey do all of Niger's ethno-linguistic groups live together. Niamey brings together the full range of "traditional" Muslim and reformist Islamist discourses, congregations, associations, beliefs, and practices found in the country. Francophone language, culture, and liberal republican values and practices as well as the reach of the state and emerging national identities are more established in Niamey than in any place in Niger. As Idrissa (2009:205,206) puts it, only Niamey (and Maradi) have sufficient "solid public spaces" to make them "full-blown sites of maximum Nigerienness."

Africanist–Traditionalist Modernities

Hausa and other ethno-linguistic communities develop their own Africanist–Traditionalist modernities. The term "Africanist–Traditionalist Modernities" highlights the blurred boundaries between tradition and modernity evident in Niamey and reflects the reality that many Nigeriens assert that their traditions can be or already have been adapted to modernity and deserve a place of equal respect alongside other cultural modernities around the world. The Hausa complex includes the language, material culture such as distinctive clothing and architectural styles, key symbols, religion and magic, and a set of core values—especially patience, generosity, reciprocity, local and global knowledge, humility, oral skill, and humor.

Hausa modernities exist in relationship to other modernities. Islam is inextricably intertwined with everything Hausa (in fact they are equated in the minds of many Nigeriens). Tens of thousands of Francophone Hausa live in Niamey. "Hausaness" is contested in various ways. Certain Muslims, especially anti-Sufi reformists, see ethnic identities and practices as a retrograde, backward tradition that is antithetical to Islam, particularly in what they see as overly flamboyant Hausa cultural expressions such as facial scarification, extravagant and expensive ceremonials, and healing and magical practices. Some Francophones, for different reasons, regard ethnicity as pre-modern, illiterate, tradition that is stuck in the past and should be left there. Hausa negotiate these oppositional discourses in various ways. Some Hausa are annoyed to be regarded as inferior. A few internalize inferiority complexes. In contrast, most Hausa regard their people and culture as modern and valid globally on account of their values, sense of meaning, and dignity. They are proud of the status of Hausa as a global language through its use by several of the world's most important international radio stations, and for conversations in cities around the world. They are proud, not ashamed, to be culturally Hausa, even if they are embarrassed at times by their poverty or perceived lack of economic modernity.

Muslimist–Islamist Modernities

Islam plays a vitally important role in the ways that virtually every Hausa thinks about local life in a global context. Various interpretations of Islam inform almost everything Hausa of Niamey think and do. Islam first arrived in what is today Niger in the 11th century.[1] Ever since, gradually, and in various forms, Hausa and their neighbors have been absorbing and practicing Islam. The French colonial regime neither felt threatened by Islam in Niger nor was it. Meanwhile, "Islam" did not feel threatened by French rule in Niger nor was it. Indeed, Idrissa (2009:184) emphasizes that, "The Islamists are as much the sons and daughters of the colony and the post-colony as are the Francophones."[2] Contemporary statistical summaries calculate that 90 to 98 percent of Hausa and Nigeriens as a whole are Muslim. While a useful starting point, these numbers reveal very little about the growth, complexity, and pluralistic nature of Islam that has emerged in postcolonial Niger, and especially in the so-called democracy era of the early 1990s to the present that is my primary concern.

The loose labels "Muslimist" and "Islamist" characterize a broad array—in a sense, a continuum—of Muslim identities, teachings, beliefs, and practices. In my usage, "Muslimist" refers to the mainstream, "traditional" Muslim that is practiced by the majority of Hausa who are affiliated—usually very loosely if at all—with Tijaniyya and Qadiriyya Sufi orders, as discussed in the previous chapter. The largest number of "Muslimist" Hausa self identify as Salalu and are unaffiliated with any congregation or sect. As Youssoufou put it, "this is the traditional Nigerien Islam of our parents and grandparents."

"Islamist" signifies a range of affiliations, teachings, and practices that contest Sufism and seek to redefine the Islamic order. The most important reformist "Islamist" group in Niamey is known in Hausa as the Izala. Anthropologist Emmanuel Grégoire (1993:111) documents that "the *Jama'at izalat al-bid'a wa iqamat al-sunna* (Movement for Supressing Innovations and restoring the Sunna) was founded in Jos,

Nigeria, in 1978 by Isma'il Abubakar Gumi, who had close ties with Saudi Arabia." From there it spread northward into Southern Niger and, by the late 1980s, to Niamey. Their influence has been very consequential, despite the very small numbers. Kala Kato emerged in Northern Nigeria in 1992 as a reformed manifestation of the Maitatsine movement led by Mohammed Marwa in the early 1980s. Similar to the Izala, though an even tinier minority, they made their way to Niger and eventually to Niamey in the last decade or so. They assert that only the Qur'an guides their theology and worship, and refer neither to the *hadith* ("the sayings of the Prophet Mohammed") nor to *ijma* ("consensus of Islamic scholars"). They mark themselves as different through particular rituals, such as washing only their faces in the performance of ablutions, following different prayer times, bowing prostrate only once during prayer, foregoing the slaughtering of sheep during Tabaski, and conducting simple funerals devoid of ritual baths, prayers, shrouds, and grave markers. They reject secular education and law, Western values and modernity, and the state. A few Wahhabi groups funded by Saudi Arabia have also emerged in Niamey.

Pluralistic articulations of Islam—including "traditional Muslimist"—among Hausa are, in fact, pluralistic articulations of modernity. Islam arrived in Niger via globalization, where it co-evolved over centuries with local cultures, encountered Francophone and nationalist cultures and politics in the 20th century, and today is in complex engagement with various global articulations of modernity, including the notion of the universal *umma* ("the global Muslim community") and the "phenomenal rise of global Islamism" (Miles 2003:51). In other words, particular manifestations of Islam emerge in relation and interaction with each other as well as various Africanist–Traditionalist and Francophoneist–Globalist forms.

The Islamic Association of Niger (AIN), established by Seyni Kountché in 1974, served as the single, permitted Islamic association in Niger until 1991. Idrissa (2009:183-84) explains,

> AIN was to be an organ of national government unifying Nigeriens through religious ideals and manners (Kountché insisted also on

> its "cultural role") and as such, it was a state organization... [with authority to manage important mosques and control the content of sermons]...Contrary to Senegal's Sufi orders, it did not claim to represent a specific path to divine blessing, requiring therefore ultimate control over the conduct of the faithful—but it did claim the central role, in Niger, as protector of the Islamic faith in its Sunni *Maliki* version, and relished the state guarantees in the accomplishment of its mission.

The state's wielding of religious power led to unresolved tensions with the people.

Niaméens have seized increasing power to disseminate diverse, and in many cases divisive, visions of Islam to a broad public, and to establish Islamic associations independent of state control and often in conflict with the state since the opening provided by democratic transition that began in early 1990s. In the last two decades, Niaméens across the traditionalist-reformist spectrum have drawn on a diverse range of technologies to disseminate their views in the public domain, including loudspeakers, private newspapers, cassette and video tapes, TV and radio programming, and occasional public protests. Charlick (2004:102) argues that since 1991, organized Islam, particularly in the form of Islamic associations, has "emerged as the most important nonstate actor in Niger today, surpassing even the unions and student groups in terms of their influence and power... By 1994, five officially recognized Islamic associations had been...established and...by the year 2000, this number had jumped to over forty" and to 50 by 2005 (Robinson 2005:2). Virtually the full range of these organizations operates in Niamey, while "only a small percentage of these associations are in fact associated with 'reformist' or Islamist movements and views" (Charlick 2004:101).

The Niger Islamic Council (Conseil Islamique du Niger [CIN]) replaced the AIN in 2006 (Idrissa 2009:192), and it

> functions as state mandated consultative and regulatory body of religious leaders representing the 10 leading Islamic associations and including 10 government representatives that regulates Islamic

> festivals, the organization of the hadj, the construction of mosques, sermons, and oversees Muslim schools and charity. The council was also charged with promoting a culture of moderation, tolerance and social peace, mediating potentially harmful Western and global modernities while countering extremist or reformist interpretations imported from, or influenced by other Islamic countries.

While its ability to carry out this broad agenda seems quite limited at times, the state has heeded CIN advice to ban certain Islamic associations just as it banned others under the suggestion of the AIN, particularly in the aftermath of violent and deadly protests and riots against the Festival International de la Mode Africaine or FIMA ("International Festival of African Fashion") led by various Islamic organizations.

Hausa of Niamey rely on Islam as a unifying principle and practice, while simultaneously they are increasingly divided by differing conceptions of Islam. Islam transcends ethno-linguistic boundaries, plays a central role in Nigerien brassage, and provides a deep sense of community solidarity. This unity is largely unstructured. That is, few Hausa "belong" to Sufi orders or brotherhoods; many more are only loosely affiliated with *malamai* or particular congregations. Most Hausa men prefer to pray primarily at home or at any informal gathering anywhere in the city. Sometimes, however, there are divisions within or between Sufi orders. For example, in the 1990s, Tijaniyya and Qadiriyya engaged in heated disputes over proper prayer posture. Nevertheless, as a general rule, the Nigerien Islam practiced "traditionally" by Hausa is personal, flexible, accommodating, syncretic, and values and promotes peace.

The core division that has emerged among Hausa of Niamey over the past 20 years is between "traditional" Islam and a range of reformist movements, the Izala being the most influential one. The following encounter illustrates this tension. When I informed my old Hausa friend Youssoufou that a mutual acquaintance invited me to attend a Thursday evening wa'izi ("sermon") sponsored by an Izala mosque, I asked him if he would like to accompany me. He not only refused, but also advised me not to go:

> You should not mix friendship and religion. The *'yan Izala* are arrogant, they think that they are better than everyone else, that they know the Qur'an best, and it is insulting. We are all trying. We *Salulu* just pray, study, respect our neighbors, and other sects and religions. We have dignity and humility.

The Salalu community (that includes many Francophones) with which Youssoufou identifies are labeled as "rationalists" by Charlick (2004:98) who draws from Meunier's (1998) categorization in that they condemn radical reformist Islam and consider Islam as a personal religion and not as a social movement. Their perspective is simultaneously wary and distrustful of the clerical control of "traditional" *malamai* and Sufi *cheikhs.* For example, Youssoufou explains that he has heard rumors the certain Sufi *cheikhs* sleep with brides (who have married other men) on their wedding nights to bring *baraka* to new marriages. He finds this ridiculous and sinful, and argues that only God can bestow *baraka*. Other examples of this longstanding distrust will be discussed later.

The Muslimists and Islamists differ in their definitions of true Islam, particular practices, and in their willingness to use violence. The Izala (and other reformers) reject "the basic norms and structure of 'traditional Hausa society'" as well as "Western-dominated modernization" and the secular Nigerien state (Charlick 2004:98). In fact the Izala agenda of "de-Africanization" (Miles 2003) is defined largely by what it opposes. Charlick (2004:103) summarizes their confrontational vision:

> It rejects the organization of Hausa society based on hierarchy, titles, and gerontocracy. It condemns traditional Hausa Muslim rituals that involve redistribution of wealth such as baptisms and naming ceremonies (*sunna*), and elaborate weddings with dances (*tam-tam*). It particularly denigrates what it sees as pagan or pre-Islamic rituals and practices such as bori (possession cults)...It rejects the idea of "marabouts" as spiritual leaders and intermediaries, as practitioners of occult arts and purveyors of mystical powers and magical medicine (charms called *gris-gris*, or *laya*), and the entire concept of the Sufi tradition and Brotherhoods.

The Izala seek to establish a new autonomous identity by practicing what they perceive as a strict, austere, and pure form of Islam based solely on the Qur'an. They differentiate themselves through a variety of practices and markers. They prefer to pray on a slightly different schedule than other Muslims in Izala congregations at their own mosques. They perform perfunctory naming ceremonies, and weddings with only small, token exchanges to promote early marriage. Izala men often wear their pants a few inches short to symbolize that they are always ready to perform ablutions for prayer. Izala preachers advocate universal Qur'anic education for men and women. Izala women face seclusion, and are expected to dress modestly when they go out of their homes—in *hijab* minimally, and increasingly in full-body covering *niqab* in Niamey. Some women choose to do this while others are pressured by men to do so.

A diverse array of Hausa in particular—and other Nigeriens as well—are affiliated with Izala congregations in Niamey, ranging from poor, disenchanted men to wealthy merchants. The Izala opposition to traditional hierarchy and the state resonates with the poor who feel excluded by each. Youth are especially drawn to Izala positions that facilitate marriage. Merchants build social networks with fellow 'yan Izala. Izala followers, in opposition to the traditional Hausa ethos of redistribution, promote "a concept of Islam that favors capitalist development and an accompanying culture of individual wealth" (Charlick 2004:105). The Izala are "responding to globalization in a new non-Western way" (Charlick 2004:105) that accommodates capitalist formation while rejecting local and Western values.

The Izala agenda and tactics are "as 'foreign' to traditional African society as 'Westernization' is. This notion is reinforced by knowledge that the ideas of Izala were in fact introduced in Nigeria by the Saudis and spread to Niger from there." (Charlick 2004:103). Izalaists sometimes counter this by asserting their reformist movement is indigenous to Niger. For example, Hassane, who has been praying at an Izala mosque and listening to Izala sermons in Hausa by a fellow Nigerien Hausa from his home village, explains, "I do not give Nigerians credit for Izala; the Qur'an has always been here." The Izala are seen as confrontational and provocative by others, and rightly so in many cases. Izala sermons are characterized by stinging attacks and relentless threats of eternal punishment. Some Izala remove themselves from engagement with non-Izala family members. And Izala have engaged in a number of protests and demonstrations in Niamey and elsewhere in Niger in which they have been ready and willing to use violence against the state, women, bars and casinos, and churches to pursue their goals that led to dozens of deaths of both Izala members and their opponents in the 1990s.

The influence and radicalism of the Izala movement should not be exaggerated. It remains a small minority, and tensions between *'yan Izala* and *'yan darika* have receded. For example, there has been no sectarian religious violence in Niamey in the last six to eight years, as far as I know. Deeply held "traditional" values and practices continue as the norm. The key point is that the Izala and other reformists have managed to get their messages "out there" in the public domain—alongside other local and global Muslim perspectives. The proper meaning and practice of Islam is now a matter of lively public debate in ways that were not possible 20 years ago.

Hausa of Niamey have reacted in various ways to the presence of Izala congregations and discourse. Some reject it as ridiculous. Many men absorb certain messages and elements (for example, ideas about money and the state), but do not participate in Izala congregations. Furthermore, contrary to separatist agendas, many Izala congregants consult with *bokaye* ("traditional healers") and are enrolled in Francophone secular schools and the Université Abdou Moumouni studying subjects such as agribusiness, accounting, and computer science. Another response, and one that merits further attention, involves efforts to reassert and redefine "traditional" Sufi Islam as valid and modern. A good example of this is the Niass Tijaniyya, "now the largest and fastest growing Sufi religious order in Niger" (Robinson 2005:1).

The Niass Tijaniyya emphasize peace, tolerance, Qur'anic scholarship, religious and secular education, and flexibility and openness to innovation. They assert that this sets them apart from Izala who lack true understanding of Islam. In the last decade the Niass Tijaniyya have entered the political arena at local and state levels. Perhaps most strikingly, as recognized in recent studies, the order stresses gender and class equality. For example, political scientist Pearl Robinson (2005:1) argues that, "in Niger, female empowerment has emerged as a significant factor in the order's global political agenda to revitalize its structures, counter the Islamists, and broaden its base." Similarly, Shailly Barnes (2009:209) documents that the Niass Tijaniyya "is a engaged in a variety of anti-poverty, empowerment and literacy programs that touch the lives of the poorest Nigeriens. Its progress in women's human, economic and reproductive rights is especially remarkable."

Francophone-ist–Globalist Modernities

Parallel to and in close interaction with Africanist–Traditionalist and Muslimist–Islamist modernities, Francophone-ist identities, practices, values, and agendas as well as a diffuse assortment of Globalist modernities constitute a third major set of cultural strands in the life worlds of Hausa and their neighbors in Niamey. The term "Francophone-ist" is used to refer to people and practices, values, perceptions, and political agendas. This complex was introduced and imposed on Niger by authoritarian French colonial rule in the early 20th century. However, in the hands of Nigeriens, contemporary Francophone-ist modernities have evolved in particular ways in postcolonial Niamey as sources of local prestige and power while also embedded in and closely identified with regional Francophone West African culture. This section concentrates on Francophone-ist modernities, because I have already discussed global modernities in some detail and will do so again in the following chapter.

The term "globalist," in my usage, refers to a broad range of images, messages, identities, and cultures from around the world—the West, the East, the South—that Hausa of Niamey draw from, negotiate, and appropriate in their attempts to understand the world and their place in it. Some are "Western" such as political ideals articulated in Western Europe and popular culture produced in the U.S., especially Hip Hop and Hollywood films. Most, however, originate from Francophone West Africa, India, Nigeria, Mexico, Brazil, China, and the global Muslim community and are consumed in Niamey via radio, Bollywood and Nollywood and Chinese films, Mexican and Brazilian telenovelas, and cassette tapes. Globalist modernities are not only experienced through mass media in Niamey but also through direct encounters as the result of migration that has led to as many Nigeriens living out of the country in diaspora as within it—as highlighted earlier. Patterns of circular migration regularly bring many Nigeriens home from West and North Africa, Europe, Mecca, and North America to Niamey with fresh infusions of ideas, fashions, languages, consumer goods, and stories.

Francophone-ist and globalist modernities are sometimes one and the same, but they can also be very different. Many Nigeriens are (still or newly) fascinated by and connected to France—where more than 50,000 live—and French culture in a love-hate relationship. France remains central to the worldviews of many Nigeriens. A substantial number of the most literate Francophones of Niamey are deeply opposed to France and its power, policies, and culture. French language skills—regardless of one's take on France—allow Niaméens access to a broad range of opportunities and globalist modernities. For example, French allows Hausa to network with other Francophone West Africans in diaspora. Most Bollywood, Nollywood, and Chinese films, and Mexican and Brazilian telenovelas are dubbed or subtitled in French for consumption in Niger. But dubbing, say a Mexican soap opera into French, does not make it French nor does it preclude critically engaged non-Francophone audiences. Indeed Francophone-ists are only somewhat more likely to engage with globalist modernities than non-Francophone-ists, traditional Africanists, and Islamists are. The majorities of Niaméens who consume global popular culture do not know French and have little or no interest in France. Many *'yan Izala* regularly play football and are avid fans of international football; Hip Hop takes a place alongside Islamic sermons and prayer from Nigeria and Saudi Arabia in their DVD collections. However, many Niaméens are not simple relativists, especially the elderly and reformist-oriented Islamists who vehemently condemn secular global modernities as contrary to local tradition, immoral, and decadent.

Two, partially related, dynamics at play are particularly important. First, the Francophone-ists and the globalists assert that they and their ideals are the only truly modern entities in Niamey. They regard ethnicity and local traditions as backward or quaint at best, and see Islamists such as the Izala as constituting a retrograde rejection of modernity. Second, across the "globalscape" with which they are engaged, Hausa of Niamey are particularly drawn to a core set of themes, including: social justice, money and wealth, individualism, love, corruption, and violence. In some cases these are the core themes that the artists, producers, and cultures intend to address, but more importantly, I argue, Hausa grapple with them in serious and fun ways because they are particularly relevant to the struggles they face to survive with dignity in their lives in Niamey.

The emergence of Francophone-ist identities and ideals in Niger vividly illustrates the contradictions and ambivalences of modernity as highlighted by social theory. The influence and power of the minority Nigerien Francophones and their vision of modernity in Niamey is remarkable given the nature of French colonial rule; that is, its short duration and hypocrisy. Idrissa (2009:181) speculates that 19th century historical factors might play a role in explaining why "the Sahelian postcolony with the shortest exposition to French ideals (about three decades, as opposed to Senegal's three centuries) should also be the most consistent in its adherence to such ideals?" Idrissa (2009:165) also emphasizes that the French colonial regime articulated liberal republican norms to justify their rule in Niger and West Africa, but in practice contradicted these ideals by imposing

> a specific subject regime, regulated by a disciplinary text called the *Indigénat* code, [that] was applied until 1945 to anyone who was not working directly for the colonial government...[Subjects] could be [and often were] imprisoned without trial, subjected to compulsory service [such as military conscription to fight on behalf of France against the menace of Nazi Germany], obligatory unpaid labor, compulsory cultivation of crops [to pay high taxes and for export], and they were barred from any form of political activity.

Although some French administrators were motivated by what they saw as a "civilizing mission" to bring modern French language and culture to Niger through secular schools, the regime as a whole was primarily concerned with "training useful auxiliaries for colonial and business administration" (Idrissa 2009:167) to facilitate the maximum extraction of wealth from Niger.

Despite the brutality and racism of French colonial rule, a distinct Nigerien Francophone culture began to emerge during the 15-year transitional period from the end of World War II and the removal of the *Indigénat* code to independence in 1960. A distinct class of Francophone politicians and bureaucrats positioned themselves to rule independent Niger; "Initially known as *commis*, that is to say petty administrative employees, they were soon also called *évolués* (the evolved ones), a concept representing their 'elevation' from inferior African cultures into the splendid spheres of French civilization [and] by the 1960s... *intellectuels*" (Idrissa 2009:168). The Hausa, including those who never learned French, refer to these Francophones as "*masu ilimi,*" meaning the "learned ones" or "the experts;" "They are in effect called the 'experts' because they are believed to possess the much valuable *ilimin zamani* (Hausa), 'modern knowledge'" (Idrissa 2009:168).

Idrissa (2009:180) documents that, "Niger's independence essentially meant that the Francophones became free to try to shape Nigerien society according to their principles of social progress, republican citizenship, and cultural modernity." These principles, based in French-style education, include capitalism, meritocracy, individualism, universal suffrage, a secular state, rule of law, a "rational" scientific perspective, and monogamy and family planning to limit fertility. In their efforts to achieve these goals, the Francophone state sought to control and exclude organized Islam from political power, by creating single corporatist institutions to regulate Islam, beginning with the Cultural Islamic Association of Niger (ACIN), and succeeded by the AIN in 1974 and the CIN in 2006 as discussed in the previous section. Traditionalists and Islamists accommodate and contest assertions of Francophone power and values; "The subjective attachment of most Francophones to such ideals—variable, contextual and strategic as it must often be—is the hallmark of their social identity, and the reason for which they are both admired and detested by other social groups, especially the Islamists" (Idrissa 2009:169). Some also admire the Francophones due to their power and wealth or achievement of "economic modernity," as Francophones are disproportionately wealthy, even though some are very poor. At the same time, many non-Francophones resent their arrogance and sense of superiority and feel that they are tainted by their connection to French colonial rule.

Particular cultural markers and performances as well as political ideas and agendas define the distinct, evolving Nigerien Francophone culture. Francophones value French literacy and fluency and many prefer to communicate with one another in French, including a small but growing segment of Niaméens who speak French almost exclusively and are teaching French as a first language to their children. Francophones prefer new, industrially manufactured French or Western clothing and hygienic products. Men of means wear coats and ties, slacks and jeans, button-down and polo shirts, and closed-toe business shoes. Women prefer dresses, skirts, blouses, jeans, and high-heeled shoes. Francophone men keep themselves cleanly shaven with their own imported razors and shaving cream topped off with generous splashes of international brand name colognes—as opposed to visiting public barbers like the masses of Niaméens. Francophone women display elaborate hairstyles free of headscarves and prefer imported perfumes. Men and women who can afford it use flush toilets and toilet paper rather than pit latrines and water. Many Francophones practice egalitarian gender relations. For example, Francophone men and women greet each other by shaking hands or exchanging kisses on cheeks, and dine together, in sharp contrast with the norms of other groups in Niamey. Many Nigerien Francophone men feel that there are shortages of Francophone women in Niger who share their behavior and values, and thus seek wives from other Francophone West African nations. In fact, I know of several wealthy families in which the majority of Francophone Muslim men have married Francophone Christian women from Togo, Benin, and Côte d'Ivoire. Their children celebrate both Muslim and Christian holidays.

Nigerien Francophone political culture emphasizes a democratic, secular constitutional form of government in which the state seeks to build a unified French-speaking nation that is neutral with respect to religion, ethnicity, and gender. These ideals have always been difficult to achieve given opposition from traditional communities, Muslimists and Islamists, the fact that only 29 percent of adults are literate in French, and a long history of authoritarian regimes.

Francophone Nigeriens capitalized on international political pressure in efforts to assert their supremacy through pushing through a liberal democratic constitution in 1991 that ushered in the current democracy era. Niaméens of all interests and persuasions are now relatively free to organize and express their opinions and visions for the future in the public domain. In the cacophonous, contentious public culture of Niamey, Francophones have managed to continue to establish a particularly broad influence. The official language of the state is French. Public education is secular and conducted only in French. French fluency is required for access to most prominent positions in the government and civil service. Nigerien nationalism based on the French language as a unifying factor is stronger in Niamey than elsewhere in Niger. All Niaméens must contend and comply with French bureaucratic structures and conventions. For example, all people must carry National Identity cards that list names according to French transliteration, such as Mohammadou, Youssoufou, and Chaibou. The independent press as well as the private television and radio stations that have emerged and flourished in the last 20 years use French primarily. A host of influential associations representing Francophone ideals has flourished in the democracy era, including the Union of Niger's Muslim Women (UFMN), the Nigerien Human Rights Defense Association (ANDDH), the Rally of Niger's Women Jurists (RFJN), and the anti-slavery organization TIMIDRIA.

Money Matters and the Occult

The moral and practical ambiguities of money and problems securing enough money are defining characteristics of Hausa lived experience in Niamey, as exemplified through mass migration that is largely driven by motivation to escape poverty, the tensions surrounding remittances, and the commoditization of communication. Hausa communities of Niamey—through various alternative modernities—endeavor to make sense of neoliberalism and other dramatic social structural transformations. Many Hausa are alarmed by deepening poverty and expanding inequality, and by the perception that increasing violent crime and immorality upset the image of Niamey as an especially tolerant and peaceful city in the midst of the turmoil of the West African sub-region. Parallel with the Kenyan communities studied by Smith (2005:141) and communities across Africa, Hausa increasingly draw on stories of occult economies that involve magic or witchcraft "to locate the sources of its conjoined moral and economic decline." The circulation of stories or rumors of nefarious methods of securing money are deployed not only to make sense of the mysteries of money, but also as an important way the poor Hausa masses assert their own dignity and morality in a chaotic world.

Many Hausa, particularly poor, mainstream Africanists, perceive that money is divisive. For them, wealth is not valued for its own sake. Wealth is only valued when tempered by generosity. This means never saying "no" to family or neighbors in need. In contrast, Islamists promote the capitalist pursuit of individual accumulation to be used for economically "rational" ends such as lodging, food, clothing, and investment in business capital, rather than for helping others or hosting elaborate naming and wedding ceremonies. Francophone-ists and globalists view money in similar ways—as a simple, matter of fact reality of modernity earned by those who deserve it.

The "new consciousness of globalization" (Geschiere, Meyer, and Pels 2008:1)—developed through appropriation of global mass media, accelerating international circular migration, and *hira*—among Hausa of Niamey includes a sharper awareness of just how poor Nigeriens are relative to other people around the world and of expanding inequality within Niger. Poverty is more difficult to bear for people who are conscious of living in a world of plenty; "the contemporary African experience is not simply that of economic deprivation. Rather it involves 'an economy of goods that are known, that may sometimes be seen, that one wants to enjoy, but to which one will never have material access'" (Mbembe 2002:271 cited in Ferguson 2006:192). The vexing paradox faced by many Hausa is this: how can Hausa be morally proper through religion, highly skilled conversation, generosity, and peace, and yet so economically disadvantaged? Their frustration and efforts to explain their situation are expressed through occult economies—alongside critiques of the global and national economy and a rising self-deprecatory attitude.

The anthropology of witchcraft and the social theory of rumor offer productive insights for understanding the types of stories about wealth accumulation that Hausa are telling with increasing frequency in recent years. Some Hausa believe that witches exist in their midst: "The witch (m. *maye*, f. *maya*) is a person possessed of the power to capture and eat the soul (kurwa) of an individual, resulting in that person's sickness and death" (Wall 1988:136). Witches' (*mayu*) power is derived from *maita* (witchcraft), "an actual physical substance present within the body of the witch" (Wall 1988:137). Witches are not consciously aware that they are witches, rather their "powers are inherent in the individual" (Wall 1998:193) as they are ingested through mothers' milk. Hausa witches are motivated by pure malice, not by the pursuit of wealth. Thus, the Hausa conception of witches and witchcraft perfectly matches classical anthropological definitions. Following recent scholarship, this analysis of the occult is concerned with explicating social processes, rather than being preoccupied by teasing out definitions and distinguishing between witchcraft, sorcery, and magic. Besides, Hausa people of Niamey are telling fewer stories about witchcraft, traditionally defined, than they did in the past. They are, instead, sharing more stories and rumors about occult economies involving volitional efforts using horrible, anti-social means to gain wealth.

"Witch-finding movements have a long history in Africa" (Smith 2005:143), and they have drawn the attention of generations of anthropologists. In recent years, "the study of 'African witchcraft' has experienced a decisive revival" (Moore and Sanders 2001:10). This renewed interest is due to dissatisfaction with earlier theories as well as "a dramatic rise in occult economies: in the deployment, real or imagined, of magical means for material ends" in postcolonial Africa and around the world (Comaroff and Comaroff 1999:279). Contemporary scholarship on witchcraft and "the occult" in general continues to: (1) address longstanding concerns to broadly interpret witchcraft and related phenomena,

(2) identify patterns of accusations and what they reveal about power and conflict, and (3) demonstrate how people draw on concepts of the occult to explain both perennial, perplexing problems such as misfortune, suffering, and death as well as hard-to-explain sudden fortune. In contrast with earlier scholarship that often depicted witchcraft as a "primitive or prelogical...static and tightly bounded tradition...[localized in] small-scale, village-level communities" (Moore and Sanders 2001:10), recent theorists strongly emphasize "the modernity of witchcraft" (Geschiere 1997). Indeed, contemporary anthropologists highlight "the historicity of witchcraft discourse and practices—suggesting that they are forever changing, alive to the basic rhythms of our world over the *longue durée*... [and thus] eminently modern...[insisting] that witchcraft operates as part and parcel of modernity itself" (Moore and Sanders 2001:10-11). Occult economies are in fact modern, even though they may appear to be quintessentially traditional or anti-modern to Islamist reformers and wealthy Francophone-ists. For those who tell these stories or pay attention to them, occult connections to money are not closed systems of beliefs and practices. They neither thwart modernity nor are they overwhelmed by it. Rather, these stories constitute a flexible and deeply ambivalent means of contemplating perplexing changes that define the contemporary moment in Niamey.

The modernity of the occult involves the dynamic interplay between the local and the global. In their important study of postcolonial South Africa, Comaroff and Comaroff (1999:282) emphasize that the rise of occult economies is simultaneously "profoundly parochial and so obviously translocal." Hausa stories of occult economies, along with Hausa analyses of these stories, are peculiarly Hausa in many ways as will be explained later. In South Africa, occult economies feature "'ritual murder,' the sale of body parts...zombies...[and] financial scams" (Comaroff and Comaroff 1999:279). The same monstrous pursuits, with the exception of the production of zombies, are also increasingly at the center of Hausa stories (and those of people around the world). These images and stories are now in global circulation. Hausaphone videos from Nigeria that have recently poured into Niamey also play a role in the construction of rumors of the occult among Hausa in Niamey. People getting wealthy quickly and then suffering all kinds of magical retributions because of their failure to redistribute their newfound riches is a common theme in these videos.

Toudou, a 40-year-old Mawri Hausa, triumphantly returned to Niamey in late 2008 after spending 12 years in New York City. Less than a month later, the brand new BMW sport utility vehicle—a key global icon of conspicuous consumption—that he purchased in the U.S., arrived after being shipped across the Atlantic Ocean to Togo and driven by a courier to Niamey. By the end of 2009, he had purchased a luxurious villa and was living in it with his new wife that he met after his return. He claimed that he had worked hard as a construction worker—a skill that he learned on the fly in New York City. His closest family and friends did not press him on this—at least not in my presence—nor did I. Toudou had regularly sent home modest remittances throughout his time abroad, but his newfound fabulous wealth must have seemed astonishing.

How Toudou earned so much money intrigues me, but I will never uncover the truth. Exploring how men who do not know Toudou explained his success and how his fortune illustrates broader themes about the mysterious nature of money in Niamey provides much more interesting anthropological insights. In describing his situation—but changing the particulars (his name, age, migratory destination, type of car) to many men who I was confident did not know him—three primary interpretations of his fortune emerged. Each explanation revealed a particular articulation of the nature of money in modernity. First, some men accepted Toudou's explanation for his riches at face value. This was supported by the common perception among Hausa in Niamey that any determined man with his wits about him can earn incredible riches in the U.S. Second, many others drew the conclusion that Toudou could only have made so much money in the drug trade. These men retained doubts, however, because I explained that Toudou did not seem like a drug dealer since he is a devout Muslim who is gentle and generous with family and friends. Third, many men suggested that Toudou must have used *dabo* ("magic") or *magani* ("medicine") to attain his riches. This explanation led to broader, detailed discussions about how money magically and mysteriously appears and disappears through occult means. Furthermore, many men who commented on Toudou's story did not see these interpretations as mutually exclusive. Rather they suggested that Toudou might have made his money through all three means.

The following reflections on the occult took place in the aftermath of discussing Toudou's story in three conversation groups. All of the discussants emphasized at the outset and throughout the gatherings that they have heard these stories, or read about them in *Le Sahel* or other popular newspapers, but that they neither personally know people who have used magic to gain riches nor have they done so themselves. Most of the men said that they believe these stories to be real in the sense that they think that some people actually are using magic in attempts to become rich and powerful. The men stated that they do not think magical techniques to get rich really work. Instead, they emphasized the depravity and desperation of those involved.

The discussions focused on three core themes: what people are said to seek through magic, the specific magical techniques they are said to use, and recounting cases through short stories. The men emphasized that clients could not act without the assistance of *bokaye* ("traditional secular healers") or *malamai* ("Muslim teacher-scholars")—sometimes referred to by the French term, *marabout.*

People use magic in pursuit of various goals. One of the most common reasons for using magic is to become rich. As Lamine, an unemployed middle-aged man, put it, "People become crazy for riches—they want money without suffering for it." Others use magic because they want to enhance their popularity, for example, politicians. Men who are jealous of neighbors, such as successful *commerçants* ("merchants"), may seek to make them poor through magic. In contrast, people use magic to prevent theft. Conflicts between co-wives are played out through the use of magic to make rivals crazy, force abortions, or to kill them. Men and women dread infertility and turn to magic to increase confidence. Magic is also used to promote many other desired outcomes, including one's children doing well in school and the marriage of sons and daughters.

The *bokaye* and *malamai* have "various jobs," as one man put it. These jobs involve duping their clients or actually seeking to satisfy their diverse requests. More strikingly and particularly in cases in which clients seek wealth, *bokaye* and *malamai* demand human blood and organs, especially from the corpses of young boys or girls. *Bokaye* and *malamai* themselves, or their clients, or acting together, are said to "bribe workers at morgues or go by night to cemeteries to cut out body parts and organs, hearts, legs, and heads" for magical uses, according to Youssoufou and many other men. Furthermore, some men said that *bokaye* and *malamai* require sacrifices of people, especially children, or animals such as horses, sheep, cattle, cocks, depending on their region of origin. They also ask their clients to bring them many relatively mundane things, including cash, perfume, kola nuts, and fabric of particular colors (especially red, black, or white). *Bokaye* and *malamai* give clients food, magical objects, and money to put in various places, such as rivers, old wells, holes in ground surrounding homes, pockets, or around the body (necks, arms, wrists, waists, or ankles). They prepare magical elixirs to be added to *hura* ("porridge"), honey, *tuwo* ("grain paste"), or put in water that is used to wash the body. Special, secret substances are put in incense that are inhaled and envelop the body.

Men also recounted many stories about the use of magic to accumulate wealth. The stories are almost always very short—just a few sentences. The stories centered on two main themes that sometimes overlap. One genre highlights ways that gullible clients are easily duped. Many of these stories are didactic, a common element in Hausa conversation in particular and in Hausa oral literature in general. Listeners learn that through *hankali* ("common sense"), they can avoid being scammed. The other theme centers on the "depraved madness" for money facilitated by *bokaye* and *malamai*. Indeed, the mediators between clients and wealth are victims of the same materialism that their clients seek. The first two stories (below) are representative of the first theme, whereas the last two are representative of the latter.

> A client who wanted to increase his wealth went to visit a *boka*. The *boka* told him to deliver a new suitcase with 5 million CFA [$10,000]

> in it and claimed that he would double it. The *boka* returned the heavy suitcase the next day and instructed his client not to open it until a few days had passed. When the client opened it, he found a brick and some old tattered clothes. The *boka* had long since moved on to the next town.
>
> A *boka* put his associate under the bed in his room. He then invited his client to visit him at night. The client heard a garbled, mysterious voice in the room. The *boka* claimed that they were having a conversation with an evil *aljan* ("jinn") and the only way to appease it would be for the client to bring money. Since the guy was crazy, he believed it was an *aljan* and brought the money. This is another way to cheat people.
>
> A Nigerien and a Nigerian were arrested for a horrible crime. They had caught a young beggar, cut off his head, took his blood, heart, and other organs. They claimed that a marabout demanded this if they wanted to get rich.
>
> To become rich, a *boka* informed a man that he would need to sacrifice one of his children. The *boka* killed the child and put him in a room in the client's compound. Whenever the father needs money, he simply goes into the room and money magically appears.

These stories of occult connections to money circulating among Hausa of Niamey are not merely pathological preoccupations or superstitions as asserted by Islamist reform movements and wealthy Francophone-ists. The social theory of rumor impels more productive directions of inquiry. Following folklorist Patricia Turner's (1993:220) analysis of rumors of mysterious lethal attacks on African American bodies, I suggest that these Hausa stories of the occult "do not cause the wounds from which...[Hausa]...suffer"—poverty and inequality do. Rumors are defined by four essential qualities that explain their emergence and perpetuation, according to Turner (1993:30). First, rumors have the "ability to explain bewildering changes in the world" (Turner 1993:30). Second, people draw on rumors to plug holes in knowledge gaps; "Rumor travels when events have importance in the lives of individuals and when the news received about them is either lacking or subjectively ambiguous" (Allport and Postman 1947:2 cited in Turner 1993:30). Third, rumors must have some degree of plausibility if they are to have an enduring existence. Fourth, rumors reveal crucial insights about worldview or conceptions of modernity. These Hausa rumors, like those considered by Moore and Sanders (2001:16) in their survey of occult economies in postcolonial Africa, are not "simply a misrecognition of capitalism or the workings of the economy, but metaphysical speculations about the origin of value." Hausa rumors are revealing whether they are "true" or not, and whether told by people who actually believe that they are true, or told by people who do not actually believe that magical techniques to get wealthy really work.

Hausa of Niamey are grappling with the theological conundrum addressed by Jewish Conservative Rabbi Harold Kushner (1978) in his influential bestseller, *When Bad Things Happen to Good People*: How can good people suffer so much pain in a world ruled by a loving and just God? Perhaps even more commonly, Hausa also invert the title by asking, "Why do good things happen to bad people?" One of the answers is that people use magic to mysteriously become instantly rich and live "First World" lifestyles in Niamey, as Toudou did. South African rumors of occult economies similarly flourish in "a world in which the *possibility* of rapid achievement, of amassing a fortune by largely invisible methods, is always palpably present" (Comaroff and Comaroff 1999:293, emphasis in original). Many Hausa men feel that these stories had some degree of plausibility because trustworthy friends had told them, they were reported in local newspapers, and because they believe that certain types of magic are honorable and efficacious. Many men who do not believe that magic can produce money, purchase *layu* ("magical amulets") from *bokaye* and *malamai*, especially ones that are affixed to their children to protect their health, and others that are placed above doorways of homes to prevent the entrance of thieves.

The desperate search for money at any cost is seen as the ultimate anti-social pursuit. What one friend called the "depraved madness" for money exhibited by others is symbolically expressed in these stories of the occult. Rumors about blood and gore and sacrifice use a special sort of exaggeration that Hausa of Niamey deploy to emphatically emphasize the connection between madness and money. As such, they constitute a "weapon of the weak" (Scott 1985). Many poor Hausa use these stories or rumors as a way of reasserting their own moral superiority. They argue that they are unsullied by money and greed. Scheper-Hughes' (2000:217) groundbreaking analysis of the global human organs trade highlights similar responses among people around the world who face daily struggles to survive: "The most vulnerable citizens will fight back with the only resources they have—gossip, rumors, urban legends, and resistance to modern laws. In this way, they act and react to the state of emergency that exists for them in this time of economic and democratic readjustments." Notably, the most horrifying manipulations, such as sacrificing children, are associated with gaining riches. A homeowner is not required to produce a fresh human heart to get an amulet to protect his home, $1 in cash suffices.

Different patterns of accusations reveal very different sorts of tensions. The central dynamic in Niamey is that poor men accuse selfish rich men of drawing wealth from magical manipulations. Furthermore, accusations against "outsiders"—however defined—have a very different meaning than accusations against "insiders." Nigerien Mawri Hausa labor migrants and smugglers from Dogondoutchi who venture south to Nigeria have long told rumors of their victimization at the hands of Nigerian Igbo headhunters and cannibals (Masquelier 2000). Masquelier (2000:88) argues that these rumors reveal "local understandings of migration, wage labor and market relations" and the vast economic gap between impoverished Niger and relatively wealthy Nigeria. Moreover, Masquelier (2000:104) contends that, "what...makes an already horrific picture of physical destruction even bleaker is that this immoral traffic of human bodies is facilitated—even promoted—by some Mawri themselves, whose own uncontrolled hunger for money leads them to actively participate in the annihilation of their kin and fellow citizens" by selling them to Igbo. In Niamey those who are associated with using nefarious magic to gain riches are primarily neighbors, not foreigners. This inward looking gaze implies that the contemporary crisis in Niger emanates from within. Hausa of Niamey do not assert that the westerners or Chinese have their own magic to attain wealth.

In addition, one of the most striking aspects of these occult stories is their sustained and deliberate assault on local *bokaye* and *malamai*—men who assist the greedy and are themselves greedy. *Bokaye* and *malamai* are not seen as uniformly bad. Furthermore, reduced access to biomedicine as a result of structural adjustment has made Niaméens increasingly reliant on medicines provided by *bokaye* and *malamai*. Accusations against *bokaye* are not surprising. They are not regarded as sacred figures. In fact, many Hausa think that all *bokaye* are charlatans. In contrast, *malamai* are typically the most revered men in Hausa communities of Niamey, which makes it ironic that some are so distrusted. The distrust of *malamai* has deep historical roots among many Hausa communities of Niger. Many Hausa of Niger are descended from people who fled Usman dan Fodio's *jihad* in Northern Nigeria in 1804 seeking freedom to practice local religions or to practice Islam without tight clerical control. Idrissa (2009:176) argues that, "an enduring trait of Nigerien rapport to religion [is] idiosyncratic judgment, opinion, 'humor'." Idrissa (2009:176) quotes a Nigerien man who reported to a French colonial official in 1919, "We do not trust clerics, for ever since we have known them, they only keep tricking and deceiving us," and emphasizes that, "the trickster cleric is still a popular theme in today's Niger."

The targeting of *malamai* today in Niamey is particularly revealing of deeper social tensions as it reflects a collision between capitalism and religion. Idrissa (2009:202) documents the monetization of their profession,

> Activities are now regulated by professional criteria, such as schedules, performance and payment. Clerics organize their time in relation to the marriages and baptisms that they will celebrate or attend, the burial prayers that they will conduct, the specific magical works that they will perform. Money and time slots are calculated in accordance to these demands. Clerics thus draw public censorship of their greed, usually contrasted with a time when they were imagined to be holy

> men who did not move about so much and instead cultivated pious poverty in a fixed abode.

By breaking the border between the profane and the sacred, in horrifically gory ways, the *malamai* represent a desperate world turned upside down.

The stories rarely cite specific named *bokaye* or *malamai*. The rumors themselves are powerful enough to serve the purposes of those who circulate them.

There are no magic courts in Niamey in which accusations can be lodged and penalties imposed that are akin to the witchcraft trials that recently emerged in parts of Cameroon (Nyamnjoh 2001). Niaméens do not physically attack *malamai*, but they do occasionally chase out of their neighborhoods or the city altogether those who have fallen out of favor with verbal insults and threats.

In conclusion, these stories of magic also reveal competing and contested conceptions of modernity. Francophone modernists dismiss them as backward, traditional superstition. Anti-Sufi reformers, such as the Izala, argue that the belief and use of magic is at the core of what is wrong with "African Islam." But for those who tell them, these widespread tales are exaggerated judgments by which people assert their own dignity in the face of the inequalities of globalization, a world full of grubby acts of greed, and an encroaching culture of materialism and money worship.

Postscript

Relentless material and symbolic striving for global connection and respect mark Hausa negotiation of alternative modernities. They desire economic and cultural modernity. The modernity at large and the alternative modernities that they pursue are difficult to define with precision. Indeed, culture and modernity are constantly changing and are generated by dynamic processes of conflict and consensus. They are defined by dialogue and contestation more so than by concord and unity. Hausa constructions are marked by hybridity, ambiguity, and contradictions—some of which are creatively resolved. Each of the key modernity strands—Africanist–Traditionalist, Muslimist–Islamist, Francophone-ist–Globalist—that have currency among Hausa of Niamey today have emerged in relation and interaction with the others. Some Hausa select from a narrow range of modernities, but many more creatively navigate multiple visions of modernity simultaneously. Hausa of Niamey draw from across the full spectrum of alternative modernities discussed—all seen most clearly in dialogue and debate over money and other contemporary matters of great concern rather than solely in the abstract—in their quest for inclusion, social justice, and dignity in a world of inequality, poverty, and greed. They navigate and attempt to reconcile the liminal spaces between the local and the global, the rural and the urban, the traditional and the modern, the fourth world and the first world, the here and the there, solidarity and impermanence, dreams and realities.

— 6 —

Growing Up Male in Niamey

Yaro da gari abokin tahiya manya:
A rich young man can become an old person's friend

Ibrahim and I met while warming ourselves around an evening street corner fire pit during the cool season of 1991. As a 25-year man from a small village near Tessaoua, he had settled in Niamey two years earlier with his wife and first-born infant son, Ismael, and was operating a fruit stand at the Petit Marché. Ismael was terrified of me because, according to Ibrahim, he had never been in close proximity to a white man. Ismael warmed up to me over the last 20 years. By the time he was five he enjoyed sitting on my lap and pulling on my long arm hairs, asking, "Are you a monkey or a man?" Over the next decade, Ismael always greeted me respectfully, avoiding eye contact. When I offered to shake hands, he awkwardly consented, then ran off blushing and laughing hysterically with his friends. In the last few years, Ismael began greeting me matter of factly with a firm handshake and sustained eye contact. He was proud to show me his high school books and notes.

Shortly after I arrived in Niamey in 2009 for five weeks of research, I made my way to the Petit Marché to greet Ibrahim who was happy to see me. His disproportionately large and strong hands were thickly calloused, rough, and weathered from a lifetime of farm work, for even though his family, now including six children, was settled in Niamey, Ibrahim returned to his village every year to farm. Ismael was there to visit his father, and offered his hand to me in greeting. Ibrahim chuckled, "You see the difference. I have the hands of a man from farm work. My son has the hands of woman from city work." Ismael was quick to respond, "Yes, this is true. I could never do farm work in the hot sun sweating all day long, nor would I ever want to do it. I respect and thank my father for being smart enough to move to the city and its civilization. But he cannot help me, he does not know how to make money." "I always made enough money to feed you and send you to school," Ibrahim retorted. We proceeded with a few more minutes of greetings and family news updates before I made arrangements to meet Ibrahim the next day at his favorite *hira* group. As I prepared to depart, Ismael informed me that he was working with friends at a shop in the Grand Marché selling cell phones and DVDs and invited me to visit him there, "This is how a man can make money in modern Niamey." He could not resist one final generational jab, "The next time you come to Niamey do not surprise my father like this as he is liable to have a heart attack. He does not know how to use a cell phone. Just call me and I will inform him." Ibrahim was still the father and thus had the last word, "These youth spend so much time on their cell phones that they have forgotten how to really talk."

My initial research focused on urban pioneers, that is, recently arrived migrants in the late 1980s that set the stage for Niamey's remarkable growth. I have kept in touch with them, and I have also seen a new generation grow up in Niamey over this time—the first substantial cohort born and reared in the city. This chapter analyzes generational links and divides generated by the extraordinary changes of the past two decades in Niamey. Adapting the model developed in the innovative work of anthropologist Karen Tranberg Hansen and a multi-disciplinary team of scholars in *Youth and the City in the Global South* (2008), the chapter is structured by consideration of four key issues: (1) Hausa youth, globalization, and the specificity of urban life in Niamey, (2) the marriage predicament, (3) the ways that youth are challenging gerontocracy, and (4) the creation of contemporary urban youth culture of Niamey.

The first large cohort of Hausa (and other Nigerien) youth born (in the late 1980s) and reared in Niamey is coming of age with bleak prospects for achieving financial security and social status as adults by traditional definitions, that is, by getting married. They have endured economic depression throughout their lifetimes as Niger has been marginalized in the neoliberal world order. Similar to millions of youths across Africa, Niamey's youths neither passively accept their predicament nor are they simply troublemakers. Rather they act with creative agency and resourcefulness in pursuing many trajectories toward the future and in their quest for empowerment, making them potentially significant catalysts for change.

Hausa Youth, Globalization, and the Specificity of Urban Life in Niamey

Young people are everywhere in Niamey. Niamey today is a city of youth with a remarkable 50% of the population less than 14 years old, and 25% aged 15-24. In contrast with rich nations where the elderly urban population is growing, the young urban population is increasing in poor nations (Hansen 2008:6) such as Niger. This urban youth bulge makes "a focus on youth particularly compelling...this simple demographic observation has complex implications for resource development, service provision, social organization, and everyday life" (Hansen 2008:5,7).

Prior to 1988 very few Hausa who lived in Niamey were born there. Most were seasonal migrants or recently settled migrants. They gave birth to a new generation, today reaching their early twenties, that is frustrated by struggles to launch their careers into social adulthood. Many face the prospect of lifelong bachelorhood. This state of limbo often creates or exacerbates another one. Many of Niamey's youth constantly ask themselves, "Should I stay or should I go?" That is, the idea of international migration as the best hope is always lurking. It is not easy to live as a young person in the city in the world's poorest nation. Many live in absolutely squalid conditions, and have no recourse to biomedical health care. One in five perish before reaching five years of age. Worse, some fall victim to various forms of forced servitude. Nevertheless, youth who were born in Niamey prefer the city. Youth talk incessantly about leaving Niamey for other cities, but never—in my experience—about moving to rural Niger.

Niamey's youth are more experienced in participating in multicultural environments than their parents were when they were young village dwellers. Nigerien *brassage* is amplified among the youth of Niamey. Niamey attracts migrants from all regions and ethnic groups of Niger, and all of its neighborhoods are ethnically integrated, as emphasized earlier. For many Niaméens, particularly the youth who are increasingly born in inter-ethnic, polyethnic, polygynous families, ethnicity is only one source—and often not the most important one—of affiliation and identity construction, alongside Islam, Francophonie, nationalism, and global hip-hop.

While Niamey and many other African cities are unique in many ways, "they have been generally shaped by some common processes: legacies of colonialism, rapid population increase, low levels of economic growth, and expansion of informal settlements. Above all, their relations with global capitalism are unequal and asymmetric" (Hansen 2008:11). The consequences of the neoliberal world order include a convergence of global youth experiences defined by "limited life opportunities and poor wage-labor prospects [that] are challenging the age and gender ideals that used to guide the social organization of households and families" (Hansen 2008:9). Furthermore, through increasing interaction between youth of the world—including Niamey's—particularly through radio, youth are ever more aware of their common plight.

Contemporary cities, such as Niamey, are "diverse, creative, modern, and distinctive with the possibility to imagine…their own futures and distinctive forms of city-ness" (Robinson 2002:545-46 cited in Hansen 2008:11). Furthermore, "all cities are global" in that they are influenced by global neoliberalism (often with dire consequences), and are "spaces of interaction that bring together people, things and ideas from around the country and around the world" (Hansen 2008:11).

Niamey is deeply embedded in contemporary globalization processes, and, far more than other places in Niger, functions as a gateway to the global world. Global flows of news, information, popular culture, images, and values are concentrated in Niamey. Niaméens have gained exponentially accelerating access to these global flows and the means to articulate their local and worldviews as a result of the democratic transition that began in 1991 and provided an opening for private media (radio, television, press), and the ensuing information and communication revolutions involving the Internet and cell phones of the late 1990s and early 2000s. This is the context in which Niamey's youth are emerging. Furthermore, tens of thousands of Niaméens—including nearly one-half of youth aged 15-24—have lived and worked abroad and have returned to Niamey with ideas, fashions, stories, and money from their sojourns. Males are much more likely to have international migration experience than girls.

The lives of Niamey's youth are embedded in local, national, and global contexts. Niamey's youth "localize global influences" (Hansen 2008:5). They craft lives within local constraints and from local resources as well as a sense of living in the world at large. Niamey's youth today are fascinated, and sometimes repulsed, by the world at large. They have grown up thinking about the world and their place in it, feeling both globally connected and globally disconnected. Youth derive satisfaction through being informed and trying to make sense of international and national news and creatively interpreting hip-hop, reggae, and other popular culture. They appreciate their power to articulate their views to wide audiences, particularly through radio. However, their inability to experience a standard of living or to share the options enjoyed by many people around the world amplifies their sense of relative material deprivation.

The Marriage Predicament

Marriage traditionally defines the passage to adulthood in Muslim Hausa culture. Many young men of Niamey are frustrated by their inability to raise the money for marriage and are reluctantly delaying marriage into their late twenties and thirties or later. The marriage predicament is a crucial contemporary reality in itself as well as a window for understanding broader changes. In addition to my own ethnography, I draw from historian Barbara Cooper's (1997) meticulous and insightful analysis, *Marriage in Maradi: Gender and Culture in a Hausa Society in Niger, 1900-1989*, and apply it to Niamey. She argues that, "Throughout the major processes the region has undergone in this century...marriage, whether fickle or merely flexible, has served as central institutional and discursive locus for the mediation of change" (Cooper 1997:xlviii). Masquelier's (2005) perspective also informs my discussion. Her research in Mawri Hausa communities of Dogondoucthi, Niger, explores how the contemporary marriage crisis involves generational and gendered divides and debates about money, conspicuous consumption, and morality.

Hausa youth in Niamey have grown up in social structural conditions very different from those experienced by their parents' generation. In contrast with their parents' rural farming roots, they have lived their lives in a cosmopolitan city oriented by labor and trade for cash. While accumulating funds for *sadaki* ("bridewealth") and other important marital expenses has long been a difficult matter for young men, new economic and social conditions are making this even more onerous. Urban youth have smaller kin networks of support to facilitate marriage than their parents did when they were coming of age in rural Niger. According to youth, the shrinking of family support is only partially offset by increasing assistance for weddings from *hira* and *fada* group members. Traditionally Hausa males needed to prove their proficiency in farming to earn their fathers' permission to marry. Youth of Niamey, while often free from these constraints, must navigate a much more individualistic economic terrain in a time of declining employment opportunities. Furthermore, in contrast with the rural Nigerien pattern of multigenerational households, today Hausa of Niamey prefer to establish new households upon marriage.

Meanwhile, despite—or perhaps because of—the dire economic conditions faced by the vast majority of Niaméens, bridewealth inflation continually spirals upward at a faster rate than overall inflation. As documented in careful detail by Cooper (1997), the items exchanged in Hausa marriage represent value at various historical moments. In the 19th century, bridewealth was paid in cowries. Through much of the 20th century and even up to the 1980s in many cases, grain, livestock, and locally woven cloth were central. Today, particularly in Niamey, cash and mass-produced consumer goods (radios, cell phones, televisions, DVD players, European cloth, refrigerators, and for the wealthy, automobiles and villas) are required to cement marital ties. Young men are also under increasing pressure to continually ply their fiancés and their fiancés' parents with gifts and to sponsor extravagant wedding events that include live music and feasts that can last for days. In addition, grooms are encouraged to purchase wedding invitations and to pay for wedding announcements in newspapers and on radio and television broadcasts. This has led to a polarization between wealthy, typically older men who are marrying polygynously, and struggling youth virtually doomed to bachelorhood. This has negative consequences for young women as well.

A repressed gay culture exists on the margins of Niamey's social life. One could live in Niamey for years without knowledge of its existence because Niameén gays are very secretive, and because most residents simply deny their existence. Ousseini expresses a typical view, "We do not have gays here because we are a Muslim country. Gays only live in Western and Christian countries." I think many gays of Niamey adapt to dominant straight norms by marrying and bearing children. However, I wonder if some youth who are postponing marriage are gay.

Elders strongly disapprove of youth who delay or refuse to marry, attributing the problem to what they perceive as the impatience and laziness of today's young people. The youth, in contrast, attribute the problem to the economic crisis in Niamey, rather than character flaws. This includes the reality of skyrocketing marital expenses that cannot be deferred until after weddings as was the case in the past (Masquelier 2005:66). Indeed, the key problematic is this: Why are Niaméens spending so much to get married in a time of economic depression and expanding inequality? "Traditionalists" and elders and potential brides assert that this simply represents the continuity of time-honored Hausa practices that mark the importance of marriage with extravagance. (In fact, over decades the colonial and the postcolonial Nigerien state have made many attempts to enforce caps on bridewealth—all of which have failed.) Islamic reformers and many young men challenge this perspective with moral and practical arguments for making marriage more accessible.

The marriage problem is also, of course, gendered. Unlike many of their parents who settled in Niamey before or after having arranged marriages in their home villages, most of Niamey's youth today are choosing their own spouses in Niamey. This is due to economic forces promoting individualism as well as perhaps the idea of love as depicted in the Bollywood, Hollywood, and Nollywood films that are so popular among Niamey's youth. However, young Hausa bachelors of Niamey seldom have good things to say about young women. For them, however, the old adage, "women, you cannot live with them and you cannot live without them" applies. Young men see young women as relentlessly materialistic. And, at least from their perspective, they are right. In contrast with their mothers who typically married in their mid-teens, young women of Niamey are increasingly resisting arranged marriages and delaying marriage until their late teens or early twenties. More young women than in previous generations want to complete high school, technical, or university educations. Small but increasing numbers of young women are staying in school after marriage. Some also use their unmarried status as an economic opportunity. Young men complain that it is nearly impossible to get a second date without giving young women of Niamey cell phones. Young women play off competing suitors, sometimes for years, demanding regular flows of extravagant gifts, particularly luxurious clothing, before finally marrying.

Young men do not necessarily reject the commoditization of love and marriage and responsibility as such, but are frustrated by their inability to compete with older, wealthy rivals. Djibo described his difficulties to me, exemplifying this point, "I was prepared to sell my motorcycle, borrow money from my father, and to work in his shop for five years to raise the bridewealth to satisfy Fatima's parents. But then Elhadji Mountari came along in his Mercedes Benz. I had no chance." Some young men are drawn to various Islamic reformist voices that reject this materialism. The Izala, for example, argue that Islamic marriage should not be hindered by local innovations, and thus argue for minimal bridewealth so as to allow devout young men and women to marry young and avoid the likely immorality that will ensue if they remain single for too long. Even when they do not agree with many other Izala perspectives, this emphasis on inexpensive weddings resonates with Hausa male youths for it opens a doorway to adulthood. A small but growing minority of Izala-inspired Hausa in Niamey is having perfunctory weddings with only small token exchanges. Many "traditionalists" regard such weddings as a somewhat illegitimate short-circuiting of custom or at least as no fun at all.

Young women, even more marginalized than young men in the world's least developed nation, see relationships pragmatically, as one of the surest ways to gain valued resources. While in their hearts many would prefer to marry young men, their brains (and their parents) tell them to choose wealthy, older husbands to facilitate social mobility. As Fatima put it, "I can live like a queen with Elhadji. I love Djibo, but I am tired of eating millet." Young women's parents have a vested interest in securing as much bridewealth and other gifts as possible, and typically do not want to wait for it, that is, they prefer their daughters to marry sooner rather than later.

In this context, it makes sense that "some Mawri elders complained to ethnographer Elaine de Latour: 'before youths obeyed their fathers, they were afraid of them! Today, they have become women and women have become whores'" (de Latour 1992:73 cited in Masquelier 2005:61). Similarly, elders in Niamey equate the "choice" of bachelorhood among youth with idleness and femininity. An unmarried young man remains dependent on his mothers or sisters to cook and clean for him, "or, worse, [must] contemplate the dire prospect of having to do these things for himself—an altogether distressingly feminizing predicament" (Masquelier 2005:76) that involves crossing the strictly defined gendered division of labor in Hausa communities. Amadou, a single man in his early twenties who is planning to migrate to Kumasi described his situation,

> I have never cooked in my life. Why would I? I am a man, not a woman. I live with my family. But I heard that I will need to cook for myself in Kumasi because street food is too expensive. My mother is going to teach me the basics of cooking. I dread this, but migration is different—I have to be a woman in order to become a man.

Elders share with Muslim reformists the belief that girls should marry young to avoid becoming prostitutes. To many of them, dating, even if it does not involve sex, is tantamount to prostitution. Their fears have some foundation, even if they often fail to recognize dire poverty, exacerbated by global neoliberaism, as the root of the problem. Many teenaged girls in Niamey have turned to sex work due to lack of opportunities and as a last resort for survival (Alidou 2005:193). Due to double standards, women bear the brunt of moral approbation for commercialized sex in Niamey.[1] Masquelier's (2005:61) conclusion regarding the marriage predicament is thus quite striking: "When men become women and women become whores [or are perceived as such by some people], the entire process of social reproduction is irremediably damaged."

In sum, in the current neoliberal moment of economic decline, urbanization, and increasing migration, middle-aged and elderly Hausa retain fairly rigid definitions of gender, marriage, and adulthood, whereas young Hausa are reconsidering and attempting to redefine them. Older men with rural roots and commitments continue to regard hard physical labor on farms—symbolized by rough, strong hands—as a key marker of true masculinity that is necessary to earn marriage and parenthood and the passage to adulthood. Younger men reared in Niamey, though generally respectfully of the difficult work of their fathers, see no future in agriculture. For them, success in the urban informal economy revolves around trading, hustling, and migrating in search of cash that leaves their hands soft. They view this as being just as arduous and unpredictable—in different ways—as the farm work of their elders. Young males' inability to afford the various costs of marriage contributes to gender conflict and their negative feelings about girls of marriage age. Their frustration is exacerbated by the rise in dating and the growing appeal of romantic love as the basis for modern marriage. In this context, in Niamey the great popularity of Mexican and Brazilian *telenovelas* that often feature story lines of anguished lovers blocked from marriage by class barriers makes perfect sense. Hausa youth—male and female—see their own conflicts in these stories, and adapt ideas about how to solve them. Some young males choose to remain at home with the mothers and sisters because they cannot face what they see as the feminizing behavior required of them—particularly cooking—if they strike out on their own without wives. Increasing numbers of young males, however, are willing to be temporarily feminized by cooking for themselves while they are labor migrants if this enables them to raise the cash needed for marriage, or as Amadou put it, "...migration is different—I have to be a woman in order to become a man." The "feminization" of masculinity has important implications for the vast majority of young men who are waiting to get married. It might lead to a blurring of gender lines and a redefinition of masculinity. Young males may come to better appreciate women and the difficulty of traditionally defined women's domestic work. For now, most young males are annoyed by feminization of masculinity. For example, upon his return from two years working alone in Lomé, Moctar explained to his *hira* mates, "Yes, I cooked for myself. It is simple. I do not know why my wife says it is difficult." Finally, increasing numbers of male youth, in large part because they are frustrated by what they see as the greedy materialism of girls and girls' parents, are rejecting the traditional standard of marriage as the sole pathway to adulthood.

I will now turn to a case study of an individual who has navigated these challenges over the past 25 years of accelerating change in Niamey. I met Aboubacar in 2005 in his capacity as a member of Niger's national committee for Les Jeux de la Francophonie. He introduced himself to me, and offered to secure a VIP pass for me. We have remained friends ever since. This will serve as a prelude to further analysis of the lives of Niamey's youth.

Coming of Age in Niamey: Aboubacar Ousmane's Experience

Aboubacar Ousmane's life history illustrates the key themes of the chapter. Aboubacar's parents felt—as tens of thousands of other Nigeriens have—that they could no longer make a secure living as rural farmers and thus decided to settle in Niamey 25 years ago when Aboubacar was an infant. His Hausa father—through family connections, charisma, a strong work ethic, and probably a little luck—established a successful career as an itinerant trader who juggled his time between Cotonou, Lomé, and Niamey. This enabled him to purchase a modest mud-brick compound in Niamey and to see to it that Aboubacar and his other son, Moussa, and daughter, Halima, completed six years of Qur'anic education and finished secondary school. Due to his father's long absences, Aboubacar was reared largely by his Zarma mother, Zeinabou, and became as comfortable speaking Zarma as Hausa. In fact his Zarma friends regard him as Zarma and his Hausa friends as Hausa, and this pleases him. After graduating from *lycée*, Aboubacar enrolled in a private institute to train to be a computer repairman.

Aboubacar and his siblings inherited the family compound six years ago when their parents died. They live relatively comfortably in part because unlike most residents of Niamey they are free from the burden of rent. Halima took over their parents' four-room quarters, as she was married with six children. She is dependent upon receiving remittances from her husband, Ibrahim, who has been working in a restaurant in Marseille for the past five years, for the maintenance of her family. Initially after their parents' death, Aboubacar and his brother took separate, smaller two-room residences. When Moussa was unable to find a job, Aboubacar invited him to move in with him. The siblings generate a small income by renting the other residence to a family of five. While all three dwellings have electricity, the compound's 14 residents share one outdoor spigot and one outdoor latrine.

The Ousmane siblings' division of their father's property involved creative manipulation of local Muslim rules of inheritance that stipulate that sons receive shares twice as large as daughters. Aboubacar and Moussa felt this was fair and practical given the number of Halima's children, the fact that Halima cooks for them, and Ibrahim's annual Tabaski gift of two large sheep. In addition, this arrangement was made possible by Halima's assertiveness. Most Nigerien wives are expected to reside with their husbands' parents while their husbands are away in diaspora working, as was discussed in Chapter 3. Halima refused to accept this, arguing that as an urbanite she could not fathom living in Ibrahim's parents' village, and that her brothers would protect her. Ibrahim reluctantly consented.

Aboubacar has worked nearly full-time over the past five years in a small computer repair shop. As a result he is relatively well to do for his age. His earnings have enabled him to buy a small motorcycle, a cell phone, a wardrobe consisting of Western-style office attire, traditional flowing gowns for Muslim holidays, and hip hop fashions, and to furnish his dwelling with a couch, two soft-cushion chairs, and a television. For several years, Halima and many friends have been encouraging Aboubacar to marry and start his own family, suggesting that it is time for him to take on the responsibilities of a Muslim adult. Many males of his age and of far lesser means have done so. Aboubacar resists even though he is sometimes irked to see non-formally educated yet married men accorded more community respect than himself. Nevertheless, he is always humble, respectful, and deferential in his interpersonal encounters with elders and with married men and women, demonstrating traditional norms. He asserts that he is respected among other unwed young men and that many married men are jealous of his lifestyle. Furthermore, due to his knowledge of the living conditions of many young married men, Aboubacar is thoroughly turned off by the prospect that marriage would lead to debt and pauperization. He insists that he will marry when the time is right, and argues that his income is not sufficient to purchase or rent his own compound to properly head a household. He says that due to the current global economic crisis he is worried that he could lose his job any day. Furthermore, he defends his Muslim credentials. One evening upon delivering his hot dinner, Halima teased him, "you know, a good Muslim man's wife would cook for him." Aboubacar responded, "I am a good Muslim, I always pray, I observe the fast, and I never drink!"

Aboubacar's willingness to delay marriage draws from careful calculations. He explained to me,

> Some days I feel like I should just get married and leave it up to Allah. I know this would make a lot of people happy. But most days I think that a good Muslim man must be prepared to raise his family in comfort. Yes, I could get married, but we would live in poverty. The way things are now; I can enjoy some luxuries, relax with my friends, and prepare for the future.

Aboubacar is, indeed, a complex, multilingual person adept at weighing the merits of multiple options and reconciling multiple articulations of modernity. Though he considers himself a mainstream, traditional Muslim, he sometimes prays with the reformist Izala congregation that meets near his workplace. He is turned off by their insults of the populace and their unwillingness to pray outside of their own mosques, but attracted by their preaching that condemns extravagant customs surrounding marriage. He is proud of his French literacy and work in a modern global industry. Yet he eschews Western biomedicine, and puts his trust in an old, traditional Hausa healer who has been affiliated with his family since before he was born. Aboubacar spends his free time at home with friends who drop by and who he invites by cell phone watching European football matches and French game shows on television and listening to radio broadcasts of world news on RFI and BBC's Hausa language programs, or meeting with his two favorite conversation groups on his neighborhood's street corners. About once every fortnight, he goes out to nightclubs with friends to watch the latest popular Nigerien rappers. Aboubacar worked for Niger's National Committee during the Francophonie Games in 2005, repairing computers and serving as a host for international guests. He explained that this was the most rewarding experience of his life, as he appreciated the honor of representing Niger and participating actively in global Francophonie.

As a lifelong resident, Niamey's specific obstacles, opportunities, and milieu have shaped Aboubacar. Simultaneously, Aboubacar has navigated Niamey's treacherous terrain with resolve and dexterity, contributing to the shaping of Niamey's modern, cosmopolitan urban culture. Within Niger, only in Niamey could Aboubacar's life—that is, his job, his friendships, his interests and opinions—have unfolded the way that it has. Living rent-free in an inherited compound with more education and a better job than most of his age peers, Aboubacar nevertheless faces a tenuous pathway to adulthood.

Challenging Gerontocracy

Hausa social structure has long been—and to a great extent remains—deeply gerontocratic, with the middle-aged and elderly holding most positions of political power, controlling community decision-making, and dominating the economy. Fathers, particularly in rural Niger, often decide when and whom sons will marry. This strict age-based hierarchy is supported by many everyday, often ritualized, norms of etiquette through which respect for elders is demonstrated. For example, younger people are expected to visit and initiate greetings with older people. Younger people limit eye contact, slightly bend their knees, and symbolically support their right hands (by holding their right arms with their left hands) when shaking hands in greetings with elders to show the weight or importance of the elders. They use honorific titles—Malam / Malama ("Mr." or "Sir" / "Mrs." or "Ma'am"), ElHadji / ElHadjiya, Mai Gida ("Homeowner"), Monsieur / Madame—rather than personal names. And younger people always surrender the best seats to older people in conversation groups.

There are key differences, however, between the generation of Hausa who arrived in Niamey as migrants in the 1980s and the generation that was born around 1990 and reared in Niamey. This generational transition is a late manifestation of a broader social transformation that has been unfolding for more than a century from a rural, communal, subsistence economy to an urban, individualistic, informal economy situated on the periphery of the global economy in which money is a key source of value. This, of course, is a huge generalization. Rural Niger has for 500 years been linked to global capitalism and trade. Urban Nigerien youth are often deeply committed to their extended families, conversation groups, and congregations. Furthermore, substantial numbers of Nigeriens are circular migrants who strive to maintain productive social networks in both villages and cities by performing "localist" and "cosmopolitan" "cultural styles" (Ferguson 1999:220) appropriate to these different contexts. The crucial point, though, is that today a few young people are able to earn (or otherwise acquire) more money—and in some cases a lot more money—than old people, even though elders retain control of the economy and political system.

Niamey is typical of cities around the world in that "within the public domain...young people tend to be depicted from two angles that leave little scope for agency: from a welfare angle, which views them as dependent and immature...and from a problem-oriented angle, which characterizes them as troublesome" (Hansen 2008:10). For example, middle aged and elderly Hausa of Niamey stereotype the *fada* groups of youth as dangerous gatherings that promote idleness, delinquency, and immoral gender mixing. From their point of view, young men should be married and living in fathers' compounds. As elders feel threatened by youth, they seek to retain their power and privilege. (Indeed, those with power never relinquish it willingly.) In Niamey and elsewhere, "it is not surprising that many young people see themselves as excluded by the institutions of the wider society and the deteriorating economic situation" (Hansen 2008:11). Representing his *fada* group in a televised broadcast, one 20-year old male declared, "We want jobs, but the government has no idea how to create them. Our parents do not really care. They would rather that we lived at home and worked for them."

Despite these constraints, many of Niamey's youth optimistically see Niamey as a portal to a wider world of hidden opportunities or as a launching pad for international migration and better lives. Hausa youth of Niamey are challenging the traditional gerontocracy of Hausa communities in various ways, namely by: gaining access to cash, developing new definitions of adulthood that do not regard marriage as the ultimate threshold, pursuing many trajectories toward the future, passionately articulating their views through electronic media, especially the radio, and seeking to become a political force.

The Hausa proverb used as the epigram for this chapter, *Yaro da gari abokin tahiya manya* ("A rich young man can become an old person's friend"), comments on the perception that in Niamey, as in much of the world, survival and value—and indeed respect and social honor—are increasingly calculated in monetary terms. The proverb also subtly acknowledges that friendships among Hausa exist almost exclusively among age-mates. In recent years, a small but influential minority of youth, typically through their own successful migration or deft use of connections in the sprawling Hausa diaspora, has amassed fortunes by local standards. They have turned the tables. In order to survive, increasing numbers of middle-aged and elderly adults now must humbly ally themselves as clients of younger men—an asymmetry that was extremely rare 20 years ago. Older Hausa chafe at the implications of this proverb.

Today in Niamey—similar to many places around the world—the meanings of youth as a life stage are more fluid and "less clearly... demarcated than in the past" (Hansen 2008:7). The continuous structural liminality of youth contributes to the uncertainty of what it means to be a youth or an adult—particularly when many must delay marriage and some confront the possibility that they may never be able to marry. Facing chronic unemployment and underemployment, many cannot find jobs that enable them to accumulate savings for the wedding costs and the financial security to marry and start families. A small but growing minority of Hausa youth—including Aboubacar—is reasonably content to remain unmarried. They feel that the benefits of this choice—free time, girlfriends, and a higher standard of living—outweigh the disadvantages.

Youth are developing new definitions of adulthood in the face of this predicament. While virtually all Hausa hope to eventually marry and have many children, some are beginning to assert that they should be regarded as adults—that is, that their voices and concerns demand respect and attention—even if they are single so long as they have demonstrated independence, initiative, education, or morality. A few—such as Aboubacar—have achieved this approbation among their single compatriots. Omar, a young Francophone bachelor, asserted, "I am a citizen of Niger. I am over 18, and I have the right to vote. Therefore, I am a man." His youthful *hira* mates agreed. In contrast, most married and elderly Hausa men do not accept these emerging definitions. Despite resistance from married and older men, young Hausa males' alternative perspective on marriage and adulthood seem to indicate a definite generational change in the making. Middle aged men, such as Youssoufou whose marital career was described in Chapter 4, cannot bear to live without wives, and in fact remarry after divorce by any means necessary. Young Hausa, such as Aboubacar, are increasingly content to remain single and do not necessarily lose respect among their age mates for this choice.

Many youth remain hopeful, see new opportunities, and are pursuing many trajectories toward the future. Most youth are eager to emigrate—at least temporarily—or have already done so as they see this as the best possibility for bettering their life chances. Meanwhile, for many reasons (including lack of resources to leave the country, parental control or support, and appreciation of the city) hundreds of thousands of youth (including more than 100,000 Hausa) stay in Niamey.

Most youth hustle to earn cash through small-scale trading or services in Niamey's informal economy. In recent years, young men have been providing security through their formal and semi-formal *fada* street gatherings that last all night long, particularly in Niamey's oldest, most densely populated neighborhoods. Residents recognize their contribution to public order by voluntarily providing them with tea, kola nuts, cigarettes, rice, and beans to fuel their discussions and keep them alert. They rarely pursue intruders or suspected criminals, because their ubiquitous presence on the streets of nocturnal Niamey is a sufficient deterrent (Gopfert 2009:10-13).

Some choose formal education in pursuit of professional employment in the private or dwindling public sectors. While a few youth—especially those with connections—achieve success, many are frustrated by their inability to find good jobs in their chosen fields. They typically feel too proud to resort to micro-commerce or manual labor, and prepare to emigrate. Military service is another important option for youth. The youth I have encountered are not enthusiastic about the military, but some see it as one of only a few stable, salaried employment opportunities.

Finally, as documented by Masquelier (2007:245), youth "point to the way that things have changed, usually for the worse, for the young people of Niger, changes that have forced them to develop new strategies for survival and even to explore alternative careers in crime [particularly smuggling and petty theft, but also the drug trade] or in the counter-culture of hip hop." Increasing numbers of youth also rely on an old strategy that is simultaneously practical and attempts to appeal to Muslim morality: begging.

All of these career-launching strategies—except for education—involve youth increasingly relying on themselves and each other, rather than their parents and family. Fluid youth networks—established through *hira* and *fada* groups—are now increasingly taking the role of sponsoring and investing in the international migrations and marriages of youth. However, youth who can draw support from both family and youth networks are best positioned to succeed.

Democratization, as seen in earlier chapters, opened the door to freedom of expression and many Niaméens were able to articulate their perspectives to wide audiences for the first time, including their take on the interplay between poverty, bridewealth, religion, and youths challenging power and redefining a better life. Since the state monopoly evaporated in 1991, Nigeriens—especially in Niamey—have created a vibrant "radio culture" that they call the "Révolution FM." This radio culture is uniquely positioned to serve as a primary mediator between the local and the global in the lives of Niamey's youths. Youths have vivaciously seized new opportunities as consumers, participants, and producers of this radio culture. Radio is important in terms of what is being said to youth by local and global voices in the two to three hours of local and global radio broadcasts they on average listen carefully to daily as well as the several more hours they hear as background noise daily. Indeed Niamey's youth are more critically informed about the leading contemporary global news stories than American youth are. Radio is also critically important in terms of how youth are using it to articulate their views to adults and to each other.

Youth use radio to disseminate religious and secular perspectives. Youths associated with a wide range of Islamic associations and movements are asserting moral positions via radio. Izala affiliated youth sharply criticize the state for being secular and corrupt, and the traditional Sufi practices of their elders, such as ostentatious ceremonials and the use of magic. Luc Peter and Stephanie Barbey, in the 2007 documentary film *Magic Radio*, argue that, particularly through rap, "youth see radio as a means for speaking out for social change...for address[ing] social evils...[for asserting youth's] and women's rights...for shedd[ing] old mindsets and embrac[ing] new ideas for development...and for speak[ing] about the problems and confusion facing youth in Niger today" (Peter, Barbey, and Tejasvi 2007:3). Similarly, the young men that Masquelier (2007:248) interviewed in Dogondoutchi,

> insist that hip hop is, above all, educational...aside from exposing the problems of youth, such as poverty and unemployment, rap songs, they claim teach young people how to survive the dangers that they face in today's unforgiving world. More so than perhaps other forms of popular culture that have become ubiquitous in Niger, rap music is both for youth and about youth.

Zara Moussa, a young woman who has established herself as one of Niger's hip-hop sensations and enjoys significant radio broadcast time, passionately raps about the situation faced by youth (Peter, Barbey, and Tejasvi 2007:2):

> I have to go, despite the peace,
> Despite the hospitality.
> I have to go.
> Too tough being young here
> To live, deadly burden,
> Doubts in our heads.
> Sad to know tomorrow will be worse.
> Tough not knowing how to end it.
>
> I have to go
> To Paris or Uncle Sam
> Aware of all the dangers
> I know that over there...
>
> I have to go to new horizons
> So that one day when I return
> My words will make sense...

Despite all its problems, there is no place like home. Most youth explain that they would strongly prefer to remain in Niamey if they could build viable futures there. Zara Moussa vividly captures this sentiment in her opening lyrics, "I have to go, despite the peace, despite the hospitality," and in her closing lyrics that express the commitment to return to Niger. In between, she describes the daunting problems confronting youth.

Muslim elders condemn hip-hop culture on various grounds. They resent the ways it challenges their authority. From their perspective the irreverent lyrics of rap, the cocky ways hip-hop inspired youth carry themselves, and the confrontational clothing styles (sagging, baggy jeans, enormous t-shirts, chain necklaces and ear piercings, baseball caps, and basketball shoes) are anti-Islamic. If nothing else, they find rap to be decidedly "unmusical" relative to other local and global musical genres. All of this only serves to inspire youth to further continue to pursue hip-hop culture as a means to assert their agency.

Youth want to be a political force, and yet are very distrustful of politics. Unmarried Hausa youth of Niamey often feel superior to their married elders, and hence are particularly frustrated by their assessment that married adults, the middle aged, and the elderly seek to maintain a "maritalocratic," gerontocracy that constrains and excludes them from economic, political, and social opportunity. They feel that they are worldlier. They think that scrambling to make a living in Niamey today requires incredible resilience, independence, and initiative. They point out their important role in providing nocturnal security. Youth who are literate in French, or computer and cell phone literate are proud of it and consider themselves more intelligent than those who are not regardless of age. Most youth identify themselves as part of the local and global Muslim community, and many consider themselves as devout if not more devout in practice as many married men.

"They cannot keep us down forever, because we outnumber them," shouted the President of a youth *fada* group, in reference to elders. Indeed, youth represent a huge and overpowering threat in elections. Furthermore, they make up a large segment of the military. Youths began asserting themselves politically in the early 1990s when "radio helped galvanize the student population in Niamey to speak out against corruption in the education sector. When radio stations publicized the report of the anticorruption committee, which exposed malpractice in the education sector, the youth in Niamey demonstrated for more transparency and better attention to student needs" (Peter, Barbey, and Tejasvi 2007:4), gaining important concessions including the release of 29 student activists. Ever since, youth have used the radio to express their justifications for opposing the state (often equated with the elders) on both secular grounds, that is for failing to provide an adequate educational infrastructure and jobs, as well as on Islamic grounds, for serving at the whim of non-Muslim foreign administrations and international financial institutions whilst ignoring the suffering of the masses, particularly of young citizens. Youth are increasingly emerging as an important political force through actively supporting the campaigns of politicians who appear to care about the crisis of poverty and unemployment faced by youth.

Tensions between generations are nearly universal, but lead to disparate, unpredictable outcomes. Whether contemporary youth challenges to gerontocracy will generate significant or long-term structural changes in the political economy, or cultural changes in the form of new definitions of youth and the passage to adulthood, remains to be seen. Goldschmidt (1990:206) views social institutions are "derivative, not formative." He argues that they derive from the actions of motivated individuals, and that institutional patterns "respond to the recurrent needs and desires of the persons who make up the society" (Goldschmidt 1990:206). However, institutional patterns do not necessarily respond promptly in contexts of dramatic—even revolutionary—change as Niamey has experienced. "Institutional lag" can last a generation or more. Perhaps in one generation's time or less, youth and the passage to adulthood will be defined very differently than they are today in Niamey.

Most married, middle-aged, and elderly Hausa of Niamey do not fear generational revolution. In fact, many Hausa parents expect and tolerate rebellion from their children, expecting that this is just a passing phase in life. "A youth who does not enjoy his youth will make up for it in old age," a proverb recorded by Masquelier (2007:249), speaks to the idea that by "sowing their wild oats" young people will come to appreciate tradition and responsibility as they age.

Many pious middle-aged men recall their own youthful rebellions and indiscretions. For example, Ousseini, a 60-year-old tailor who wears only traditional Muslim Hausa attire and is seldom seen without his prayer mat draped over his shoulder, once showed me an old photo album circa 1970 that he kept hidden in his cupboard featuring him drinking beer in nightclubs with several girlfriends at a time in clothing straight out of African American soul-funk culture. Lamine, an unemployed 55-year-old man who keeps his hair closely cropped and prefers conservative Nigerien "business suits" (of the sort that became fashionable among civil servants in the 1970s), has preserved a few photos of himself from the same era holding his favorite James Brown album and sporting a large afro, a shiny silk body-hugging shirt tucked into his flare-bottom slacks, and 5-inch high platform shoes. He developed a taste for beer and could not resist pork in various forms "out of curiosity" when he worked in the U.S. for 18 months in the 1980s, but quit these habits upon his return to Niger and probably has not missed a single prayer since.

Men like Ousseini and Lamine can see a bit of themselves in the hip-hop culture of today's youth. While they certainly do not approve of it, they do their best to ignore it. Simultaneously, youth can imagine themselves becoming like Ousseini and Lamine; "they justify their immersion in rap culture by claiming that 'it is what youth do,' they just as quickly point out that when they grow up—that is when they marry, produce children, and are granted the authority that comes with maturity—they will leave rap culture behind to focus on more 'serious' things. Like Islam" (Masquelier 2007:248).

The unprecedented challenges that today's youth face in finding jobs that will support their passage to adulthood suggest that their challenges to traditional norms have the possibility of enduring as more than just passing fancies. In any case, Niamey's youth are constructing a distinctive and creative culture.

Contemporary Urban Youth Culture of Niamey

The emerging youth culture of Niamey involves much more than marriage frustrations, conflicts with elders, and assertions of power. Youth find joy as well. One evening, as I was traveling across the city by taxi, the middle-aged taximan nearly ran over a young man who was strolling across the street. He yelled, "Life is not a game, you only get one chance!" The young man who was sharing the back seat with me overheard this, but disagreed, "Life is a game. It is too short. We must take chances and enjoy ourselves." Indeed, Niamey's youth value and seek out opportunities to have fun. They relish laughing with their *hira* and *fada* mates. Virtually all boys and youth love football and play on streets and sandlots daily. Many enjoy dating, despite its tribulations, partly because they feel it is a freedom their parents did not enjoy. Some sneak into the shadows to smoke marijuana and hashish.

The complex interplay between local, national, and global forces involved in the dramatic changes in Niamey over the last 20 years have led to generation gaps and the emergence of new articulations of meaning and affiliation, "new forms of Muslim religiosity...new models of personhood and public life, new modes of production, and new patterns of consumption" (Masquelier 2007:245). The core worldviews and visions of modernity that Hausa and other youth of Niamey are negotiating and experimenting with include what I call Africanist–Traditionalist, Muslimist–Islamist, and Francophone-ist–Globalist. None is monolithic. Each has gendered and multiple varieties and nuances. Many of Niamey's youths—like Aboubacar—accommodate differences across most of this entire spectrum. In fact, this flexible, open-mindedness is one of the key ways that youth see themselves as different from previous generations, even though evidence suggests that this difference may be only a matter of degree.

Niamey's dynamic youth are integral to the accelerating transitions that define the city's cosmopolitanism as they navigate a world that is increasingly and fluidly unconstrained by spatiotemporal, ethnic, linguistic, and ideological boundaries—even if it is a world rigidly constrained by boundaries of capital. They are building an emerging urban youth culture that consists of a vortex made up of fragments that converge and whirl without ever settling into a single pattern. Indeed, urban youth culture of Niamey is defined by tensions between local and global connections and disconnections, freedom and constraints, inclusion and exclusion, accommodation and contestation. Hansen (2008:11) argues that this dynamic is commonly experienced among urban youth of the world, "rather than being mutually exclusive, these two experiences pertain to different, yet simultaneous, levels of interaction; for instance, the realms of formal employment and of popular culture and electronic media." That is, Niamey's youth are constrained by being excluded from employment and authority, but free to explore global news, images, and entertainment and to strive for a sense of global cultural connection and inclusion.

The emerging youth culture of Niamey involves accommodation and contestation that are expressed in various ways. Niamey's youth strategically navigate lives back and forth from accommodation to contestation and in the spaces in between: "*Flexibility*, then, is the key to securing the often contradictory and increasingly tenuous promises of the current neoliberal moment when one lives in one of the world's poorest nations" (Masquelier 2007:252, emphasis in original). In the end youth seek traditional access to adulthood—that is, through marriage—even as they carve out their own more global worldview. Youth are using a more wide-open world to find ways to save parts of tradition. An enormous and diverse range of specific global youth cultures expressed through mass media attracts the attention of Niamey's youth. Each has something to say about marriage; even those that exclude it are communicating an important message. Global hip-hop culture, including its Niaméen variants, expresses the struggles and grievances against power of Black, African American, African, and African diaspora youth, and calls for rebellion, social justice, and freedom, but rarely addresses marriage. Bollywood films, in contrast, that feature the beauty of falling in love and marriage (in opposition to caste barriers and arranged marriages) have long been enormously popular among Niamey's youth. These have inspired a wave of new love dramas in the vast Hausa videofilm industry that have recently flooded the markets of Niamey. Roughly equal in popularity are Brazilian and Mexican *telenovelas* that often highlight how family, tradition, and social class stand between sympathetic young people who fall in love. The one thing this vast, culturally diverse, multi-polar, global ecuneme of perspectives seems to share is an emphasis on the autonomy of (or the struggle for the autonomy of) individual young people who challenge gerontocracy and other barriers to their self-assertion and fulfillment.

Niamey's youth, with a few exceptions, have not rejected the religion of their parents. Islam and the sense of being part of the global Muslim community are central to their identities. Many see Muslim identity and religiosity as compatible with enjoying hip hop music and attire, soap operas, and dance parties.

In this context of rapid sociocultural change in the midst of sustained economic crisis, increasing numbers of Niamey's youth are asserting that marriage should not be the only threshold to be passed for achieving adulthood—unless "the rules" are changed or jobs become available enabling more to afford grand affairs. Other youth simply want to redefine "youth-hood" itself, as consisting of people with the right to be different from their parents, worthy of respect and attention, and whose demands for economic security and political participation must be met. In the meantime, many do not care if their rapping and shady ways of "circumventing conventional circuits of exchange to ensure economic survival" (Masquelier 2007:257) repulse elders, as they navigate the margins of the cash-driven, inherently individualist, neoliberal world order.

Youth contestation of traditional norms, including gerontocracy, takes many forms. Like Aboubacar, most Niaméen youth remain humble, respectful and deferential in face-to-face interactions with elders. But this does not mean that the emerging youth "revolution" is silent. Through radio, youth voices on Islam, the state, and social justice have entered the public domain. Hip hop, particularly the creative ways that Niamey's youth have vernacularized it, has emerged as a particularly potent and popular means of consciousness raising, critiquing of social problems and injustice, and expressing struggles to survive. This strategy of identity making involving the performance of a worldwide culture style redefines youth as global citizens who can imagine a better future.

Conclusion: Uncertain Futures

Sani gaibu sai Allah: Only God knows what will happen

Surviving with Dignity focuses on the lived experience of two generations of migrant Hausa men in Niamey, Niger's capital city, set in a larger social matrix of national and global transformations. Most Hausa of Niamey live on the precipice, one lost job or one annual round of inflation of staple foods or one curable illness from death. Their extraordinary ability to maintain their dignity despite their daily struggles to eke out a living in the face of structural violence and unrelenting hardship reveals a tremendously powerful will and capacity to keep going.

Chapter 1 defined structural violence, suffering, and surviving with dignity as the core themes of the book. Chapter 2 reviewed the history of Niamey, emphasizing key demographic, economic, political, and technological transformations of the past two decades. Chapter 3 focused on migration as a core adaptive strategy for dealing with poverty, highlighting the important roles played by Hausa communities in Niamey in the maintenance and ongoing creation of the global Hausa diaspora. Chapter 4 addressed the central economic and symbolic strategies—particularly *hira*, *fada*, and *foyandi* groups—employed by Hausa on the ground in Niamey in their struggles to survive with dignity. Chapter 5 summarized several alternative articulations of modernity that have currency among Hausa of Niamey today. Chapter 6 considered the links and divides between the first generation Hausa migrants I met some 20 years ago, and the young generation born and reared in Niamey who are establishing a new urban youth culture.

—

One day more than a decade ago, an American friend who knew of my work in Niger offered me the telephone number of a Hausa man he had met by chance who was living within a manageable drive from my home. I called him immediately, explained my research interests in Niger, and my desire for a conversation partner to keep the rust off my Hausa language skills. He graciously invited me to his home for several visits. Bizo Oumarou informed me that he was granted a full scholarship by the government of Niger for graduate studies in agriculture at a prominent university in the U.S. These scholarships, as I knew from other cases, require recipients to sign contracts agreeing to return home to Niger to work for several years for relevant government ministries. During our conversations Bizo spoke very fondly of his home and family, and we shared sumptuous Nigerien meals prepared by Saratou, his wife. When I informed him of my impending trip to Niamey, he asked if I would be willing to bring some gifts to his sister. I consented, and delivered a huge suitcase filled primarily with beauty products to her when she met me at Niamey's Hamani Diori International Airport.

I mentioned my relationship with Bizo to three old friends in Niamey over coffee a few days later. They informed me that they knew Bizo, and asked me if I had noticed the thick scar around his neck. I said that I had, but out of politeness I did not ask Bizo about it. They informed me that they had heard from government workers that Bizo had attempted suicide because he could not bear the thought of returning to Niger. Issaka explained, "One day while Bizo was at home with his wife and two young children he locked himself in the bathroom and slit his throat from ear to ear. By the grace of God, amen, his wife saw blood flowing out from under the door and called an ambulance and the doctors saved his life." Salou added, "Bizo is too ashamed to come home now, as suicide is a grave sin in Islam, perhaps even worse than murdering another person. Suicide is totally unacceptable. Why did he do this? He signed the contract. Niger is a very nice place to live, especially if a man has money. He could have lived luxuriously on his government salary." Amadou compared his experience with Bizo's, "I had a similar scholarship to study engineering in France. I could have easily defected and lived an easy life there, but I wanted to come home to help my country.

Even though I was laid off more than a decade ago, I have no regrets. I love my people and the life in Niamey."

A few years later, Issaka, Salou, and Amadou were told that Bizo's father had died in his home village about 400 kilometers east of Niamey. They heard that Bizo bought a roundtrip plane ticket to Kano, Nigeria, travelled clandestinely across the porous border into Niger to offer his condolences to family, returned secretly to Kano, and flew back to the U.S. They explained that Bizo could never show his face in Niamey again as he would be too embarrassed to encounter his high school and university classmates and would risk arrest.

I cannot confirm the details of Bizo's life story, but my friends' take on it constitutes a very interesting parable that addresses Hausa men's complex and often mixed feelings about home, a core theme of the book. As highlighted earlier, most young Hausa men are eager to emigrate. A small minority who leave the country is never heard from again, but most migrants remain committed to family and friends while away from home, live frugally in diaspora in order to send home as much money as possible, and seek to eventually return home.

Bizo apparently struggles with a love – hate relationship with home. On the one hand, he expresses nostalgia for home and retained his preference for Nigerien cuisine while living in the U.S. He sent home many gifts for his family. Despite the risks, Bizo felt compelled to participate in his family's funeral process. On the other hand, after experiencing the comforts of living in the U.S. and imagining the opportunities available to him there, he could not bear the thought of returning to Niger and took drastic measures to avoid it. Irrespective of whether or not their psychoanalysis of Bizo's motivations is valid, Issaka, Salou, and Amadou believe this story to be true. Their reactions are reflective of the majority of Hausa men's attitudes about home. They reassert the positive aspects of life in Niamey, even though all three men spent several years abroad. They do not empathize with Bizo. Similar to other examples described in the book—such as the men's long discussions deploring migrants who do not keep in touch and rumors of occult economies—Hausa men criticize others as part of their multidimensional strategies for surviving with dignity.

Why would Hausa men, or anyone else, want to live in Niamey? Hausa are drawn to Niamey for practical, material reasons. Niamey offers more job opportunities than rural Niger, especially during long dry seasons, and it is the best place in the country to plot international migrations. More importantly, this book has shown that many Nigeriens find the vibrant social life of Niamey very attractive. Most Hausa and their neighbors live joyfully, purposefully, and peacefully together. All together, their deep Muslim faith, commitment to and love of family, community solidarity, sophisticated humor and exuberant laughter, friendliness and hospitality, incredible creative energy and activism exhibited in *fada* groups, worker and student unions, and incessant, clever, funny and serious conversation enable them to endure and survive brutal material conditions with grace and dignity. Their complex conceptualizations of globalization and their place in it through the creation of alternative modernities constitute another important strategy for maintaining their dignity. They achieve different kinds of dignity through different articulations of modernity.

Niamey is also very attractive to Hausa due to the perpetuation of hope among its residents. Youssoufou, my Hausa friend of 20 years, explained, "If Israel turned a desert into a prosperous country, then I do not see why we cannot do the same in Niger." When I suggested that this sounded unrealistically optimistic to me, Youssoufou explained that it is not that simple: "We are not really optimists because of religion. We wish that life will become better than it is now, *inchallah*. Everything comes from God."

Bolstered by strong faith, Hausa men of Niamey demonstrate strong initiative and resolve, and ready willingness to take considerable physical and intellectual risks to improve their standard of living and to find meaning and dignity. Most men, like Youssoufou, are neither paralyzed with fatalism nor do most simply wish that their lives will improve. (Even though Youssoufou used the phrase "we wish that life will become better," he continuously looks for new job opportunities and does not sit waiting for a windfall to come from the sky.) *Surviving with Dignity* has shown many examples of this agency, including the daily hustling in the informal economy on the hardscrabble streets of Niamey, the smuggling of goods—petrol, food, plastic bowls, flip-flops, and in rare cases, illegal drugs—into the country, and the millions of Nigeriens who have left the country seeking to improve their life chances, including many who knowingly risk their lives in the process, particularly those who embark on perilous journeys across the Sahara. As the journalist George Monbiot (2011:1) put it, "If wealth was the inevitable result of hard work and enterprise, every African woman [and man] would be a millionaire"

Other forms of risk taking involve different kinds of choices and an element of fun. Hausa youth typically think that taking risks is necessary precisely because they perceive of life as very short. This attitude is expressed even through mundane, everyday behaviors such as studied, casual indifference to traffic, as described in my road story in the previous chapter. Most significantly, recent years have seen the survival of longstanding forms of gambling (horse racing), and the steady rise in various newer types of gambling (lotteries and casinos) in Niamey that defy simple explanation.

I greeted a group of middle-aged men in 2010 gathered in the shade under a tree, poring over off-track horse race betting cards from France. Two of the men asked me to pick their horses for the day. I explained that I know little about horse racing, and nothing about the particular horses, but they replied, "We think you will bring us good luck, and besides you cannot do worse than we have been doing of late," before doubling over in laughter. I consented, despite some reservations. This popular pastime among Nigerien men functions as a subtle mechanism for the neocolonial extraction of wealth from Niger for it involves the transfer of wealth from the poorest country in the world to its former colonial ruler and one of the richest countries in the world. For some Nigeriens the fact that it lures men into gambling—a violation of Muslim norms—adds insult to injury.

This encounter reveals important yet different attitudes about money, life, and morality. I have long wondered why Hausa men rarely comment on the exploitative nature of betting on horses in France, and what explains their eagerness to gamble on horses they almost never get to see, even on television. (Hausa and other Niaméens also bet on local horse races at Niamey's Hippodrome. Furthermore, many simply enjoy watching the races, and never place bets.) They are spurred by the same goal that motivates poor men the world over to take risks with their money, the desire to do something, even something quite unrealistic, to get ahead. Many Hausa men derive satisfaction from careful study of racing forms and place small bets daily. I think their comment followed by laughter that, "you cannot do worse than we have been doing of late," is not just about picking horses but can be extended to express their attitudes about money and their current life predicament. Finally, some men regard gambling on horses as a silly form of wasting money, and others reject it on religious grounds. In contrast, avid horse racing gamblers who enjoy the combination of skill and chance involved are typically devout Muslims who see no contradiction in their behavior.

Niger launched its first national lottery, Tambola Nationale, in 1966. Loterie Nationale du Niger was established in 1983 to regulate the lottery industry, and now has offices in six Nigerien cities. A new law in 1993 eliminated the state monopoly on lotteries, and legalized private operators. From its inception nearly 50 years ago, Tambola leaders have made consistent efforts to differentiate the lottery from gambling to draw wide Muslim participation (NLRC 2012). The success of their public advertising campaigns inspired a visit in 2011 from the National Lottery Regulatory Commission of Nigeria to learn how to promote the lottery in largely Muslim Northern Nigeria where heretofore people have been reluctant to buy lottery tickets due to their interpretation of it as sinful. Despite—or because of—the dire economic situation in Niger, recent years have seen a substantial rise in the numbers of lottery participants, according to *hira* groups and my observations. In 2010 the Loterie Nationale du Niger constructed a new building, one of the tallest and most expensive on Niamey's skyline, reflecting rising revenues. The national lottery's popularity has prevented private operators from gaining a foothold in the lottery industry. However, private casinos have seen substantial growth in the past few years. A few years ago only a couple of casinos existed in Niamey. Today more than two dozen casinos in Niamey lure easy money seeking patrons, including several posh 3,000 square meter operations adorned with gaudy, flashing neon lights.

Hausa men also take bold intellectual risks in negotiating and reconciling a range of alternative modernities. For example, Africanists assert that tradition deserves a prominent place in modernity, Islamist reformers contest longstanding Sufi norms even when it often means alienating family and friends, and youth challenge old definitions of adulthood and the sensibilities of older men and women with their hip hop styles. Most strikingly, many men, especially young ones, find ways of balancing Africanist–Traditionalist, Muslim–Islamist, and Francophone-ist–Globalist modernities. Indeed, this book examined the vibrant creative energy of Niamey's youth in the face of incredibly difficult conditions.

Several crises have reemerged in the past few years, including: the famines of 2005, 2010, and 2012; the re-ignition of civil war in 2008 linked to the predatory capitalism of a new uranium mining rush that continues to exclude the masses of the poor Nigeriens; the toppling of Muammar Gaddafi's regime in Libya in 2011 that forced roughly 100,000 Nigerien workers—upon which many Hausa and other Nigeriens relied for their substantial remittances—to return home and ultimately led to a civil war in Mali that has sent tens of thousands of refugees streaming across the border into Niger; and the loss of the Petit Marché—Niamey's most important produce and meat market—to fire in 2012.

Hausa men's buoyancy and unconquerable spirit enable them to "keep on keeping on" even though the prospects for a stable, secure, prosperous future in Niamey and Niger as a whole seem tenuous at best. This is revealed in reactions to these recent tragedies. Reflecting the opinions of the vast majority of Hausa in Niamey, Youssoufou declared "Even though we are poor country that is currently enduring a famine, Malians are our neighbors and our brothers, we must allow them into our country and treat them with hospitality." Doudou, who lost his water and ice business in the Petit Marché fire and did not own an insurance policy, stated matter of factly, "This is another misfortune for the country. It is nothing. One day I will have bigger and better refrigerators, *inchallah*."

Hausa men of Niamey navigate complex, multiple challenges of continuous liminality, betwixt and between: inclusion and exclusion, home and away, tradition and modernity, joy and pain, surviving and dying, dignity and suffering. In this context of uncertainty, they continue to strive relentlessly to enjoy their lives on a daily basis, and for material and symbolic global connection. Through intelligent conversation and analysis of radio, television, and video culture, they actively seek to understand the complexity of the local and global worlds in which they live, but they also want what they see as the purported fruits of globalization—economic security, consumer goods, and health care. Growing weary of grinding poverty and daily struggles to survive, they want socioeconomic justice and the right to participate in the world as global citizens.

Notes

Chapter 1

1. As a polite and mutually humorous way of including me, Hausa often say that I am a Hausa man. After all, I speak Hausa reasonably well and, depending on the context, respond affirmatively when people ask me if I am Hausa.

Chapter 2

1. I believe I am the first to report this demographic shift. This is an educated estimate, drawing from discussions with local scholars, the opinions of a wide range of migrants, and my own observations. I have encountered no recent published estimates of the ethnic composition of Niamey.

2. The most popular websites among Hausa and other Niaméens, include: "Agadez-Niger.com (set up by a Frenchman and located in France)…Tamtaminfo.com (set up by a Nigerien student living in the USA)" (Alzouma 2009:493), aernusa@yahoogroups.com (created by l'Association des Ressortissante Nigéreins aux USA [AERNUSA]), Nigerdiaspora.info (established by a Nigerien living in Brussels), and nigeriendelexterieur.net (operated in collaboration with the Organisation Internationale pour les Migrations [OIM]).

3. Smith (2007:307) explains that, "to 'flash' someone means to call the recipient's line and allow the phone to ring just once, so that the incoming number is displayed to the recipient, but the caller hangs up before the recipient answers. This way, the recipient knows the number of the person trying to reach him or her, and hopefully has enough credit to call back." This is possible due to the fact that the caller is not charged if the recipient does not answer.

4. For example, Catholic Relief Services (CRS) and the Center for Information Technology Research in the Interest of Society (CITRIS) have implemented an innovative project targeting 7,000 adults in 140 villages of Niger, using multimedia phones and cell phone literacy primers in Hausa and Zarma as well as French (Aker and Lybbert 2009).

5. The current rates for calls in Zain's most basic plan in Niamey include: 25 cents per minute between Zain subscribers, 39 cents per minute to other mobile subscribers and fixed lines, 16 cents per minute for a family and friends plan, 30 cents per

minute for international calls within the ECOWAS zone, and 60 cents per minute for international calls to the rest of the world. Zain's SMS rates are 5 cents per text message between Zain subscribers, 15 cents per text message to other mobile subscribers, and 24 cents per text message to the rest of the world (Zain 2010).

Chapter 3

1. The interview schedule began by collecting basic demographic information on age, gender, and occupation. Then, it included five sets of questions. 1) Where are you from? Why and how did you come to Niamey? How has your stay been in Niamey? 2) Since when have you lived in Niamey? What makes you feel happy and what are your problems in Niamey? Has it met your expectations? 3) Have you ever lived in a foreign country? Which country or countries? When? How many years did you live in a foreign country? Why did you return to Niger? 4) Do you intend to migrate to a foreign country? Why? Where? How? When? 5) Do you have family or friends living in a foreign country? Where? Do you receive news from them? Do they send you money? How much in a year? Have they solved your problems?

2. The typical Hausa male of Niger enters the world in a small village. He spends the first 16 years of his life there embedded in a close-knit community of extended family and friends, learning from his father how to cultivate millet and beans. He learns the core beliefs and practices of Islam as a boy attending a local Qur'anic school. Simultaneously, assuming his village is not too distant from a larger town, he completes primary school at a state-run secular school. By about the time he is 16 years old—following his elder brothers, cousins, and friends—he begins a path of circular migration that will continue for the next two to five years. That is, he spends the long dry seasons as a small-scale trader in Niamey, and returns home to farm each rainy season. While he loves the feeling of being at home, at the age of 20 years he begins staying in Niamey year-round so as to earn enough money for marriage and to live more comfortably. During his next two to five years as a settled migrant in Niamey, he expands his trading business or learns a new occupation such as repairing motorcycles, saving enough money to occasionally send small remittances to his parents at home. Meanwhile, he spends hours in street corner conversation groups daily, learning about possibilities for earning more money in another West African city. If he is deemed responsible, personable, clever, and linguistically adept, his family or his friends will loan him money for transportation and to help him get settled in Lomé, Accra, or Cotonou or another African city. (Otherwise he remains in Niamey or continues circular migration.) During the next 20 years, from the time he is about 25 until he is 45, he spends about half of his years abroad living frugally in order to save money to pay back those who sponsored him and for bridewealth. By the time he is in his early 30s, he has saved enough money for bridewealth and returns home to marry a Nigerien woman and start a family. But he does not stay in Niger for longer than a few months at a time, preferring to return to, say, Accra where he knows that he can earn more money. By the time he is about 45, unless his business is unusually successful,

his homesickness inspires him to return to Niger. Having grown accustomed to city life, he spends his first several years in Niamey, before returning to his village to retire.

3. Indeed, dependence on remittances leads some unemployed Hausa of Niamey to stop looking for work.

Chapter 4

1. Hausa *hira* groups are unique, but all ethnic groups in Niamey enjoy their own conversation groups that seem to serve purposes similar to those of Hausa *hira* groups. Furthermore, conversation groups in Niamey are increasing ethnically integrated. Informal conversation groups are key institutions throughout West Africa, and are a classic phenomenon around the world. *Hira* groups must also be considered in the context of two patterns in globalization processes: conversation groups are most common in the periphery, where social life is less formally organized by enterprises and states (because the periphery is stuck with the least profitable activities of the world-economy); and conversation groups are common among recent immigrants in the core states due to racism and exclusion. In short, informal social organization is a way of coping with marginalization, but is conditioned in historically and culturally specific ways.

2. Hausa subgroups in Niger include: Aderawa, Arawa, Damagarawa, Gobiriwa or Maradawa, Mawri, Katsinawa, Kourfeyawa. Neighborhoods in the study include: Abidjan, Bayan Ruwa, Boukoki, Katako, Nouveau Marché, Yantala, and Zongo.

3. Given its overwhelming significance, the dearth of scholarly analysis of *hira* is mysterious. I would be surprised to find any Hausa community anywhere over the last few centuries where *hira* groups were not central to everyday social life. I suspect that others see *hira* as "low culture"; an everyday, taken for granted, seemingly mundane way of killing time unworthy of serious analysis. There is now a vast ethno-linguistic and formal linguistic literature on such "high culture" themes as the extraordinarily rich Hausa verbal arts (poetry, folk tales, praise singing), the spread of Hausa as a lingua franca in West Africa, multilingualism, grammar, greetings, and the role of silence (Adamu 1978; Furniss 1996; Hunter and Oumarou 1998; Yanco 1983).

4. Many men, across *hira* groups, comment negatively about the perceived ugliness of Hausa women based on their "blackness" relative to other women around the world they have seen on television or in videos. Not all men feel this way however. For example, Aboubacar comments on Nigerien women's beautification strategies: "It is very good to be curious about the rest of the world, but not good to imitate; for example, Niger women are now using skin lightening creams. They believe the racism of the first world." Indeed in recent years skin lightening creams have become widely available in Niamey's markets, and women are the primary customers. Their appeal among women seems to indicate a response to local men's derogatory remarks as well as both men's and women's own active (though damaging) interpretations of media images emphasizing the beauty of fair-skinned women, whether Indian, Chinese, European, or American. In contrast, there appears to be a gender-based, double

standard regarding complexion, as Mohammadou explained to the agreeing men of his *hira* group: "Michael Jackson and all black men should be proud to be black."

5. It is memorialized in the title and chorus of one of the most popular songs heard in Niamey during the 1990s and early 2000s performed by Taya. His voice and music are joyous. Taya's song is played during *hira* gatherings, at weddings, in nightclubs, and as background music for spectators entering the National Stadium to watch football games.

6. In addition, local artists are now appropriating and reinterpreting global popular music. After years of listening to African American rap, men are now rapping in Hausa and Zarma, telling their own stories about the difficulties of life on the streets of Niamey. In the past few years, young Nigerien rappers have performed in Niamey's top venues, including single group performances and well-organized Hip Hop Festivals.

Chapter 5

1. For detailed histories of Islam in Niger see Brenner (1993), Idrissa (2009), Fuglestad (1983), Nicolas (1981), Trimingham (1962).

2. Idrissas's use of the term "Islamist" here is very broad.

Chapter 6

1. Alidou (2005:193) exposes the fact that "ironically even the new Islamism with its claimed 'purity' also is implicated in the trafficking of women to Islamic countries or Islamic communities located in the West...a good number of Nigerien Muslim women now travel to places like Nigeria, Dubai, Saudi Arabia, and Western countries to serve as 'comfort' women for a very temporary period for the new Islamist men located or traveling abroad."

Bibliography

Abdou, Mahaman Sani. 1984. *Impact de la television sur le milieu rural (cas de Zinder)*. Bamako, Mali: Ministère des Sports des Arts et de la Culture.

Adamu, Mahdi. 1978. *The Hausa Factor in West African History*. Zaria, Nigeria: Ahmadu Bello University Press and Oxford University Press Nigeria.

Adesida, Olugbenga and Arunma Oteh, eds. 2001. *African Voices African Visions*. Stockholm: The Nordic Africa Institute.

African Press. 2007. "Nigerien Girls Are More and More Resorting to the Old Braids, amongst Other Tricks, to Look after Their Looks," last modified March 18, 2007, http://africanpress.wordpress.com/2007/05/18/.

Agier, Michel. *Commerce et sociabilité: les négociants soudanais du quartier zongo de Lomé (Togo)*. Paris: OSTROM (Éditions de l'Office de la Recherche Scientifique Outre-Mer), 1983.

Aker, Jenny C. 2008a. "Does Digital Divide or Provide? The Impact of Cell Phones on Grain Markets in Niger," last modified October 27, 2008, www.dgdev.org/content/publications.detail/894410/

———. 2008b. "Can You Hear Me Now?' How Cell Phones are Transforming Markets in Sub-Saharan Africa. Center for Global Development," last modified October 27, 2008, http://us.oneworld.net article/358288- niger- cell- phones- bring-down- food-prices.

Aker, Jenny C. and Travis J. Lybbert. 2009. "Can You Text Me Now? Using Cell Phones as a Platform for Adult Literacy." Center for Information Technology Research in the Interest of Society, last modified July 12, 2009, www.citris-uc.org/research/projects/mobile_phones_literacy_platform_niger.

Alidou, Ousseina. 2005. *Engaging Modernity: Muslim Women and the Politics of Agency in Postcolonial Niger*. Madison: University of Wisconsin Press.

———. 2009. Personal communication.

———. 2010. Personal communication.

Allport, Gordon W. and Leo Postman. 1947. *The Psychology of Rumor*. New York: Henry Holt.

Alzouma, Gado. 2009. "The State and the Rebel: Online Nationalisms in Niger." *Journal of Contemporary African Studies* 27(4):483-500.

Anderson, Benedict. 1991. *Imagined Communities: Reflections on the Origins and Spread of Nationalism (Revised Edition)*. London: Verso.

Appadurai, Arjun. 1990. "Disjuncture and Difference in the Global Cultural Economy." *Public Culture* 2(2):1-24.

———. 1996. *Modernity at Large: Cultural Dimensions of Globalization*. Minneapolis: University of Minnesota Press.

Appadurai, Arjun and Carol A. Breckenridge. 1995. "Public Modernity in India." In *Public Culture in a South Asian World*, edited by Carol A. Breckenridge, 1-20. Minneapolis: University of Minnesota Press.

Argenti, Nicolas. 2002. "Youth in Africa: A Major Resource for Change." In *Young Africa: Realising the Rights of Children and Youth*, edited by Alex de Waal and Nicolas Argenti, 123-154. Trenton, NJ: African World Press.

Baker, Jonathan, ed. 1997. *Rural-Urban Dynamics in Francophone Africa*. Uppsala, Sweden: Nordiska Afrikainstitutet.

Baker, Jonathan and Tade Akin Aina, eds. 1995. *The Migration Experience in Africa*. Uppsala, Sweden: Nordiska Afrikainstitutet.

Barber, Karin. 1997. "Introduction." In *Readings in African Popular Culture*, edited by Karin Barber, 1-12. Bloomington: Indiana University Press.

Barnes, Shailly. 2009. "Religion, Social Capital and Development in the Sahel: The Niass Tijaniyya in Niger." *Journal of International Affairs* 62(2):209-21.

Bastian, Misty L. 2001. "Vulture Men, Campus Cultists, and Teenaged Witches." In *Magical Interpretations, Material Realities: Modernity, Witchcraft, and the Occult in Postcolonial Africa*, edited by Henrietta L. Moore and Todd Sanders, 71-96. London: Routledge.

Bauman, Richard and Charles L. Briggs. 1990. "Poetics and Performance as Critical Perspectives on Language and Social Life." *Annual Review of Anthropology* 19:59-88.

Bernus, Suzanne. 1962. *Niamey: population et habitat*. (*Études Nigériennes*, Document Number 11.) Niamey, Niger: IFAN-CNRS.

———. 1969. *Particularismes Ethnique en Milieu Urbain: L'Example de Niamey*. Paris: Université de Paris, Institut d'Ethnologie, Musée de l'Homme.

Beynon, John and David Dunkerley. 2000. "General Introduction." In *Globalization: The Reader*, edited by John Beynon and David Dunkerley, 1-38. New York: Routledge.

Brenner, Louis. 1993. *Muslim Identity and Social Change in Sub-Saharan Africa*. Bloomington: Indiana University Press.

Brujin, Mirjam de, Francis Nyamnjoh, and Inge Brinkman, eds. 2009. *Mobile Phones: The New Talking Drums of Africa*. Leiden, The Netherlands: African Studies Centre.

Castles, Stephen and Mark J. Miller. 2008. "Introduction." In *The Age of Migration: International Population Movements in the Modern World (Fourth Edition)*, edited by Stephen Castles and Mark J. Miller, 1-18. New York: The Guilford Press.

Cellular-News. 2008. "Africa's Niger Announces Plans to Award Two Mobile Operator Licenses," last modified October 10, 2007, www.cellular-news.com/story/26616.php.

Charlick, Robert B. 2004. "Islamism in West Africa: Niger." *African Studies Quarterly* 47(2):97-108.

Cisse, Amadou. 1983. *L'Éxode rural à Niamey: causes et consequences*. Bamako, Mali: Ministère des Sports des Arts et de la Culture.

Clifford, James. 1997. *Routes: Travel and Translation in the Late Twentieth Century*. Cambridge, MA: Harvard University Press.

Cohen, Abner. 1969. *Custom and Politics in Urban Africa: A Study of Hausa Migrants in Yoruba Towns*. Berkeley: University of California Press.

Cohen, Michael A. 1989. "Urban Growth and Economic Development in the Sahel." World Bank: Staff Working Paper No. 315. Washington, DC: The World Bank.

Cohen, Robin 1997. *Global Diasporas: An Introduction*. Seattle: University of Washington Press.

Comaroff, Jean and John L. Comaroff. 1999. "Occult Economies and the Violence of Abstraction: Notes from the South African Postcolony." *American Ethnologist* 26(2):279-303.

Comaroff, John L. and Jean L. Comaroff. 1997. *Of Revelation and Revolution: The Dialectics of Modernity on a South African Frontier, Volume 2*. Chicago: University of Chicago Press.

Communauté Urbaine de Niamey. 1991. *Guide: Niamey, Capital of Niger*. Niamey, Niger: Les Éditions du Sahel.

Cooper, Barbara M. 1997. *Marriage in Maradi: Gender and Culture in a Hausa Society in Niger, 1900-1989*. Portsmouth, NH: Heinemann.

———. 1999. "The Strength in the Song: Muslim Personhood, Audible Capital, and Hausa Women's Performance of the Hajj." *Social Text* 17(3):87-109.

———. 2003. "Anatomy of a Riot: Single Women and Religious Violence in Niger." *Canadian Journal of African Studies* 37(2-3):467-512.

Coquery-Vidrovitch. 2005. *The History of African Cities South of the Sahara: From the Origins to Colonization*. Princeton, NJ: Markus Weiner.

Dearden, Nick. 2012. "Greece Can Do without the 'Sympathy' the IMF Has Shown Niger." *The Guardian*, last modified May 29, 2012. www.guardian.co.uk/.

Decalo, Samuel. 1989. *Historical Dictionary of Niger (Second Edition)*. London: Scarecrow Press.

de Latour, Elaine 1992. *Les temps du pouvoir*. Paris: Éditions de l'École des Hautes Études en Sciences Sociales.

Desjarlais, Robert. 1997. *Shelter Blues*. Philadelphia: University of Pennsylvania Press.

Diawara, Manthia. 1998. *In Search of Africa*. Cambridge: Harvard University Press.

Falola, Toyin and Steven J. Salm, eds. 2004. *Globalization and Urbanization in Africa*. Trenton, NJ: Africa World Press.

Fardon, Richard and Graham Furniss, eds. 2000. *African Broadcast Cultures: Radio in Transition*. Oxford: James Currey.

Farmer, Paul. 2003. *Pathologies of Power: Health, Human Rights, and the New War on the Poor*. Berkeley: University of California Press.

Ferguson, James. 1999. *Expectations of Modernity: Myths and Meanings of Urban Life on the Zambian Copperbelt*. Berkeley: University of California Press.

———. 2006. *Global Shadows: African in the Neoliberal World Order*. Durham: Duke University Press.

Friedland, Roger and Deirdre Borden. 1994. "NowHere: An Introduction to Space, Time, and Modernity." In *NowHere: Space, Time, and Modernity*, edited by Roger Friedland and Deirdre Borden, 1-60. Berkeley: University of California Press.

Fuglestad, Finn. 1983. *A History of Niger, 1850-1960*. New York: Cambridge University Press.

Furniss, Graham. 1996. *Poetry, Prose and Popular Culture in Hausa*. Washington, DC: Smithsonian Institution Press.

Gado, Boureima Alpha. 1997. *Niamey: garin Kaptan Salma (histoire d'une ville)*. Niamey, Niger: Nouvelle Imprimerie du Niger.

Gaonkar, Dilip Parameshwar. 1999. "On Alternative Modernities." *Public Culture* 11(1):1-18.

Gavin, Michelle. 2007. "Africa's Restless Youth. " *Current History* (May): 220-26.

Geschiere, Peter. 1997. *The Modernity of Witchcraft: Politics and the Occult in Postcolonial Africa*. Charlottesville: University of Virginia Press.

Geschiere, Peter, Birgit Meyer, and Peter Pels, eds. 2008. *Readings in Modernity in Africa*. Bloomington: Indiana University Press.

Giddens, Anthony. 1994. "Forward." In *NowHere: Space, Time, and Modernity*, edited by Roger Friedland and Deirdre Borden, xi-xiii. Berkeley: University of California Press.

Global Gini Index. 2010. "Global Gini Index (Distribution of Family Income) Ranking by Country," last modified, January 25, 2010, www.mongabay.com/reference/stats/rankings/2172.html

Gluckman, Max. 1963. *Order and Rebellion in Tribal Africa*. Cambridge: Cambridge University Press.

Goldschmidt, Walter. 1990. *The Human Career: The Self in the Symbolic World*. Cambridge, MA: Basil Blackwell.

Gomni. 2009. "Gomni." Niamey, Niger: Gomni.

Goodwin, Charles and John Heritage. 1990. "Conversation Analysis." *Annual Review of Anthropology* 19:283-307.

Gopfert, Micro. 2009. "Security in nocturnal Niamey—Preliminary reflections and conceptual outlook." Working Papers, No. 103, Department of Anthropology and African Studies, Gutenberg Universitat, Germany.

Grégoire, Emmanuel. 1993. "Islam and the Identity of Merchants in Maradi (Niger)." In *Muslim Identity and Social Change in Sub-Saharan Africa*, edited by Louis Brenner, 106-15. Bloomington: Indiana University Press.

Grosz-Ngaté, Maria. 1997. "Introduction." In *Gendered Encounters: Challenging Cultural Boundaries and Social Hierarchies in Africa*, edited by Maria Grosz-Ngaté and Omari H. Kokole, 1-21. New York: Routledge.

Gupta, Akhil and James Ferguson. 1997. "Beyond 'Culture': Space, Identity, and the Politics of Difference." In *Culture, Power, Place: Explorations in Critical Anthropology*, edited by Akhil Gupta and James Ferguson, 33-51. Durham, NC: Duke University Press.

Hamidou, Issaka Maga and Sani Ali. 2005. *Impacts Sectoriels de la Croissance Démographique dans un Contexte de Stratagie de Réduction de la Pauverté: Perspectives Dérivées 2005-2050.* Niamey: République du Niger, Ministère de la Population et de l'Action Sociale.

Hamidou , Sidikou A. 1980. *Niamey, étude de geographie socio-urbaine.* Thèse pour le Doctorat, Université de Rouen Haute-Normandie.

Hansen, Karen Tranberg in collaboration with Anne Line Dalsgaard, Katherine V. Gough, Ulla Ambrosius Madsen, Karen Valentin, and Norbert Wildermuth. 2008. *Youth and the City in the Global South.* Bloomington: Indiana University Press.

Hartill, Lane 2008. "Cell Phones Boost Nigerien Literacy, Profits." Catholic Relief Services, http://crs.org/niger/cell-phone-literacy/ (accessed March 13, 2010).

Haour, Anne and Benedetta Rossi, eds. 2010. *Being and Becoming Hausa.* Leiden, The Netherlands: Brill.

Hill, Kathleen. 1999. *Still Waters in Niger.* Evanston: TriQuarterly Books/Northwestern University Press.

Hill, Polly. 1972. *Rural Hausa: A Village and a Setting.* Cambridge: Cambridge University Press.

Hodgson, Dorothy L. 2001. "Introduction: Of Modernity/Modernities, Gender, and Ethnography." In *Gendered Modernities: Ethnographic Perspectives,* edited by Dorothy L. Hodgson, 1-23. New York: Palgrave.

Hunter, Linda and Chaibou Elhadji Oumarou. 1998. "Towards a Hausa Verbal Aesthetic: Aspects of Language about Using Language." *Journal of African Cultural Studies* 11(2):157-70.

Idrissa, Abdourahmane. 2009. *The Invention of Order: Republican Codes and Islamic Law in Niger.* Ph.D. dissertation, University of Florida.

Idrissa, Cheifou. 2010. Personal communication.

Inda, Jonathan Xavier and Renato Rosaldo, eds. 2008. *The Anthropology of Globalization: A Reader (Second Edition).* Malden, MA: Blackwell.

Isbrandt. Scott. 2009. "Cell Phones in Niger (West Africa)," http://isbradt.com/, (accessed December 5, 2009).

Jamal, Vali and John Weeks. 1993. *African Misunderstood: Or Whatever Happened to the Rural-Urban Gap?* London: The Macmillan Press.

Jankowsky, Richard. 2001. "The Globalization of Music in Tunisia." Paper presented at Fulbright-Hays Seminars Abroad Program: The Challenges of Globalization in Morocco and Tunisia, Tunis, Tunisia, July 17.

Kirk-Greene, Anthony H.M. 1974. "*Mutumin Kirki*: The Concept of the Good Man in Hausa." The Third Annual Hans Wolff Memorial Lecture. Bloomington, IN: African Studies Program.

Kleinman, Arthur. 1996. "Suffering." In *Blackwell Dictionary of Anthropology,* edited by Thomas Barfield, 396-99. Cambridge, MA: Basil Blackwell.

Kleinman, Arthur, Veena Das, and Margaret Lock. 1997. "Introduction." In *Social Suffering,* edited by Arthur Kleinman, Veena Das, and Margaret Lock, ix-xxvii. Berkeley: University of California Press.

Koudize, Aboubakari Kio. 1983. *La crise du logement à Niamey: une realité vivante.* Dakar, Senegal: Université de Dakar.

Kushner, Harold S. 1978. *When Bad Things Happen to Good People.* New York: Random House.

Larkin, Brian. 1997. "Indian Films and Nigerian Lovers: Media and the Creation of Parallel Modernities." *Africa* 67(3):406-40.

Loftsdottir, Kristin. 2008. *The Bush is Sweet: Identity, Power and Development among WoDaaBe Fulani in Niger.* Uppsala, Sweden: Nordiska Afrikainstitutet.

Lycett, J.E., and Dunbar, R. 2000. "Mobile Phones as Lekking Devices among Human Males." *Human Nature* 11(1):93-104.

Maazou, Souleymane Saddi. 2009. "Les tontines de la réussite." Presse de la Nation, last modified January 5, 2009, http://pressedelanation.com.

MacGaffey, Janet and Rémy Bazenguissa-Ganga. 2000. *Congo-Paris: Transnational Traders on the Margins of the Law.* Bloomington: Indiana University Press.

Maghnia, Abdeljalil. 2001. "The Musical Tradition of the Gnaoua in the Age of World Music." Paper presented at Fulbright-Hays Seminars Abroad Program: The Challenges of Globalization in Morocco and Tunisia, Essaouira, Morocco, July 10.

Manger, Leif and Munzoul A.M. Assal. 2006. "Diasporas within and without Africa—Dynamism, Heterogeneity, Variation." In *Diasporas within and without Africa—Dynamism, Heterogeneity, Variation*, edited by Leif Manger and Munzoul A.M. Assal, 7-31. Uppsala, Sweden: Nordiska Afrikainstitutet.

Marcus, George E. 1998. *Ethnography through Thick and Thin.* Princeton: Princeton University Press.

Masquelier, Adeline. 1996. "Identity, Alterity, and Ambiguity in a Nigerien Community: Competing Definitions of 'True' Islam." In *Postcolonial Identities in Africa*, edited by Richard Werbner and Terence Ranger, 222-44. Atlantic Heights, NJ: Zed Books.

———. 2000. "Of Headhunters and Cannibals: Migrancy, Labor, and Consumption in the Mawri Imagination." *Cultural Anthropology* 15(1):84-126.

———. 2001. *Prayer Has Spoiled Everything: Possession, Power, and Identity in an Islamic Town of Niger.* Durham: Duke University Press.

———. 2005. "The Scorpion's Sting: Youth, Marriage, and the Struggle for Social Maturity in Niger." *Journal of the Royal Anthropological Institute* 11:59-83.

———. 2007. "Negotiating Futures: Islam, Youth, and the State in Niger." In *Islam and Muslim Politics in Africa*, edited by Benjamin F. Soares and René Otayek, 243-262. New York: Palgrave Macmillan.

———. 2009. *Women and Islamic Revival in a West African Town.* Bloomington: Indiana University Press.

Mbembe, Achille. 2002. "On the Power of the False." *Public Culture* 14(3):629-41.

Meunier, Olivier. 1998. *Les voies de l'islam au Niger dans le Katsina indépendant du XIXe au XXe siècle (Maradi, pays hawsa).* Paris: Musée de l'histoire naturelle.

Miescher, Stephan. 2005. *Making Men in Ghana.* Bloomington: Indiana University Press.

Miles, William F. S. 1994. *Hausaland Divided: Colonialism and Independence in Nigeria and Niger*. Ithaca, NY: Cornell University Press.

———. 2003. "*Shari'a* as De-Africanization: Evidence from Hausaland." *Africa Today* 50(1)51-75.

———. 2004. "Islamism in West Africa: Introduction and Conclusions." *African Studies Quarterly* 47(2): 55-60, 109-18.

Miles, William F. S. with Samuel Benjamin Miles. 2008. *My African Horse Problem*. Amherst: University of Massachusetts Press.

Mills, C. Wright. 1961. *The Sociological Imagination*. New York: Grove Press.

Monbiot, George. 2011. "The Self-Attribution Fallacy." *The Guardian*, last modified November 8, 2011, www.monbiot.com/2011/11/07/the-self-attribution-fallacy/.

Moore, Henrietta L. and Todd Sanders. 2001. "Magical Interpretations and Material Realities: An Introduction." In *Magical Interpretations, Material Realities: Modernity, Witchcraft, and the Occult in Postcolonial Africa*, edited by Henrietta L. Moore and Todd Sanders, 1-27. London: Routledge.

Motcho, M. Kokou Henri. 1992. "Problèmes de Croissance Urbaine dans la Communauté Urbaine de Niamey." Niamey, Niger: Colloque de Niamey: "L'Environment Urbain," Association Internationale des Maires et Responsables des Capitales et Métropoles Partièllement ou Entièrement Francophones.

Murray, Martin J. and Garth A. Myers, eds. 2005. *Cities in Contemporary Africa*. New York: Palgrave MacMillan.

Nicolas, Guy. 1981. *Dynamique de l'Islam au sud du Sahara*. Paris: Publications Orientalistes de France.

NLRC (National Lottery Regulatory Commission of Nigeria). 2012. "NLRC Visits Niger Republic." www.nlrc.org.ng/about-nlrc/management-team/144-nlcr-visits-niger-republic (accessed July 12, 2012).

Nyamnjoh, Francis B. 2001. "Delusions of Development and the Enrichment of Witchcraft Discourses in Cameroon." In *Magical Interpretations, Material Realities: Modernity, Witchcraft, and the Occult in Postcolonial Africa*, edited by Henrietta L. Moore and Todd Sanders, 28-49. London: Routledge.

Olivier de Sardan, Jean Pierre. 2007. "Analyse rétrospective de la crise alimentaire au Niger en 2005." *Document de Travail* 45. Niamey: LASDEL and Paris: Agence Francaise de Développement.

———. (avec la participation de M. Ali Bako, E. Guillermet, O. Hamani, Y. Issa, M. Koné et M. Moha). 2007. "Analyse rétrospective de la crise alimentaire au Niger en 2005." *Document de Travail* 45 (août 2007). Niamey: LASDEL and Paris: Agence Française de Développement.

Olofson, Harold. 1975. "Cultural Values, Communication, and Urban Image in Hausaland." *Urban Anthropology* 4(2):145-60.

Oring, Elliott. 1983. "The People of the Joke: On the Conceptualization of Jewish Humor." *Western Folklore* 42(4):261-71.

Painter, Thomas M. 1987. *Migrations, Social Reproduction and Development in Africa: Critical Notes from a Case Study in the West African Sahel.* Working Paper Number

7, Sahel Development Policy and Practice Research Group, The Open University, UK.

———. 1992. *Migrations et SIDA en Afrique de l'Ouest*. New York: Care.

Pellow, Deborah. 1991. "From Accra to Kano: One Woman's Experience." In *Hausa Women in the Twentieth Century*, edited by Catherine Coles and Beverly Mack, 50-68. Madison: University of Wisconsin Press.

———. 1999. "The Power of Space in the Evolution of an Accra Zongo." In *Theorizing the City: The New Urban Anthropology Reader*, edited by Setha M. Low, 277-314. New Brunswick, NJ: Rutgers University Press.

———. 2008. *Landlords and Lodgers: Socio-Spatial Organization in an Accra Community*. Chicago: University of Chicago Press.

Perry, Donna L. 1997. "Rural Ideologies and Urban Imaginings: Wolof Immigrants in New York City." *Africa Today* 44(2):229-60.

Peter, Luc and Stéphenie Barbey. 2007. *Magic Radio*. Geneva: Intermezzo Films. Filmstrip, 83 min.

Peter, Luc, Stéphenie Barbey, and Ajay Tejasvi. 2007. "The FM Revolution in Niger: Radio's Impact on Capacity Development." *Capacity Development Briefs*, World Bank Institute, October 2007, No. 24, 1-4.

Piot, Charles. 1999. *Remotely Global: Village Modernity in West Africa*. Chicago: University of Chicago Press.

Pollock, Sheldon. 2000. "Cosmopolitan and Vernacular in History." *Public Culture* 12(3):591-625.

———, Homi K. Bhabha, Carol Breckenridge, and Dipesh Chakrabarty. 2000. "Cosmopolitanisms." *Public Culture* 12(3):577-90.

Potts, Deborah. 1995. "Shall We Go Home? Increasing Urban Poverty in African Cities and Migration Processes." *The Geographical Journal* 16:245-64.

Regis, Helen A. 2003. *Fulbe Voices: Marriage, Islam, and Medicine in Northern Cameroon*. Boulder, CO: Westview Press.

République du Niger. 1990. *Migration, urbanisation, emploi amenagement du territoire*. Niamey, Niger: Comité Technique Interministèriel Sur la Population.

———. 2010. *La population du Niger en 2010*. Niamey, Niger: L'Institut National de la Statitistique, Ministère de l'Économie et des Finances.

Robinson, Pearl. 2005. "Islam and Female Empowerment among the Tijaniyya in Niger." Unpublished manuscript, Research Note: September 2005.

Robinson, 2002. "Global and World Cities: A View from Off the Map." *International Journal of Urban and Regional Research* 26(3): 531-54.

Rouse, Roger. 1991. "Mexican Migration and the Social Space of Postmodernism." *Diaspora* 1(1):8-23.

Sabo, Mahaman Lawan. 1996. *Résultats de l'enquete sur les besions et aspirations des jeunes au Niger*. Niamey, Niger: République du Niger, Ministèère de la Communication de la Culture de la Jeunesse et des Sports.

Safran. 1991. "Diasporas in Modern Societies: Myths of Homeland and Return." *Diaspora* 1(1):83-99.

Sanjek, Roger. 2003. "Rethinking Migration, Ancient to Future." *Global Networks* 3(3):315-36.

Sassen, Saskia. 1998. *Globalization and Its Discontents: Essays on the New Mobility of People and Money*. New York: The New Press.

———. 2007. *Deciphering the Global: Its Scales, Spaces and Subjects*. London: Routledge.

———. 2009. *A Sociology of Globalization*. New York: W. W. Norton & Company.

Scheper-Hughes, Nancy. 2000. "The Global Traffic in Human Organs." *Current Anthropology* 41(2):191-224.

Schildkrout, Enid. 1978. *People of the Zongo: The Transformation of Ethnic Identities in Ghana*. New York: Cambridge University Press.

Scott, James. 1985. *Weapons of the Weak*. New Haven: Yale University Press.

Simmel, George. 1949. "The Sociology of Sociability." Translated by Everett C. Hughes. *The American Journal of Sociology* 55(3):254-61.

Simone, Abdoumaliq and Abdelghani Abouhani, eds. 2004. *Urban Africa: Changing Contours of Survival in the City*. London: Zed.

Smith, Daniel Jordan. 2007. "Cell Phones, Sharing, and Social Status in an African Society. In *Applying Anthropology: An Introductory Reader (Eighth Edition)*, edited by Aaron Podolefsky and Peter J. Brown, 305-12. New York: McGraw Hill, 2007.

Smith, James H. 2005. "Buying a Better Witch Doctor: Witch-Finding, Neoliberalism, and the Development Imagination in the Taita Hills, Kenya." *American Ethnologist* 32(1):141-58.

Smith, M.G. 1954. "Introduction and Notes." In Mary F. Smith, *Baba of Karo: A Woman of the Muslim Hausa*, 11-36. London: Faber and Faber.

Soumana, Assane. 2010. "L'Air du temps—Foyandi à Niamey: dépenses et derives." Sahel Dimanche. Posted to the Web March 5. www.nigerdiaspora.info.

Stoller, Paul. 1999. *Jaguar: A Story of Africans in America*. Chicago: University of Chicago Press.

———. 2002. *Money Has No Smell: The Africanization of New York City*. Chicago: University of Chicago Press.

———. 2009. *The Power of the Between: An Anthropological Odyssey*. Chicago: University of Chicago Press.

Thomas, Dominic. 2006. *Black France: Colonialism, Immigration, and Transnationalism*. Bloomington: Indiana University Press.

Tostensen, Arne, Inge Tvedten, and Mariken Vaa, eds. 2001. *Associational Life in African Cities: Popular Responses to the Urban Crisis*. Stockholm: The Nordic Africa Institute.

Toure, Adamou. 1990. *Sacrifices dans la ville: le citadin chez le Devin en Côte d'Ivoire*. Abidjan, Côte d'Ivoire and St. Maur, France: Éditions Douga.

Trager, Lillian. 1995."Women Migrants and Rural-Urban Linkages in South-Western Nigeria." In *The Migration Experience in Africa*, edited by Jonathan Baker and Tade Akin Aina, 269-88. Uppsala, Sweden: Nordika Afrikainstitutet.

Trimingham, John S. 1962. *A History of Islam in West Africa*. New York: Oxford University Press.

Turner, Patricia A. 1993. *I Heard it Through the Grapevine: Rumor in African-American Culture*. Berkeley: University of California Press.

(UNHDP) United Nations Human Development Programme. 2002. "Human Development Report 2002: Human Development Index." www.undp.org/hdr 2002/.

(UNHDP) United Nations Human Development Programme. 2012. "Human Development Report 2011: Human Development Index." www.undp.org/en/statistics.

van Dijk, Teun A. 1985. "Introduction: Dialogue as Discourse and Interaction." In *Handbook of Discourse Analysis, Volume 3: Discourse and Dialogue*, edited by Teun A. van Dijk, 1-12. London: Academic Press.

Van Hear, Nicholas. 1998. *New Diasporas: The Mass Exodus, Dispersal, and Regrouping of Migrant Communities*. Seattle: University of Washington Press.

Verrips, Jojada and Birgit Meyer. 2008. "Kwaku's Car: The Struggles and Stories of a Ghanian Long-distance Taxi Driver. In *Readings in Modernity in Africa*, edited by Peter Geschiere, Birgit Meyer, and Peter Pels, 155-64. Bloomington: The International African Institute in Association with Indiana University Press.

Wall, L. Lewis. 1988. *Hausa Medicine: Illness and Well-Being in a West African Culture*. Durham, NC: Duke University Press.

Wanner, Zukiswa. 2009. "Madam Zukiswa Wanner," last modified November 9, 2009, http://creativew09.wordpress.com/2009/11/09/madam-zukiswa-wanner/.

Waterman, Christopher A. 1997. "'Our Tradition Is a Very Modern Tradition': Popular Music and the Construction of Pan-Yoruba Identity." In *Readings in African Popular Culture*, edited by Karin Barber, 49-53. Bloomington: The International African Institute in Association with Indiana University Press.

Weiss, Brad. 2009. *Street Dreams and Hip Hop Barbershops: Global Fantasy in Urban Tanzania*. Bloomington: Indiana University Press.

Winchester, Norris Brian. 1976. *Strangers and Politics in Urban Africa: A Study of the Hausa in Kumasi, Ghana*. Ph.D. dissertation, Indiana University.

Works, John Arthur, Jr. 1976. *Pilgrims in a Strange Land: The Hausa Community in Chad*. New York: Columbia University Press.

World Bank. 2006. "Niger." Migration and Remittances Factbook, www.worldbank.org/prospects/migrationandremittances, (accessed April 13, 2009).

———. 2009. "Niger: Data Profile." World Bank Development Database, last modified September 2009, http://ddp-ext.worldbank.org/ddpreports/.

Worstall, Tim. 2008. "Mobile Phones and Prices," last modified February 10, 2008. www.adamsmith.org/blog/technology/mobile-phones-and-prices-20080210887.

Yahaya, Ibrahim Yaro. 1973. "Kishi: Feeling among Hausa Co-Wives." *Kano Studies* 1(1):83-98.

Yamba, C. Bawa. 1995. *Permanent Pilgrims: The Role of Pilgrimage in the Lives of West African Muslims in Sudan*. Washington, DC: Smithsonian Institution Press.

Yanco, Jennifer J. 1983. "Language Attitudes and Bilingualism in Niamey, Niger." *Africana Journal* 14:1-9.

Youngstedt, Scott M. 2004a. "The New Nigerien Hausa Diaspora in the U.S.: Surviving and Building Community on the Margins of the Global Economy." *City & Society* 16(1):39-67.

———. 2004b. "Creating Modernities through Conversation Groups: The Everyday Worlds of Hausa Migrants in Niamey, Niger." *African Studies Review* 47(3):91-118.

———. 2004c. Household Forms and Composition: Sub-Saharan Africa. In *Encyclopedia of Women and Islamic Cultures*, Volume 2, edited by Suad Joseph, 58-60. Leiden, The Netherlands: Brill Academic Publishers.

———. 2008. "The 5th Francophonie Sports and Arts Festival: Niamey, Niger Hosts a Global Community." *African Studies Quarterly* 10 (2 & 3):1-46.

Yusuf, Ahmed Beitallah. 1974. "A Reconsideration of Urban Conceptions: Hausa Urbanization and the Hausa Rural-Urban Continuum." *Urban Anthropology* 3(2):200-221.

Zain. 2010. "Un Monde Merveilleux," last modified March 16, 2010, www.ne.zain.com.

Index

About the Author

Scott M. Youngstedt earned his Ph.D. in Anthropology at UCLA in 1993, and is currently Professor of Anthropology at Saginaw Valley State University. His ethnographic research in Niger over the past 24 years is primarily concerned with exploring the ways by which migrant Hausa construct communities in diaspora, create modernities, and negotiate personal identities in the context of neoliberal globalization. His work has been published in *Africa Insight*, *African Studies Quarterly*, *African Studies Review*, and *City and Society*, among other places. Youngstedt currently serves as Vice President of the West African Research Association and is in line to become its President in November 2012.

www.ingramcontent.com/pod-product-compliance
Ingram Content Group UK Ltd.
Pitfield, Milton Keynes, MK11 3LW, UK
UKHW012037150926
475560UK00001B/61